D1187542

THE VISION OF PIERS PLOWMAN

WILLIAM LANGLAND

* * *

THE VISION OF PIERS PLOWMAN

NEWLY RENDERED INTO MODERN ENGLISH BY

HENRY W. WELLS

WITH AN INTRODUCTION
BY NEVILL COGHILL AND
NOTES BY THE TRANSLATOR

SHEED AND WARD
LONDON AND NEW YORK

SHEED AND WARD LTD.
33 MAIDEN LANE
LONDON W.C.2

FIRST PUBLISHED 1935
CHEAP EDITION 1938
THIS EDITION 1959

THIS BOOK IS SET IN
13 POINT POLIPHILUS AND BLADO ITALIC
REPRODUCED AND PRINTED BY
LOWE AND BRYDONE (PRINTERS) LTD., LONDON

CONTENTS

AUTHORSHIP

IT is not known who were the architects of our ancient cathedrals; they rise anonymously, and on them the signature of style, carried by every work of genius, is the signature of a people and a Faith. *Piers Plowman*, which of all poems is most like an English cathedral, is also virtually anonymous; it is the poem of a Catholic people, written from below; a whole nation's way of thinking and feeling finds voice in it; indeed, it speaks for all Christendom, though with an English accent.

A long tradition, springing from the fifteenth century, assigns it to William Langland, but this attribution tells us little, for it is not certainly known who William Langland was. A Dublin manuscript of the fifteenth century has the note that he was the son of Eustace de Rokayle, a gentleman; another source of later origin says he was born in Shropshire near the Malvern Hills; a number of like jottings, some of which are palpably mistaken, makes the sum of our information about him, apart from that which seems to be given in the poem itself: yet this poem was undoubtedly among the most famous of its day in England, as we may judge by the multiplicity of manuscripts, some three score of which survive from the fifteenth century; only ballads or miracle plays could have been more widely known; it was even alluded to by a popular agitator; John Ball wrote in his celebrated letter of encouragement to the insurgents under Wat Tyler:

" . . . . and biddeth Peres Plowman go to his werk . . .
And do wel and bettre, and fleeth synne,
And seketh pees, and hold you therinne . . ."

For the most part John Ball's hearers, being serfs, were illiterate; but still the poem had somehow found home in their hearts. An allusion could stir them.

Still, notwithstanding the wide and rapid popularity of his work, William Langland the author remained in an obscurity almost as deep as oblivion itself. No contemporary record of any such man has come down to posterity except what may be gleaned from his poem; his name, for instance, is said to be concealed in the line:

> I have lived *long* in the *land*; Long W*ill* men call me . . .
> (Passus XV, 161)

Beside this, in the margin of one manuscript, are added the words: "Nota the name of thauc (tour)"; but this anagrammatic hint cannot by itself carry much weight; it is merely an item in a tradition, undisputed until the twentieth century, that William Langland wrote *Piers Plowman*.

INTERNAL EVIDENCE

The story of the poem is told in the first person; it is told in the form of a series of dreams related by a dreamer. There can be no absolute certainty that this dreamer is the author himself, but it is a reasonable presumption that Langland is talking quite simply about himself, when he says:

> On a May morning on a Malvern hillside . . .
> . . . As I lay and leaned and looked on the water
> I slumbered and slept, so sweetly it murmured.
> (Induction, lines 5, 9, 10)

Scattered through the poem, there are quasi-biographical asides, the longest and most interesting of which occurs in Passus V of the present translation. When all our information is gathered together we may believe the picture seen in the mind's eye of a grim and lanky figure, coarsely dressed as a shepherd, wandering in the Malvern foothills in solitary rumination, and thinking, as largely as he might, of the whole

universe under God, and of man's part in it; or later in his life
we may imagine him living poorly in Cornhill, in mediaeval
London, with his wife and daughter; by then he was in Minor
Orders and plucking a livelihood from the pockets of the rich
by saying psalms for their souls.

He was born in 1332; so much may be inferred from Passus XII, where he speaks of himself as being forty-five years old;
other internal evidence proves this part of the poem to have
been written towards 1377, and in this way the date of his
birth is deduced. If his own name was Langland and the
name of his father de Rokayle, it would seem that he was a
bastard; perhaps, as Mr Bright suggests in his book *New Light
on Piers Plowman*, the son of some peasant bond-woman living
near the great field that is to this day called Longland, in the
parish of Colwell, by Ledbury, under the Malvern Hills.
Eustace de Rokayle had business in those parts, for he was a
friend and tenant of the Despenser family, which resided at
Hanley Castle, between the Malvern Hills and the Severn; it
seems he combined business with pleasure.

Of the bond-woman who became Langland's mother,
nothing is known; her boy was sent to school, probably at
Great Malvern Priory, by the father and his friends:

> My father and my friends furnished my schooling
>   (Passus V, 37)

By learning his letters and taking Minor Orders in the Church
he would escape the life of a serf; the facts that he wandered to
London and could earn a pittance by prayer and psalm-
singing prove that he cannot have been bound to the soil, if
further proof were needed than what is supplied in his poem,
which is clearly the work of a Churchman familiar with Bible
and Prayer-book; still inasmuch as he was married he cannot
have been priested; he can never have risen higher than minor
orders.

It may well have been his bastardy that was the first
obstacle to his clerical advancement; seeing in the neighbour-
hood of Malvern no chance of employment, to say nothing of
preferment, he found his way at some unknown date to
London, in the hope of making his fortune. He was still young,
and the excitements of the city inflamed his violent nature to a
life of dissoluteness, if his own report of himself is to be believed. Pride of perfect living, covetousness of eyes and con-
cupiscentia carnis were in the train of Fortune whom he followed,
and "caressed me about the shoulders . . ." (Passus XI, 17),
while Recklessness bade him defy the thought of old age.
Some time, not much later than the early seventies of the century, he married, for it is clear that he had a daughter, Calote,
old enough to be taken to church, in 1377. They lived together in a hovel in Cornhill, his wife, Kit, Calote, and he,
and continued there, it may be supposed, until his death. The
date of his death is even more doubtful than that of his birth,
but it cannot have been earlier than 1395, for, as will be seen,
he was still revising his poem in that year.

All this time he was slowly beating out the measure of his
great vision-sequence, turning it over in his mind, correcting,
adding and inserting, extending his conceptions, choosing
and making symbols and images to contain them. In a sense it
went against the moral grain in him to do so; some element in
his conscience, fortunately not a strong one, accused him of
wasting his time with his verse-writing; poetry was no occupa-
tion for a man of religion, so his Imagination told him:

> But you meddle with making poems when you might
>   say your psalter
> And pray for them who give you bread . . .
>   (Passus XII, 11-12)

But the visions worked themselves through him in spite of this
self-administered rebuke, and the poem grew. It was, in the

truest sense, his life-companion, the instrument and product of his thoughts for five and thirty years: the instrument in that it is contrived from a whole traditional system which directed his thinking about the Universe; the product in that it is his personal embodiment of that traditional system.

STYLE

The style of his writing is, like that of a cathedral, easy and difficult to describe; it follows and is servant to the plan and range of his ideas. This plan or scheme is laid out in roughly proportionate dimensions under four great headings: *The Vision of Piers Plowman, The Life of Do Well, The Life of Do Better,* and *The Life of Do Best*; each of these locks as naturally with the others as nave locks with transepts and transepts with choir. Together they make a complete edifice of thought about man's life in God's world.

ALLITERATION

The significance of these four headings will be discussed presently; for the moment the quality of his style which adorns the structural plan may be considered. Langland used the alliterative measure, as it had come down to him from Old English times. Five hundred years before, that measure in its hey-day was complicated by subtleties of rhythm, stress and initial rhyme, which would astonish any modern reader led to expect barbarities from his remote and primitive ancestry. But by the fourteenth century the delicate metrical system of the Anglo-Saxons had become a rougher medium; the nice laws of the courtly scansion such as are to be discerned in Beowulf, had given way before the continental system, more courtly still, of rhymes and syllable-courting, and the alliterative metre fell chiefly to the blunt use of popular poets; but poets of the people can put life into their bluntness, and for the nuances they lose, there are compensating directnesses. The essentials

of the alliterative structure, however, were roughly remembered. Each line was to be divided in the middle by a pause,
corresponding to a pause in the sense, and in each half-line so
formed, there were to be at least two strong beats falling upon
important words, heavy syllables. The thud of these syllables,
two in each half-line, was further emphasized by alliteration;
at least two of these important words (one on either side of the
pause) had to begin with the same initial letter. More usually
there were three syllables so linked; two in the first half-line, and
one in the second. Apart from these rules there was little to
govern the handling of a line except the poet's sense of what
was fitting, and this he must have derived partly from tradition
itself and partly from an instinct brought up in that tradition.

Langland was not strictly faithful even to these few metrical
precepts; his alliteration is sometimes deficient, sometimes
excessive, the number of his stresses borders upon uncertainty;
it is usually clear where he means his stresses to fall, but often
the unstressed syllables demand more emphasis and attention
than would have been permitted in the classic times of alliteration. But in effect his poem is easy to read; if his knowledge of
metre was faulty, his sense of rhythm was fine; his verses never
want for a vigorous cadence. In the present translation the old
rhythms have been as far as possible preserved together with
the sense and feeling; if they are read with that emphasis which
the meaning seems to dictate, and if the medial pause be
observed, the spring and tension of the verse will quickly
make themselves felt. An example taken from the original
and printed together with the corresponding passage from the
translation will show the relation of ancient to modern: the
lines are also chosen for the pathos and beauty of their descrip-
tion of the life of the poor:

> The most needy aren oure neighebores . and we nyme good
>   hede
> As prisones in puttes . and poure folke in cotes,

Charged with children . and chef lordes rente,
That thei with spynnynge may spare . spenen hit in houshyre
Bothe in mylke and in mele . to make with papelotes,
To a-glotye with here gurles . that greden after fode.
Al-so hemselve . suffren muche hunger.
And wo in winter-tyme . with wakynge a nyghtes
To ryse to the ruel . to rocke the cradel,
Bothe to karde and to kembe . to clouten and to wasche,
To rubbe and to rely . russhes to pilie
That reuthe is to rede . othere in ryme shewe
The wo of these women . that wonyeth in cotes:
An of meny other men . that muche wo suffren,
Bothe a-fyngred and a-furst . to turn the fayre outwarde,
And beth abasshed for to begge . and wolle nat be aknowe
What hem needeth at here neihebores . at non and at even ...
There is payn and peny-ale . as for pytaunce y-take,
Colde flessh and cold fyssh . for veneson y-bake;
Frydayes and fastyng-dayes . a ferthyng-worth of muscles
Were a feste for suche folke . other so fele cockes.
These were almes to helpe . that han suche charges,
And to comfortie such cotyers . and crokede men and
  blynde.

(C Text. Passus x, lines 71-97)

(*nyme*: take. *prisones in puttes*: prisoners in pits. *cotes*: cots,
hovels. *papelotes*: porridge. *to a-glotye with here gurles,* to glut
their children with. *greden*: cry aloud. *ruel*: space between
bed and wall. *karde and kemb*: card and comb wool. *clouten*:
patch. *rely*: wind yarn on a reel. *pilie*: peel rushes to make
rushlights. *That reuthe is to rede*: so that it is sad to think of.
Wonyeth: dwell. *a-fyngrede and a-furst*: hungry and thirsty.
payn: bread. *other so fele cockes*: or as many cockles).

The movement and feeling of this original comes easily
through in the modern translation:

The needy are our neighbours, if we note rightly;
As prisoners in cells, or poor folk in hovels,
Charged with children and overcharged by landlords.
What they may spare in spinning they spend on rental,
On milk, or on meal to make porridge
To still the sobbing of the children at meal-time.
Also they themselves suffer much hunger.
They have woe in winter time, and wake at mid-night
To rise and rock the cradle at the bedside,
To card and to comb, to darn clouts and wash them,
To rub and to reel and to put rushes on the paving.
The woe of these women who dwell in hovels,
Is too sad to speak of or to say in rhyme.
And many other men have much to suffer
From hunger and from thirst; they turn the fair side outward,
For they are abashed to beg, lest it should be acknowledged
At their neighbours what they need at noon and even . . .
They have bread and penny ale in place of a pittance,
And cold flesh and cold fish for venison from the butcher.
On Fridays and fast days a farthing-worth of mussels
Would be a feast for such poor folk, with a few cockles.
It were an alms to help all with such burdens,
And to comfort such cottagers and crooked men and blind
    folk.

(Passus VII, 96-122)

LANGLAND'S POETIC RANGE

The style within the style—Langland's personal voice speaking through the traditional form—is less easy to describe; it
varies wonderfully with the thought he is trying to express; his
phrases answer the helm of his mood. His poem was written
for Christendom, and especially for the English part of
Christendom; for the man in the fields, the man in the street,
the shop-keeper, and the government official; for the King and
his Commons; for the priests and bishops of the Church. If it

was principally a poem for Tom, Dick and Harry, Margery and Rose, there was matter in it for lords and ladies, Cardinals and Popes. It is one of the great Christian poems about humanity, and differs from what might be called a Humanist poem about humanity (such as are Chaucer's *Troilus and Criseyde*, Shakespeare's *Romeo and Juliet*, or Byron's *Don Juan*) in one essential spiritual particular. In these last-named poems the relations among men and women are treated for their intrinsic interest; they have no reference beyond themselves, and are substantial and complete, human interchanges in a mortal world. But in *Piers Plowman* no human relationship is thought of as an isolated thing in itself; for Langland all dealings between people are functions of a prior relationship with God; every man's act and thought conforms with or disturbs the love and justice of God, and has eternal consequences that cannot be evaded. The road to your neighbour lies through Calvary and there are no short cuts. Nothing can be considered in detachment from God. Herein lies that sense of the Holy which distinguishes *Piers Plowman* from the idiom of thought to which Renaissance poetry has accustomed us.

From this central fire of Christian perception in Langland the light strikes outward or downward upon the sensible world and is refracted into all the colours of a poet's feeling; he can be zealous, sardonic, compassionate, lyrical, realistic, visionary, light and dark, angry, humorous, sublime. The prophetic nature gave him rage and pity, and a clear sense of doom and glory; he had a mystical mind that was still eminently practical, never far from the thought of God, yet never caught away from the sober knowledge of this world and its people; a mind which was continually and richly poetic in a strong vernacular vein, able well to use the undainty speech of the countryside or the powerful language of the Bible to embody the images that were present to it.

Alliteration, the prophetic mood, and the thought that our

B

dealings with each other cannot be separated from our
dealings with God are to-day somewhat rare in literature; but
if the Langlandian manner is still a little strange to the
modern reader by reason of the fundamental differences that
have been noted there is a further gulf between the twentieth
and the fourteenth century that must be crossed to reach *Piers
Plowman*. A total falling away in the use and understanding of
Allegory has come about; that whole system of poetic thinking
has virtually disappeared.

ALLEGORY

Allegory is not a mere trick of writing, a device to twist simple
stories into moral shapes; it is not even excogitated in separate
pieces and then assembled like a motor car; it is the form of
thought and poetry that arises from the deep intuition of the
seamless coat of the Universe. Man is in the image of God,
Nature is the instrument of God; one Divine Mind created,
sustains, informs, and is everywhere capable of interpretation,
because nothing is that does not proceed from and express it.
Experience in such a Universe is full of meanings, for lesser
things are microcosms of greater, and meditation will bring
the understanding of one problem to light by the looking-
glass of another. This gift of transferred and simultaneous
thinking has something of the qualities of metaphor and
parable; the manifest meaning is a type of secondary meanings,
which in the end are seen to be the richer, the more important.
But just as they were not imagined in separate pieces by the
poet, but imagined simultaneously on all planes of meaning at
once, so they cannot be understood analytically by the reader,
but synthetically. Analysis is possible, but it tends to constrict
and prevent that fluidity of meanings which, in a fully developed allegorical poem like *Piers Plowman*, are everywhere in
ambience. What follows here is an analytical explanation; but
the living flavours of the poem will come, not when the

analysis has been mastered, but when it has been mastered and forgotten; the meanings are to be heard together, like the voices of a fugue. It is an admirable thing to know the intellectual map of a fugue, the sequences of key, the episodes, the introduction and reintroduction of voices, because this formal knowledge is valuable in preparing the ear for sounds it might otherwise have missed; but music is to be heard not argued; and in a similar way allegory is to be perceived and not dissected.

FOUR MEANINGS

There had grown up during the Dark and Middle ages a system of meditation on religious subjects, which was already fully developed and expounded in the writings of St Thomas Aquinas. Proper meditation and exposition of the meanings latent in a given passage of the Bible followed four parallel lines of interpretation. These were: (1) The simple, manifest meaning of the story as such; (2) the transferred meaning, whereby the reader sees in a simple story a reflection of his own state or condition; (3) the moral meaning, or ethical abstract of the story, which the reader can apply to himself in maxim form, and (4) the meaning that the story can have, not as shadowing what goes on in this world, but as shadowing the life in eternal glory. Put more simply, there is the Story; its Meaning on Earth; its Moral meaning, and its meaning in Heaven. Inasmuch as Man is made in the image of God, it is not unnatural that what has meaning when applied to man will also have meaning when applied to God. All these meanings are to be found in *Piers Plowman*. They are sometimes simultaneous, sometimes interlinked, sometimes single; but on all four planes the poem is complete, and all understanding of it must move poetically among them all.

SUBJECT OF THE POEM: MAN AND THE GOOD LIFE

I have said that this is a Christian Poem about humanity,

and it deals entirely with the most important of all questions possible to the Christian, namely "How can a Man win Salvation?" In other words, the poem is an enquiry into the nature of the Good Life, judged by Christian criteria, that is, *sub specie aeternitatis*. Langland conducts this enquiry first by means of a consideration of the actual world of men and their behaviour; and it is this aspect of the book that supplies so many vivid scenes of strife, debauchery, cozening, magnificence, bragging, idleness, and destitution; scenes that have the vigour and authenticity of an Jan Steen or a Hogarth, and which, in consequence, have been largely drawn upon by social historians in search of local colour. This consideration of the active world is chiefly centred in the first seven Passus, but it is seldom very far from Langland's imagination, and he will break off in the middle of a theological discussion to satirize a brewer or a doctor of divinity, or to describe some scene of pity in a poor man's cottage, or to damn the Friars' treachery, lechery, sophistry, lying, and grabbing.

MAN AND GOD

But it is not only in this world that his enquiry is centred. Man's origin and home is God; he is made in God's image; therefore, to reach that home after his wandering through this foreign world, he has only to show forth in his life those qualities in him which are the images of the attributes of God. God is true and faithful in His dealings with men: therefore, men can be true and faithful in their dealings with each other; God is charity: therefore, men can be loving to one another. Jesus taught, healed, and suffered, and was the true type for all priests; the Holy Ghost came to inspire, sustain, and govern the Church of God; that is work for the Princes of the Church to follow.

Meditating on these parallels, which will seem stranger to us than they did to Langland (who would have been more surprised not to find them than we to find), he perceived that in the Holy Trinity was present the right nature of man; there were three kinds of men, as there were three aspects of God. There were laymen, there were priests, and there were Bishops. In this essential parallel Langland found the means of writing a poem about Man which was also a poem about God; he could write allegorically of the actual world, with simultaneous meanings in his mind about the "world of eternal glory," to use the phrase of St Thomas. The poem grew according to careful plan; but there is in it a certain wildness and roughness and a tendency to sudden digression which proceeds from his unselfconsciousness as a writer. The work of great writers would seem in general to be partly automatic; a thing not originating in the conscious mind, but submitting to a light control from it; there is a sense that it is not the writer that is writing, but something within him, other than his known self, whether this be called a Daemon, a Muse, an Inspiration, or the Sub-conscious. Langland does not lay claim to any such affable familiar ghost as the source or companion of his composition, but the ease and copiousness of his sentence, the quick inventions and transitions, the mysterious emblems and symbols whose significance deepens like an incoming tide as the poem advances, suggest what is known to be true of other great poets, Shakespeare and Milton for example, that his work welled up in him with a dream's uncommanded quickness and fullness, and he wrote luckily, with the light guidance of his conscious mind; so his thoughts came to lie in their logical shape with all the rambling symmetry of a cathedral.

ANALYSIS

The plan may here be given; it is no entertainment to read, but it is a necessary aid for the reviving of a way of thought that has perished.

THE VISION OF PIERS PLOWMAN
(Induction to Passus VII, inclusive)

The World of Affairs. The world is seen as a field full of folk, in mortal predicament, between the Tower of Heaven, and the Pit of Hell; yet that folk appears oblivious of all considerations except those of money-making. Could that be the true meaning and purpose of Life? Should life be professional or vocational? This question is answered by Holy Church (to Langland the only possible authority for such a problem); a reasonable care for the business of the world is right, inasmuch as God himself provides man with the raw material of food, drink, and clothing; but a profession is not a vocation; men may earn a living, but are more importantly called to Truth and Love, which are at once the Way and End of Life, for they are God himself; Truth and Love are implanted in man as instincts which the simplest can recognize and follow in themselves, for they too are made in God's image, and therefore by their nature can reflect those divine virtues. Langland then shifts his ground from human life in general to the life of secular Government, and in the allegory of Lady Meed, and later, of Wrong, shows that justice is corrupted and oppression is unchecked; the remedy is that the King should rule by Conscience and Reason, spiritual remedies for practical ills, just as are Truth and Love. Langland then returns from the Court to the Field of Folk to consider the evils at large in society; against them is Penance, with its three parts, Contrition, Confession and Reparation.

The reparation imposed—to seek Saint Truth—leads Langland into a consideration of the economic troubles of his day, famine and unemployment. For these he proposes the remedies of hard work and charity. It is our duty to support even those who decline to work, for they are our blood-brothers in Christ. It is in this section that Piers Plowman first enters the poem; he it is that propounds the solution of Work for All and Food for

All. To him, therefore, is entrusted a Pardon sent from Truth, in token that whoever in this world of affairs lives according to Truth and Love, Conscience, and Reason, Penance and Labour, is in a state of Grace and will win to Salvation. This is to "Do Well." That phrase sets the Dreamer thinking on a new line, and he passes from the first great section of the poem to the second.

THE LIFE OF DO WELL
(Passus VIII to XV inclusive)

The World of Moral Interpretation. Here the Dreamer, under the form of his own educational autobiography, meets with a number of phantoms, Thought, Wit, Study, Clergy, Scrip-ture, Imagination, and so forth, to each of whom he puts the question, "What is Do Well?" And each of them supplies a part of the answer, not only to that question, but also to the question, "What Are Do Better and Do Best?" This section, then, is the moral elucidation of the whole allegory. The ac-cumulating answers he gets from these ghostly informants make up the maxims for living upon which Do Well, Do Better, and Do Best are based. In brief, the maxims for Do Well are: to be honest, God-fearing, neighbourly, hard-working, and obedient to the Church. For Do Better: to be all these and, in addition, to teach and heal the ignorant and suffering, to practise what you preach, and to endure. For Do Best: to be perfect in all the foregoing virtues, and also to guide and ad-minister the Church with that authority by which others may be saved from Hell, even in spite of themselves.

This section of the poem tells us much of the history of Lang-land's mind, his gruff ruminations, his comments on the more disgraceful ecclesiastics, his fears that Haukin, the Active Man, worthy by comparison with them, is not so worthy upon closer inspection; town life is too much for his virtue; his cloak is spotted with the seven sins. Other matters, too, are broached;

as the wonder and beauty of Nature, the obedience to their kind, and to the laws God gave them, of all birds and beasts and the fishes of the flood; Man alone is perverse. Again there is the matter of Jews and Saracens, and of noble pagans like Plato and Aristotle; the former believe in one God; the latter taught virtue, even if a pagan virtue, to mankind; are all these to be damned? If the simple life of an ignorant farmer may win salvation, how is the life of learning and clerkship any better? Yet how could the ignorant be saved if they had not the learned to teach them the Gospel? These and other problems diversify the main enquiry into the virtues that should underlie the lives of layman, priest, and bishop.

THE LIFE OF DO BETTER
(Passus XVI to XVIII inclusive)

The Priestly Life. Just as the first great section (The Vision of Piers Plowman) uses the thought of God the Father (Truth and Love), for a foundation and standard of rightness in human affairs, so this section uses the thought of God the Son; Faith and Hope (Abraham and Moses), are shown to us as necessary but insufficient; Charity (the Good Samaritan), is greater than both. The Good Samaritan journeys with the Dreamer, expounding to him the nature of the Trinity, after having taken care for the man who fell among thieves, and, as on the journey to Emmaus, it is not until afterwards that the Dreamer realizes that the Good Samaritan is Piers Plowman and that both are Jesus. Then follows the central sublimity of the poem, the great Passus XVIII, in which Christ's trial and crucifixion and descent into Hell are told. This section of Do Better has thus exemplified the teaching, healing, and suffering that are the marks of the true Priest, as of Christ.

THE LIFE OF DO BEST
(Passus XIX, XX)

The Episcopal Life. This, the last section, begins with the vic-

torious return of Christ from Death and Hell, by which he
won that authority which true conquest confers; and this He
delegates to Piers Plowman, whose form, human nature, He
had undertaken and now discards. In His life, He had lived
Do Well, Do Better, and Do Best. And then, after His ascen-
sion, the coming of the Holy Ghost is told, and how He
taught Piers to build a great Barn for the garnering of the
wheat of Christendom, "the crop of Truth"; the barn is called
Unity, "Holy Church in English." But the order established
under Piers by the Holy Spirit was not to endure; for next
Langland tells of the coming of man's ancient adversaries
from within, Pride and the other sins; while from without the
forces of Evil under the banner of Anti-Christ are mustered
against the Barn. Conscience calls in vain for a rallying into
Unity; none hear her but the fools; the rest hasten to join with
the enemy. In this last crisis Piers, the builder of the Barn, has
vanished, and the poem ends with the Dreamer awaking to
hear Conscience setting out on a quest for Piers, seeking for
Grace. This enigmatic and defeated climax can only be understood through the meaning of the symbol Piers himself.

PIERS PLOWMAN'S CHARACTER

Piers is the embodiment of the central thought of the poem; he
embodies the ways of life that shall win Salvation. Do Well,
Do Better, and Do Best are ungainly moral abstractions, but
Piers is a figure to lend them the nearness and charm of a
human example. When he first thrusts forth his head into the
poem, Piers seems to be a fine and honest farmer, a servant of
Truth, well-trusted; friendly and serviceable to his neighbours;
considerate to all men for Christ's sake; a payer of all his debts,
a man with a wife and family, who lives humbly in hard work
and who is firm and prompt in his obedience to the Church.
Such a man leads the world of secular men, for it is upon his
labour and goodwill that all states at last depend, his politics

and his economics are Christian ethics and these, in Langland's faith, were the only basis of practical life. It is not
difficult to see in this portrait the embodiment of the virtues of
Do Well, a symbol of true laity.

At his next appearance in the poem (Passus XVI), Piers is a
man who can tell of the nature of the Tree of Charity, and can
expound the mystery of the Trinity; he is recognizable in the
Good Samaritan, healer of the helpless, and in Jesus who
suffered at the hands of Pilate; he is the same character as before,
but there have been added unto him the virtues of teaching,
healing and suffering, in other words the virtues of Do Better;
he has become a symbol for the way of true Priesthood.

At his last appearance he is entrusted with the building of the
Church of Christ, whose authority is committed to him, to
save Christendom from the forces of wickedness within and
without the soul; he is faithful to his commission and builds
the Barn of Unity; but thereafter vanishes and is nowhere to be
found when, in the day of Anti-Christ, his presence is most
needed. It is not difficult to see in this embodiment of the life of
Church authority, the Bishop's life, Do Best; and the dis-
appearance of Piers in the day of reckoning is Langland's
bitter way of showing how in the fourteenth century, the
century of the captivity of the Popes at Avignon under a
French Monarchy, the century of the Great Schism, when
Pope and Anti-Pope were struggling for supremacy, that the
Episcopal Authority committed to the Princes of the Church
by Christ after the Resurrection, had in his opinion vanished
from the earth; the Life of Do Best was no longer being lived in
the world.

LITERARY SOURCES

The foregoing analysis tells as much and no more of the poem
than a skeleton would tell of a man that owned it; but shows at
least that there is a governing shape and construction, planned,

as it were, in four dimensions; it is not, as has been commonly
supposed, a set of haphazardly divagating visions. It may
well be asked where so much learning, so firm a hold on a full
system of thought, so vast a scope and so ready a symbolism
can have come from to the bastard son of a bond woman.
How could any man invent so much? Langland did not
invent it; no one mind could have done so. Apart from this
impossibility, it is also impossible for a great poet to give
utterance without that stream of assisting energy that comes
from the body of dumb men that people a land and feel as he
does, but who have not the inner Muse or automatic power to
help their thoughts out. Shakespeare had an Elizabethan audience to give him that assent; Milton had the impulse of militant
Puritanism all about him and the memory of days that had been
great in the service of a Puritan state. Without a public a poet is
in danger to fail of expression; he loses greatness without a
people behind him, for the stuff of great poetry is corporate and
communicable. Langland had a long Catholic tradition at his
back; his scheme of allegory belonged not to him but to Europe.
Fourfold meaning was a commonplace of interpretation: St
Thomas speaks of it; Dante describes it. The Three Lives,
Do Well, Do Better, and Do Best, were also known to St
Thomas. The figure of the Plowman, in a sense Langland's
greatest creation, was already in use as a symbol of hard-
working Christ-like simplicity in the pulpits of his day. The
opening vision of the Malvern Hills, with the Field of Folk,
the Tower of Truth, and the Pit of Falsehood, presents a
setting already in essence familiar to his hearers from the
Miracle Play stage. So, too, his greatest scene, when Christ
descends to harrow Hell, is taken from the contemporary
theatre, as is also the coming of Anti-Christ. The form of his
metre, as has been said, was also traditional; he did not create
any of his material. But he abundantly created a poem in
which all these and other traditional elements were fired

together; his utterance was the strong voice of what was ambient in Catholic thought and feeling; his greatness is a summing up of the Catholic Age in England, and in particular of that part of it that often lacks a spokesman, the common men of the people.

THE THREE TEXTS

The form in which the poem is here presented is not exactly that in which Langland himself seems to have published it; he was working at it over many years and it was issued in three successive versions, of which some details may be briefly given. The first version was comparatively short, going no further than to the end of Passus X in the present translation. This version, generally known as the A Text, must have been composed towards the year 1362, when the author was thirty or so; for there is a chance allusion to the celebrated storm that swept up through England from the south on Saturday, January 15th of that year. Many chroniclers report this storm, and also the pestilences for which the year was sadly remembered. The A Text speaks thus of these occurrences:

> He proved that the pestilences were for penance only,
> And that the south-west wind on a Saturday at even
> Was plainly to punish the pride of sinners.
> Pear trees and plum trees were puffed to splinters,
> In meaning, you men, that you must do better ...
> (Passus V, 119-123)

The next version (the B Text) was being written fourteen years later; no doubt during the intervening years the poem seldom left his imagination, and possibly he was still at work on this revision even after 1377, but the only certain allusion to contemporary events occurs in the fable of belling the cat (Induction, lines 182-192), which must refer to a time when an old King was on the throne, and a child the heir-apparent.

This can only have been after the death of Edward the Black Prince in June, 1376, and before the death of his aged father, Edward III, in June, 1377, during which time the Prince of Wales, Richard, was a boy in his eleventh year. The B Text is about three times as long as the A Text. In it Langland has re-handled many lines, excised and inserted others, and added some ten passus which bring to full fruit the notions of doing well, doing better, and doing best, which were already in seed in the A Text. This, in the opinion of many, is the finest of all the texts, written when Langland was in the full power of his maturity, a man of five and forty.

The C Text cannot have been earlier than 1394, though once more we may suppose that the author was pondering his revision in the years between. He made many alterations of individual line and phrase, and transposed long passages from one part of the poem to another; in length it is about a hundred lines longer than the B Text. The date is fixed by a curiously significant change in one of the passages re-handled from the B Text. In a mood of threatening prophecy the poet was foretelling the doom that would fall upon monks who broke the rules of their Order when Christ, at His Second Coming, came to judge the World.

> But a King shall come and confess the orders
> And punish you, as the Bible tells, for breaking your
> ordinances...
> Then the Abbot of Abbington and all his issue for ever
> Shall have a knock from a King and an incurable injury...
> (Passus X, 332)

This fine alliterative phrase "the Abbot of Abyndoun," as the original has it, is what appears in the B Text. In the C Text it is changed to the weaker image, "the abbot of Engelonde." The reason for this change can hardly be other than fear of the powerful Abbot of Abingdon. We know from other sources that this ecclesiastic had a violent quarrel with the Crown of England in the year 1393-34. The dispute was over the owner-ship of certain poor tenants of the village of Winkfield. Ultimately the Crown won its case; the tenants were adjudged to belong to the King, not to the Abbot; but before the latter received this 'knock', he had forcibly imprisoned the ring-leaders of the tenantry for some months in the Fleet prison. A pure instinct for alliteration had thus led Langland in 1377 to an accidental but astonishing prediction of the Abbot's humbling in 1394, some seventeen years later; consequently when he came to revise the line, having before him the sad example of the imprisoned tenants, he changed it to the col-ourless and inoffensive "Abbot of England," thereby stumb-ling no less accidentally on a second prediction, in which sense the passage has often been interpreted of the dissolution of the monasteries under Henry VIII.

In the present translation Mr Wells has attempted to com-bine the excellencies of all three texts by a judicious confla-tion; those who have studied his originals will be the first to acknowledge how admirably he has succeeded in a difficult task. Here is presented in modern language all the B Text except passages obviously improved in the C Text, all the improvements and more important additions of the C Text, and even a few of the most brilliant lines which Langland wrote in the A Text, but which he later preferred to discard. It will be seen that this treatment presupposes that all three versions were the work of one man, namely William Lang-land, and that this is substantially true a continuous tradition from the fifteenth century asserts and the most recent scholar-ship confirms. Another view, namely that *Piers Plowman* is not the work of one man, but of five, working in succession, was very brilliantly advanced some thirty years ago by Professor Manly of Chicago University, and this view is still enter-tained by some scholars. The arguments for and against this theory are too long and too particular to be repeated here; the most careful consideration of the evidence however seems certainly to support the traditional view that "*William Langland made pers plowman.*"

NEVILL COGHILL

Exeter College,
Oxford.

PIERS PLOWMAN

N a summer season when the sun was softest,
Shrouded in a smock, in shepherd's clothing,
In the habit of a hermit of unholy living
I went through this world to witness wonders.
On a May morning on a Malvern hillside
I saw strange sights like scenes of Faerie.
I was weary of wandering and went to rest
By the bank of a brook in a broad meadow.
As I lay and leaned and looked on the water
I slumbered and slept, so sweetly it murmured.　　　10

Then I met with marvellous visions.
I was in a wilderness; where, I knew not.
I looked up at the East at the high sun,
And saw a tower on a toft artfully fashioned.
A deep dale was beneath with a dungeon in it,
And deep ditches and dark, dreadful to see.

A fair field full of folk I found between them,
With all manner of men, the meanest and the richest,
Working and wandering as the world demanded.
Some put them to the plough and practised hardship　　20
In setting and sowing and seldom had leisure;
They won what wasters consumed in gluttony.
Some practised pride and quaint behaviour,
And came disguised in clothes and features.
Prayer and penance prevailed with many.
For the love of our Lord they lived in strictness,
To have bliss hereafter and heavenly riches.
Hermits and anchorites held to their dwellings,
Gave up the course of country roving
And all lusty living that delights the body.　　30
Some turned to trade; they tried barter;

3

And seëmed in our sight to succeed better.
Some men were mirthful, learned minstrelsies,
And got gold as gleemen—a guiltless practice.
Yet jesters and janglers, Judas' children,
Feigned idle fancies and wore fools' clothing,
But had wit if they wished to work as others.
What Paul has preached I proffer without glossing:
Qui loquitur turpiloquium, is Lucifer's servant.

Bidders and beggars ride about the country   40
With bread to the brim in their bags and bellies;
They feign that they are famished and fight in the ale-house.
God wot, they go in gluttony to their chambers
And rise with ribaldry, like Robert's children.
Sleep and sloth pursue them always.

Pilgrims and palmers were plighted together
To seek Saint James and saints in Rome.
They went on their way with many wise stories,
And had leave to lie for a lifetime after.
I saw some who said that they sought for relics;   50
In each tale that they told their tongue would always
Speak more than was so, it seemed to my thinking.

A host of hermits with hocked staves
Went to Walsingham with their wenches behind them.
These great lubbers and long, who were loath to labour,
Clothed themselves in copes to be distinguished from others,
And robed themselves as hermits to roam at their leisure.
There I found friars of all the four orders,
Who preached to the people for the profit of their bellies,
And glossed the gospel to their own good pleasure;   60
They coveted their copes, and construed it to their liking.
Many master-brothers may clothe themselves to their fancy,

For their money and their merchandise multiply together.
Since charity has turned chapman to shrive lords and ladies,
Strange sights have been seen in a few short years.
Unless they and Holy Church hold closer together
The worst misery of man will mount up quickly.

There a pardoner preached as priest of the parish,
And brought out a bull with a bishop's signet,
Said that he himself might assoil all men   70
Of all falsehood in fasting and vows that were broken.
Common folk confided in him and liked his preaching,
And crept up on cowed knees and kissed his pardons.
He abused them with brevets and blinded their eyesight;
His devil's devices drew rings and brooches.
They gave their gold to keep gluttons,
And believed in liars and lovers of lechery.
If the bishop were blessed and worth both his ears
His seal would not be sent to deceive the people.
But the power of the bishop is not this preacher's licence, 80
For the parish priest and the pardoner share the profits together
Which the poor of the parish would have if these were honest.

Because parishes were poor since the pestilence season,
Parsons and parish priests petitioned the bishops
For a licence to leave and live in London
And sing there for simony, for silver is sweet.

Bishops and bachelors, both masters and doctors,
Who have cures under Christ and are crowned with the tonsure,
In sign of their service to shrive the parish,
To pray and preach and give the poor nourishment,   90
Lodge in London in Lent and the long year after,
Some are counting coins in the king's chamber,
Or in exchequer and chancery challenging his debts

From wards and wardmotes, waifs and strays.
Some serve as servants to lords and ladies
And sit in the seats of steward and butler.
They hear mass and matins and many of their hours
Are done without devotion. There is danger that at last
Christ in his consistory will curse many.

I pondered on the power which Peter was given   100
To bind and to unbind as the Book tells us.
He left it with love at our Lord's commandment
And in care of four virtues, which are fairest of all virtues,
These are called cardinal, or hinges to the gateway
Where Christ is in his kingdom; they close it to many
And open it to many others and show them heaven's glory.
Yet I dare not deny that the dignity of Peter
Is in cardinals at court who command this title
And presume on its power in the pontiff's election.
The election belongs to love and to learning.   110
I might but I must not speak more of their college.

Then there came a king in the company of knighthood.
The might of the Commune made him a ruler.
Common Wit came after and created advisers,
As a council for the king and for the common safety.
The king and the clergy and the company of knighthood
Decreed that the commons should contrive their welfare.
Common Wit and the Commune made craftsmen and
    tradesmen,
And put others to the plough for the peoples' profit,
To till and to toil as true life bade them.   120
The king and the Commune and Common Wit also
Ordained loyalty and law, and each man knew his own.

Then a fool came forth, a long lean fellow,

And knelt to the king and spoke like a cleric:
"Christ keep you, my king, and all your kingdom also,
So live in your land that loyalty may love you,
And righteous rule be rewarded in heaven!"

Then high in the air an angel from heaven
Spoke loudly in Latin, that laymen might never   130
Either judge or justify or object to opinions,
But suffer and serve; and thus spoke the angel:
Sum rex, sum Princeps; neutrum fortasse deinceps;
O qui jura regis Christi specialia regis,
Hoc quod agas melius, justus es, esto pius!
Nudum jus a te vestiri vult pietate;
Qualia vis metere, talia grana sere.
Si jus nudatur, nudo de jure metatur;
Si seritur pietas, de pietate metas!

Then a glutton of language, a scandalous jester,
Answered the angel, who hovered above them: 140
Dum rex a regere dicatur nomen habere;
Nomen habet sine re, nisi studet jura tenere.

Then the crowd of the commons cried out in Latin
To the king's council for all to construe it:
Praecepta regis sunt nobis vincula legis.

A rabble of rats ran suddenly hither
With a swarm of small mice sporting among them.
They came to a council for the common profit.
A cat of the court would come at his pleasure
Sport and spring and seize whom he fancied.   150
Play with them perilously and push them before him.
"We dread the danger and dare not come forward,
And if we grudge him his game he will grieve us further,

Scratch us or claw us or take us in his clutches,
And make life loathsome before he leave us.
If we had the wit to withstand his pleasure
We might be lords aloft and live at our leisure."

A rat of renown, a ready speaker,
Sought for the sovereign salve for his people:
"I have seen men," he said, "in the city of London   160
Bearing bright chains about their shoulders,
On cunning collars; they go at random
Through warren and waste as their will inclines them.
And at other times elsewhere, as I hear reported.
If they bore bells, I believe, by heaven,
One might hear where they went and run away!
So," said the speaker, "reason shows clearly
That we should buy a bell of brass, or bright silver,
Clasp it on a collar, and for the common profit
Hang it on the cat's head, and then we may hear him   170
When he roams or is at rest or runs to frolic.
When his mood is mild we may move at pleasure,
And appear in his presence when he is playfully minded,
And be ware of his wrath and wary of his coming."

The rabble of rats thought his reasons clever;
But when the bell was brought and bound to the collar,
There was no rat in all the rout, for the realm of Louis,
Who dared bind the bell about the cat's shoulders,
Nor hang it on the cat's head to win all England.
They granted themselves cowards and their counsel feeble,
And their labour was lost and all their long sessions.   181

Then a mouse of importance, and of merit, as I thought him,
Strode forth sternly and stood before the council,
And with the rout of rats reasoned as follows:

"If we killed the cat there would still come another,
To catch us and all our kin, though we crept under benches.
So I counsel the commune to let the cat wander,
And never be bold to bring him the collar.
For my sire said, seven years past,
Where the cat is a kitten the court is in sorrow.   190
So Holywrit witnesses; who will may read it:
V*ae terrae ubi puer rex est, etc.*
For no one could rest for rats in the night.
While the cat catches rabbits he cares for us little,
But feeds wholly on that venison—never defame him!
A little loss is better than a long sorrow,
And the raids of a robber than ruin forever.
We mice would demolish the malt of many,
And the rout of rats rend men's clothing,
If that cat of the court could not control you.   200
For if you rats had your way you could not rule yourselves.
For my part," said the mouse, "I see so much further,
That neither the cat nor the kitten should be grieved at my
        counsel.
Neither complain I at the collar that cost me nothing.
If it had cost me a crown I should never confess it.
We must suffer our rulers to roam at their pleasure
Uncoupled or coupled, and catch what they will.
And I warn the wise to watch out for themselves."
What this dream may mean, you men who are clever,
Divine, for I dare not, by dear God in heaven!   210

Hundreds in silk hoods hovered about me,
They seemed to be sergeants who served in the court rooms,
Took pounds for pence, and pled for justice,
Nor for the love of our Lord unlocked their lips ever.
Better measure the mist on Malvern hillsides,
Than hear a mumble from their mouths till money is promised.

I saw in the press, as you shall hear hereafter,
Barons and burgesses and village bondmen,
Bakers and butchers and brewers without number,
Wool-websters and weavers of linen,   220
Tailors and tinkers and tollmen in markets,
Masons and miners and many other craftsmen.
All lived in labour. But others leapt forward,
Dykemen and diggers who do their work badly,
And drive out the long day with *Dieu vous save, dame Emme!*
Cooks and their knaves cried, "Hot pies, hot!
Good geese and bacon! Come dine, Come!"
Taverners too were tossed in the turmoil,
"White wine of Alsace and red wine of Gascony,
Rhine and Rochelle digest the roast!"—   230
I saw all this sleeping, and seven times more.

THE meaning of the mountain, of the murky valley
And of the field full of folk, I shall first show you.
A lovely lady in linen garments
Came down from the castle and greeted me softly,
And said, "Son, do you sleep? do you see this people,
How busy they are about the meadow?
Most of the men who move in this meadow
Have their worship in this world and wish no better;
No heaven but here holds their fancy."

I was afraid of her face, for all her beauty,   10
And said, "Mercy, Madam, what is your meaning?"
"The tower on the toft," she said, "is Truth's dwelling;
Would that you worked as his word teaches!
He is father of faith, and fashioned you wholly,
Blood and bone, and bestowed five wits
To worship him here while you are mortal.
He has willed the world to yield to all men
Woollen, linen, and life's sustenance.
He has measured the mean of a moderate comfort,
And bestowed from his bounty three blessings in common; 20
None are needful but these. Now I shall name them—
Though I know their natures—and do you name them after.
The first is clothing to keep out the cold;
Meat at meal-time to maintain the body,
And drink to the thirsty; but do not drink always.
You are the worse for that when the work hour calls you.—
Lo, Lot in his lifetime, from love of drinking,
Did the devil's work with his two daughters.
He delighted in drink, as the devil bad him,
Lechery laid hold on him, and he lay by his offspring.   30
Wine defeated wit, and wickedness had the mastery.

Inebriamus eum vino, dormiamusque cum eo, ut servare possimus
    de patre nostro semen.
Wine and women were Lot's undoing,
He begat in his gluttony cursed children.—
Dread delicate drink, and do what is prudent;
Moderation is a medicine for men of yearning,
All is not safe for the soul that the stomach calls for,
Nor best for the body, best for the spirit.

Believe not the body, for a liar is his teacher,
The wretched world,—he would betray you!   40
For the fiend and the flesh follow you together,
And seduce the soul with soft whispers.
I warn men to beware and to watch warily."
"Mercy, Madam," I said, "your words delight me;
But the wealth of this world, that men hold so fiercely,
Tell me, Madam, to whom this treasure belongs."
"Go to the gospel," she said, "where God answered
The people who pressed him with a penny in the temple,
Asking him whether they should worship Caesar.
God asked them whose was the inscription,   50
And whose the sign that stood within it.
"Caesar's," they said, "we see it clearly."
"*Reddite Caesari*," said God, "what belongs to Caesar,
Et quae sunt Dei deo, or else you do evil."
For good counsel should govern you always,
Common Wit be warden of wealth's treasure,
And tell when the time to dispense arises;
Counsel and Common Wit are companions of husbandry."

Then I humbly asked by him who made me,
"Madam, may I know what meaning is hidden   60
In the dismal dungeon of the dale beneath us?"
"That is the castle of Care. Who comes within it

May ban his birth in body and soul.
Wrong is the name of the wretch who lives there:
The Father of Falsehood was first to build it.
He egged Adam and Eve to mischief,
And counselled Cain to kill his brother.
He jested with Judas for Jewish silver,
And afterwards hung him high on an elder.
He is the leader of liars and love's traitor,   70
Yet betrays the soonest all who trust in his treasure."

When I heard this I wondered who was this woman,
Whose words were weighed in the wisdom of Scripture,
I hailed her on the high name, and asked that she tell me
What title she bore, who taught me so mildly.

"I am Holy Church," she said, "and you should know me.
I first found you. My faith I taught you.
You brought me pledges to be at my bidding.
And to love me loyally while life lasted."

Then I kissed the ground, and cried her mercy,   80
And piteously I prayed her to pray for a sinner,
And tenderly teach me to believe in Christ,
That I might work his will who wrought me to man!
"Tell me of no treasure, but teach me only
How I may save my soul, O Sainted Lady!"

"When all treasures are tried," she said, "Truth is the fairest.
It is as dear a dowry as the dear God himself.

He who is true of tongue and with his two hands,
Who works with this will, and wishes no evil,
Is a God, says the gospel, on our ground and in heaven,   90
And likened to our Lord in Saint Luke's teaching.

Clerks who comprehend this should convey it to the people,
For christian and unchristian folk claim it equally.

Kings and knights should keep it before them,
Ride and rule in realms about them,
Take transgressors and tie them in bondage,
Till truth has determined their trespass fully.
This is the perfect practice appertaining to knighthood,
And not to fast one Friday in five score winters:
To stand with him or with her who upholds truth,   100
And never leave them for the lust and liking of silver.

David in his days dubbed champions,
Made them swear on their swords to serve Truth forever,—
Whoever passed that point was *apostata* in the order.
Christ, the king of kings, knighted ten,
Cherubim and Seraphim, such seven, and one other,
Gave them majesty and might and the mirth of heaven;
He ordained archangels over the under legions,
Taught them Truth by knowledge of the Trinity,
And obedience to his bidding; and bad nothing further. 110
Lucifer and his legions learned it in heaven.
But when he lost his loyalty his bliss left him.
He fell from that fellowship in a fiend's likeness
Into a deep dark hell to dwell there forever.
More fell with him than man can number.
They leapt forth with Lucifer in loathsome bodies,
For they believed in his lies who spoke as follows:
Ponam pedem in aquilone, et similis ero altissimo.
No heaven might hold any who hoped so,
All fell like fiends for nine days together,   120
Till God in his goodness granted a respite,
Gave the heavens quiet and girded them fast.

When the wicked went out in the wondrous exile,
Some to air, some to earth, some to hell's dungeon,
Lucifer fell lowest and lies beneath all others;
For pride that he practised his pain is immortal.
All whose works are with Wrong shall wend downwards
After their death⁄day to dwell with that villain.
But those who work well as Holywrit teaches
And die, as I declared, in Truth, as is wisest,   130
May be sure that their souls shall rise to heaven,
Where the Tri⁄une Truth has ordained their triumph.
I say now as I said first, with such texts to witness,
When all treasures are tried, Truth is the fairest.
Let laymen learn it, for the lettered know it;
Truth is the dearest of all treasures of the living."

"But I have no natural knowledge," said I, "to teach me
How Truth descends and dwells in my body."

"You are a blunt blockhead and a blind pupil,
You learnt too little Latin, lad, in your schooldays.   140
Heu michi! quia sterilem duxi vitam juvenilem.
By the common gift of Nature hearts acknowledge
The love of the Lord above the love of self,
And dread to do evil though death may follow.
This I trust is true. Who teaches you better,
You must suffer to speak, and pursue his teaching.
God's word is the witness; work in that doctrine.
For Truth tells that love is the treacle of heaven,
No sin may be seen where that spice preserves you.
All his works are wrought with love and freedom;   150
He taught love in the law of Moses; it is most like heaven,
The plant of peace, the most precious of virtues.

Heaven might not hold it, it was itself so heavy,

Till it had eaten heartily of the earth beneath it.
In the flesh of the fold, in the blood of your body,
No leaf of the linden was lighter on the branches;
It was as piercing and poignant as the point of a needle;
No walls nor armour withheld its passage.

So Love is leader of the Lord's folk in heaven,
And a mean, as the mayor, between the king and the commune.
So love is a leader, and takes law upon him   161
For the amerciament of men in the mischief they practise.
The Might of the Maker begat it in Nature;
Its head⁄spring is the heart, where all arises.
The Might that is moving in a man's conscience
Fell from the Father who fashioned all men.
He looked on us with love, and let his son
Die in meekness for our misdeeds, to amend us all.
Yet he wished no evil to the wretches who pained him,
But meekly murmured that Mercy might hear him   170
And have pity on the people who pained him and slew him.
Here may we mark the main example
Of the meekness of the Almighty, whose mercy was granted
To those who hung him on high and pierced his heart.

Therefore I warn you rich, have ruth on poor folk;
Though you are mighty in the moot⁄hall be meek in your
     judgements;
For the measures that you mete shall be meted to you;
Your weights shall weigh you when the hour is ready.

Though you are true of tongue and true in dealing,
And as chaste as children weeping in the churches,   180
If you love disloyalty and never lend the poor,
Nor give the good that God has sent you,
You have no more merit in masses and devotions

Than Malkin in a maidenhood whom no man wishes.

James the gentle has judged in his letters
That faith without works is vain and idle,
And as dead as a door-sill unless deeds follow.
Fides sine operibus mortua est, etc.

Therefore chastity without charity will be chained in hell.
It is as lifeless as a lamp whose light is out.   190
Many chaplains are chaste but charity is absent;
No men are so avarous as they, when advancement meets
   them,—
Unkind to their kin and to all Christian people!
Gorging their gifts and crying after others!
Such chastity without charity will be chained in hell.

Many curates keep themselves clean in body,
But are crushed under covetousness and cannot leave it,
So hard have they and avarice clasped themselves together.
This is no truth of the Trinity, but treachery of Satan,
And a lesson to laymen to love evil.   200

Therefore these words are written in the gospel:
Date, et dabitur vobis; for I deal you all things.
This is the key of grace, and the keyword is loving,
To comfort the careworn crushed under evil.

Love is leach of life, and our Lord is with him,
It is the wicket gate that goes to heaven.
I say now as I said first, with these texts to witness,
When all treasures are tried, Truth is the fairest.
Love it," said the lady, "I may not linger
With my lesson of love,"—and she left me gently.   210

C

THEN I begged her blessing on bended knees,
And said, "Mercy, Madam, for Mary's love in heaven,
Who bore the blessed child who bought us on the [roodtree,
Show me some skill to perceive falsehood."

"Look on thy left side; lo, where he is standing,
Both Falsehood and Flattery and all their folk with them."

I looked on my left side as the lady bad me,
And was aware of a woman wonderfully apparelled.
The finest of furs were affixed to her garments.
She was crowned with a coronet that a king might envy,   10
Her fine fingers were fretted with gold wiring
And red rubies upon it red as coal brands:
Dazzling diamonds, double sapphires,
And blue beryls from the East to ban diseases.
Her robe was rich, ingrained with red scarlet,
And ribands of red gold, and rich jewels.
Her raiment ravished me; its richness amazed me.
I wondered who she was, and who was her husband.

"Who is this woman," I asked, "so worthily apparelled?"
"She is Mede the Maid," she answered, "who wrongs me often.
She lies to the lords who have law in keeping,   21
And libels Loyalty, my lord and master.
In the pope's palace she is as privy as I am.
But Truth surely would not so, for she is a bastard.

Flattery is her father, who has a fickle tongue
Which seldom touches truth unless deception guide it.
Mede is mannered after him, as may well be by Nature:
Qualis pater talis filius, Bonus arbor bonum fructum facit.

But I ought to be the higher, for my origin is higher;
My father is the Great God, the ground of all graces,   30
God without beginning, and I his godchild in christening.
He gave to me mercy for a marriage portion;
And the man who is merciful and loves me truly
Shall be my lord and my lover in the high heaven.
He who marries Mede, I lay my head at wager,
Shall lose with her love a lapful of charity.
King David teaches of meed-takers,
And of mortal men who maintain truth;
He shows in his psalter how souls are blessed:
Domine, quis habitabit in tabernaculo tuo, etc.   40
Now Mede will marry a miserable villain,
False Fickle-Tongue, of fiend's begetting.
The fair speech of Flattery leaves the folk bewildered,
And Liar alone has led her to this wedding.
They have made to-morrow the maiden's bridal,
And then you may witness, if you will, who are the people
Who belong to this lordship, both the low and the mighty.
Know them there if you can, and keep silence.
Do not blame them, but let them be, till loyalty be justice,
And have power to punish them; and then put forth   50
     your reasons.
Now I commit you to Christ and to his clean mother,
And let no love of Mede allure your conscience."—
So that lady left me, as I lay in slumber,
And I dreamed of Mede's marriage in a marvellous vision.
All the rich retinue that ranged about Falsehood,
All manner of men, the mean and the richest,
Were bidden to the bridal from both parties.
For the marriage of this maiden the multitude assembled:
Knights and clerics and commons, and such others
As sizars and sompnours, sheriffs and their servants,   60
Beadles and bailiffs, brokers and tradesmen,

Victualers and foragers and advocates of the arches,
No one could number the rout that ran about her.
But Simony and Civil and the assizers in court rooms
Were most privy with Mede of all men around her.
Flattery was the first who fetched her from her chamber,
And like a broker brought her to be the bride of Falsehood.
When Simony and Civil saw what each was seeking
They assented for silver to say what was wanted.
Then Liar leapt forth and cried "Look! Here! A charter 70
That Guile with his great oaths has given the lovers."
He prayed Civil to see it and Simony to read it.
Then Simony and Civil stepped out together
And unfolded the enfeoffment that Falsehood had granted,
And thus these scoundrels cried and declaimed it to the people:
Sciant praesentes et futuri, etc.
"Know ye and witness all people of all nations,
That Mede is married more for possessions
Than for virtue or fairness or any free affection.
Falsehood feigns to love her, for he knows her riches,   80
And Flattery with his fickle tongue enfeoffs them by this
    charter:
To be princes in pride and to despise poverty,
To backbite and boast and bear false witness,
To scorn and to scold and slander others,
To be disobedient and bold and break God's commandments.

The earldom of Envy and Wrath, its neighbour,
With the castles of Chiding and Chattering-out-of-reason,
The county of Covetousness and all the grounds about it,
As Usury and Avarice—I grant them freely
With Bargain and Brokerage, and all the borough of
    Thieving.   90

All the lordship of Lechery in length and breath,

As Words and Works and wandering glances,
Wearing and Wishing and Idle Fancies,
Where Will would go but wants the chances.

He gave them Gluttony, and great Oaths with him,
And to drink all day in dingy taverns,
There to jest and jangle and judge their fellow Christians;
To feast on fastdays before evening,
And then to sit and swill till sleep assail them,
Breed as the borough swine, and bed at pleasure;   100
While sloth and sleep slick their haunches,
Till they wake in despair with no desire for amendment.
And believe themselves lost, and look for death.

To have and to hold, and their heirs forever,
A dwelling with the devil and to be damned to eternity,
With all appurtenances of purgatory and pains of hell.
And to yield for this, when a year is over,
Their souls to Satan to suffer with him in torment,
And to dwell with him in woe, while God is in heaven."

In witness whereof Wrong was the first,   110
And Piers the pardoner, of Pauline doctrine,
Bet the beadle of Buckingham Shire,
Rainald the reve of the Rutland marches,
Mund the miller, and many others.
In the date of the devil was this deed sealed,
In witness of Sir Simony, and with Civil's permit.

This affixing of the enfeoffment vexed Theology,
And he said to Civil: "Sorrow upon you,
To meddle with such marriages and make Truth angry!
Before this marriage is made may woe betide thee!   120

Mede is a maiden; Amends is her Mother.
God grant us to give her at Truth's direction!
But you have given her with guile, and God give you sorrow!
I, Theology, teach the text, and the true lesson.
Lazarus the Levite, lying on the gridiron,
Looked up to our Lord, and with a loud cry
Said, 'God, be gracious, open the gates of heaven!
For I, a man, have merited the meed of thy mercy.'
Dignus est operarius to have his wages,
And you have affixed Mede to Falsehood! Now fie upon you!
You live by lying and lecherous teaching!   131
Simony and yourself shame Holy Church!
You and the notaries annoy the people!
Both shall grieve for it, by God who made me!
Well you know, you wretches, unless your wits are wandering,
That Falsehood is faithless and fickle in his working,
He was born a bastard of Beelzebub's children,
But Mede is a maiden, a mistress of station,
And might kiss the king as a cousin at pleasure.

Therefore deal discreetly and do as I bid you,   140
Lead her to London where the lawyers will tell you
If law will allow them to live together.
And though Justices judge her and join her to Falsehood,
Yet beware of that wedding, for Truth is wily,
And Conscience is in his council, and knows each of you,
And if he finds you in fault or in Falsehood's company,
Your souls will smart for it sorely hereafter."

Then Civil assented; but Simony was unwilling
Till he had had silver for his service, and so, too, the notaries.
Next Flattery fetched his florins by the purseful,   150
And bad Guile give the gold freely,
And notably to the notaries, that none should fail him.

"And give florins freely to False Witness,
For he can master Mede and make her agreeable."
Then gold was given; and great were the compliments
To Falsehood and to Flattery for their fair presents!
All swore their services in aid of Sir Falsehood,
And said, "Never, Sir, shall we cease to serve you,
Till Mede be your wedded wife, and all through our
    friendship.
We have moved Mede with our merry talking   160
Gladly to grant us to go with her to London
And learn if the law will link you forever."
Then Flattery and Falsehood laughed together
And bad summon all servants from the shires about them,
And made all agree, helpers and beggars,
To go with them to Westminster, and witness the charter.

But all their hackneys were hackneys for hire.
So Guile got horses from many great masters,
Mede sat on a sheriff shod for the journey;
Falsehood sat on an assizer who trotted softly;   170
And Flattery on a flatterer fastidiously harnessed.

The notaries were annoyed, for they had no horses:
Sir Simony and Sir Civil would have gone afoot,
But Simony and Civil swore together
That sompnours should be saddled and serve them in
    common.—
"Apparel these provisors," said Civil, "in the palfries'
    trappings;
Sir Simony himself shall sit on their shoulders.
You deans and subdeans, draw there in one harness!
You archdeacons and officials, and all you registrars,
Be saddled with the silver that our sins win you: 180
With adulteries, with divorces and with hidden usury,—

Go, bear the bishops abroad in their visiting.

You Pauline people for complaints in the consistory
Shall serve myself. My name is Civil!—
A carriage saddle there for Commissary! He shall guide the
    wagon,
And fetch us our food from *fornicatores*.
Make a long cart for Liar to lead all the others,
As these friars and feigners who follow barefoot."

So Falsehood and Flattery rode forth together,
With Mede in the midst and the mass behind them.   190
I want tongue and time to tell who followed.
Multitudes of men of all moulds under heaven:—
But one Guile was their guard, and guided them onward.

Soothness saw them well and said but little.
He pricked his palfrey, passed beyond them,
And came to the king's court, where Conscience heard him,
And Conscience recounted it to the king after.
"Now by Christ," said the king, "if I ever capture
Falsehood or Flattery or any of their *confrères*,
I shall deal with these devils and their dishonest practice, 200
And hang them in a halter, and all who help them!
No one in the world will bail them a title,
But the letter of the law shall light on them together."
He commanded a constable to come before him,
And said, "Attach the traitors; let no man touch you!
Fetter Falsehood and defy his presents,
Cut off Guile's head! Let him go no farther.
If you light upon Liar never let him from you
Till you place him in the pillory, petition or no petition.
And bring Mede to me, maugre them all."   210

Dread standing at the door heard the doom of the traitors,
And the king commanding his constables and servants
To fetter Falsehood and put his friends in bondage.
Dread was soon on his way, and warned Falsehood
To flee with his fellows and fear justice.

Falsehood in a fright fled to the friars.
As Guile was going aghast for his life,
Merchants met him and made him a lodging;
They apparelled him as a prentice to practise on the people,
And set him in their shops to show their wares.   220

Lightly Liar leapt into hedges,
And lurked through lanes, belaboured by many.
He was nowhere welcome for his wily talking,
But everywhere hooted and hustled about.
Yet pardoners had pity on him and put him in their houses,
Washed him and wiped him and wound him in tatters,
And sent him with seals to service on Sundays
To give pardons for pennies, at partial payments.
Then letters of the leaches, who lowered in envy,
Invited him to visit them and view their waters.   230
Grocers commended him to come to their houses;
He was acquainted with their goods and with their customers
    also.
Minstrels and messengers met him on a season
And held him an half year and eleven days longer.
Friars fetched him thence with their fine talking,
And robed him as a brother for his broad acquaintance.
Yet he has leave at his liking to leap from them,
And is welcome where he will, and dwells with them often.
Sir Simony and Civil sent to Rome
And put themselves through appeals into the pope's favour.
But Conscience accused them in the king's presence.   241

C*

All fled for fear and flew to hiding.
None but Mede maintained her station.
And to tell you truly, she trembled with terror,
Wept and wrung her hands when the guard attached her.

NOW Mede the Maid, with no more of her comrades
Than beadles and bailiffs, was brought to the
council.
 The king called a clerk—whom I cannot tell you—
To take Mede the Maid and minister to her comfort.
"I shall myself," said the king, "discover
Whom in the world she would love most dearly.
If she will do as I decree and take my counsel
I will forgive her her guilt, as God shall help me."

The clerk was courteous, and as the king bad him
Embraced Mede and brought her to her chamber,   10
Where mirth and minstrelsy were at Mede's pleasure.
Those who wait in Westminster worshipped her wholly.
All the gentle justices were joyous at her coming,
And bustled to the bower where their bride was dwelling,
To comfort her and be kind to her, with Clergy's permission.
They said, "Do not mourn, Mede, and make yourself wretched
We will commend you to the king, and procure his promise
To wed you where you will and whenever you wish it,
For all the craft and cunning of Conscience, I assure you!"
Mede was mild, and cried mercy to all of them.   20
For their great goodness the gave them severally
Cups of pure gold, goblets of silver,
Rings with rubies, and riches so numerous
That the least of her lovers had a golden crown piece.—
And then the lords took leave of their lady mistress.

Clerks came after to comfort her further
And bad her be blithe, "For we shall be your servants,
And as long as mede shall last be led by your wishes."
Then she promised and pledged them in polite speeches:
"I shall love you loyally; I shall lord you freely;   30

27

And in the consistory at court I shall call you by your titles.
No ignorance shall injure the initiates whom I favour.
I shall advance them first; for I am privy
Where the subtlest scholar struggles dishonoured."

Then a false confessor in friar's clothing
Bespoke her very softly like a shriving parson,
"Though the laity and the learned had lain with you always;
Though Falsehood had followed you fifty winters;
I should assoil you myself for a sackful of flour,
And be your faithful beadsman and bear your messages   40
To counsellors and clerics for Conscience' undoing."

Then Mede knelt for her misdeeds in the man's presence,
Shrived herself shamelessly for her sin's offences,
Told her tale, and made him take a noble
To be her beadsman and her broker also.

He assoiled her speedily and spoke as follows:
"We are working at a window that will cost us dearly.
If you would glaze the gable and engrave your name in it,
Easily would your soul ascend to heaven."
"If I were sure of that," she said, "I should never be wanting 50
As a friend, good friar, nor fail you ever
While you love lords who love lechery,
And blame no ladies who love it also.
It is a frailty of the flesh, your volumes tell you.
It is the course of kind by which we come hither.
Escape the slander, the sore is healed quickly;
Of the deadly seven it is the soonest pardoned.
Have mercy," said Mede, "on men who haunt it,
And I shall give you your cloister, gable your churches,
Whiten your walls, glaze windows,   60
Paint and picture and pay the workmen,

So that all men will say that I am a sister of your convent."

—But good men are not gravers. God has forbidden them
To write in windows of their worthy actions,
Lest pomp and pride of man should be painted in his churches.
Christ knows your conscience and the secret purpose,
The will and the way and to whom the wealth is owing.
Look well, you lords, and leave such practice,
This writing in windows of your worthy actions
And calling the witness of God's men when you give a beggar!
You may have your hire here and your heaven also: 71
N*esciat sinistra quid faciat dextra.*
Let not the left hand, late or early,
Discern the deed done by the right hand.
Thus the gospel commands that good men do almsdeeds.

Mayors and mace-men, who are means conjoining
The king and the commune in keeping the statutes,
Should punish in pillories and with the pains of press chairs
Brewers and bakers, butchers and cooks.
Of all mischievous men these are most harmful   80
To the poor people who buy at retail.

They poison the people with privy dealing;
They are retail robbers and rent wrackers;
They eat what poor people should put in their bellies.
If their traffic were true they would not timber so boldly,
Nor buy their great buildings—of that be certain.
Many misfortunes may fall on cities
Both by fire and flood, and all through false people
Who beguile good men and grieve them wrongly.
These cry on their knees that Christ may punish,   90
Here on earth or in hell hereafter,

Those who beguile them of their goods. And God plagues
   them
With fevers or foul evils or fire in their houses,
Or murrain, or other misfortune; and many times it happens
That the innocent are heard by the saints in heaven
Who pray for them to our Lord and our Lady with him
To grant the guilty the grace of amendment,
And to pass penance on earth without hell pains hereafter.
Then fire falls on false men's houses;
And for their guilt good men glow also.   100
We have often seen that because of a brewer
Buildings are burnt and bodies in them.
A candle guttered in an evil corner,
Flickered, and fell, and fired the alley.
Therefore mayors who make freemen should mind their duties,
Not hear the speech of silver, but spy and question,
Before a man were made free and a member of the city,
What manner of mystery or merchandise he practised.
It is surely dishonest that in city or borough
Usurers and wrackers for gifts and bribery   110
Should be enfranchised as freemen, and bear false titles.
But Mede the Maid has admonished the mayor
To take silver solace from all such merchants,
Or presents without pence, as pieces of silver,
Or rings, or other riches, for the wrackers' protection.—

"If you love me," said that lady, "love them all,
And suffer them to sell somewhat against reason."

—Solomon was a sage and spoke to the people
On the amendment of mayors and men of justice.
He gave them a good text, and I give it you: 120
Ignis devorabit tabernacula eorum, qui libenter accipiunt munera, etc.
To men of learning the meaning of this Latin

Is that fire shall fall and burn to blue ashes
The houses and the homes of all who covet
Gifts and concessions because of their offices.—

The king came from council and called for Mede,
And sent for her as speedily as his servants could take her
And lead her to their lord with heart's lightness.
The greeting of the king was given kindly.
To Mede the Maid he commenced as follows: 130
"Your works, woman, have been unwise often,
But they were never worse than when you embraced Falsehood.
Yet I forgive you your guilt and grant you my favour:
From now to your death-day do so no longer.
I have a knight called Conscience, come lately from beyond.
If he will have you for his wife, will you have him?"

"Yes, lord," said that lady, "the Lord forbid otherwise!
Hang me on high if I am not wholly at your bidding."
Then Conscience was called to come in the presence
Of the king and his council of clerks and laymen.   140
Conscience kneeled to the king and inquired humbly
What was his will and how he could serve him.
"Will you wed this woman," asked the king, "if I wish it?
She is fain of your fellowship and would live as your lady."

Conscience cried to the king, "Christ forbid it!
If I wed such a wife woe betide me!
Her faith is frail, and there is fickleness in her language,
She urges men to evil and to endless error,
And trust in her treasure has betrayed many.
Wives and widows and wantons are her pupils,   150
Who learn from her lechery and the love of presents.
Your father fell through her false counsel.
It has poisoned popes and impaired Holychurch.

There is no better bawd, by him who made me,
Though men sought all earth between hell and heaven!
She is loose in living and lavish in talking,
And as common as a cartway is to common villains,
To monks, to minstrels and to lepers in hedges.
Assizers and sompnours and such men praise her;   160
Sheriffs of shires would be shorn without her;
She loses men's lands and their lives after.
She lets prisoners pass, paying for them often,
And gives gold to the keepers, or groats at random
To unfetter the false to flee at pleasure.
She takes true men by the hair and ties them firmly
And hangs them in hatred, when they have harmed no man.
Curses in the consistory she accounts as rushes,
For she copes the commissary and clothes his servants.
She is assoiled as soon as she herself wishes,
And may do as much in a month only   170
As your secret seal in six score days.
She is privy with the pope; provisors know it;
And Sir Simony himself seals bulls and pardons.
She blesses bishops of debased learning,
She provides for parsons and gives priests permission
To have lewd lemans for their whole lifetime
Who beget beggars forbid by justice.
Where the king commends her the country is in peril;
For she is favourable to falsehood, and defiles truth often.

By Jesus, with her jewels your justices are ruined!   180
She lies against law and beleaguers him at his doorsill,
And faith may not come forth, her florins fly so thickly.
She leads the law at will, and has love-days at pleasure.
Sometimes men lose through her love what law might win
    them;
Sometimes poverty is perplexed, though he plead forever.

Without presents or pence she pleases no man,
For law lords it, and is loath to make an ending.

She brings great barons and burgesses to sorrow,
And care to all the commons who covet honour.
She couples Clergy and Covetousness together: 190
Such is the life of this lady! Now Lord give her sorrow!
And all maintainers of her men meet with ruin!
Poor men may have no power to complain, though they are
     smarting.
Such a mistress is Mede among men and angels."

Then Mede mourned and moaned to the sovereign
For a space to speak and soften his sentence.

The king granted it in gracious language:
"Excuse yourself if you can; I can speak no further;
For Conscience accuses you to condemn you forever."

"No, lord," said that lady, "believe him the less,   200
When the injury is judged as justice teaches.
Mede may help you when misfortune presses;
And you know, Conscience, that I care for no chiding,
Nor to hurt your honour with arrogant behaviour.
You know well, deceiver, if you would dare admit it,
That you have hung on my arm in an hundred places,
Or grasped for my gold, to give it at your pleasure.
—Now why you are wrathful is a wonder to me.

I might serve you still with a shower of presents,
And advance your honour beyond your dreaming.   210
But you have defamed me vilely before the sovereign,
Yet I never killed a king, nor counselled treason,
But saved myself and sixty thousand,

Here and elsewhere and in all nations.
If I dare tell it, the truth is that you
Have awed the hardy who would have fought bravely
And burnt and broken and beat down strongholds.
The king came to France, and Conscience checked him
From felling foes when fortune willed it
And destiny ordained, with our dear Lord's favour.   220
Conscience like a caitiff counselled the leaving
Of the heritage of France in the hands of the enemy.
Conscience had no cunning in the selling of a kingdom
Conquered by the commons; a kingdom or a duchy
May not be ransomed; for many are the portions
Of the folk who fought for it and followed the king's will.
The least lad who belongs to him, when the land is conquered,
Looks for a lordship or a large bounty,
And forever after to live a freeman.
Show me the sovereign who so robs his enemies   230
To help his army; or else orders
That his men may own what each captures.
If a king covets to conquer a people
I counsel him never to consult Conscience.
Never should Conscience be a constable of mine
Were I a crowned king," quoth Mede, "by Mary!
Nor marshal men of mine in the midst of battle.

I stayed by the sovereign to save his life,
And made mirth among his men to moderate their hardship.
I slapped them between the shoulders and strengthened   240
   their courage.
And they danced in the hope of having me at pleasure.
Had I been marshal of his men, by Mary in heaven,
I durst have laid my life—no less a wager—
He should have been lord of that land in length and breadth,
King of that country for his kindred's profit,

Each bright drop of his blood a baron's equal!

But Conscience like a coward counselled him hither,
To leave a lordship for a little silver,—
The richest realm that rain moistens!

It becomes the king to keep his people,   250
And to give meed to the men who meekly serve him,
To honor them all, and aliens, with his favours.
Meed makes him beloved and multiplies his power.
Emperors and earls and all knighthood
Have young squires and runners and reward them truly.
Popes and prelates take presents from others
And give meed to men to maintain their statutes.
We see how servants for service rendered
Take meed from masters who make pledges.
Beggars in bidding beg meed also;   260
Minstrels have mirth at meed's pleasure;
A king's men give meed to make peace in the kingdom;
Tutors and teachers take meed from their pupils;
Priests who preach to the people ask meed of heaven
And meat at meal time and mass-pennies;
All crafts and kinds crave meed for the prentice;
Merchants and meed must walk together;
And no meedless man may live longer."

Then the king said to Conscience, "By Christ, in my
     judgment,
Mede in justice must have the mastery!"   270

"No," said Conscience to the king, kneeling before him:
"There are two manners of meed, my lord, believe me!
God of his grace grants one in heaven
To all who do good works while life is with them.

Thus the prophet preaches and puts it in the psalter:
Domine, quis habitabit in tabernaculo tuo?
'Lord, who shall dwell in thy dwelling with thy dear saints
   in heaven,
Or rest on thy holy hill,' asks king David.
And David answers it himself, as the psalter tells us:
Qui ingreditur sine macula et operatur justitiam.   280
He who is of one colour and of one will,
He whose works are ruled by right and reason,
Who never uses the life of usury,
And lends poor men and pursues truth:
Qui pecuniam suam non dedit ad usuram, et munera super innocentem.
And all who help the innocent and hold with just men,
Who do them good without meed, and help the truthful,
Such men, my lord, shall have meed soonest
From God, at their great need, when they go hence.

But the other meed is measureless; masters desire it,   290
And maintain misdoers for meed's profit.
And thus says the psalter at the psalm's conclusion:
In quorum manibus iniquitates sunt, dextra eorum repleta est muneribus.
He who grasps for gold, so God help me,
Shall pay for it bitterly, or the Book lies.
Priests and parsons who are pleasure-seeking,
Who take meed and money for masses offered,
Take their hire here, as Matthew teaches:
Amen, Amen, recipiebant mercedem suam.
What labourers and the lowly take from their masters   300
Is by no means meed, but measurable wages.
There is no meed in merchandise, I make bold to say it;
But that is mere mutation, so much for so much.

Thus merit and meed are two modes or relations,
As direct and indirect differing, but moving

Safely and surely in sympathy with each other.
So adjective and substantive call for agreement
According to kind, case and number;
Each helps the other, and hence comes retribution,
The gift of God to all his creatures in loyalty,   310
The grace of a good end, and great joy hereafter:
Retribuere dignare, domine deus, omnibus nobis, etc.

Then the king asked Conscience to comment further
On the relations of direct and indirect action,
And on adjective and substantive, unknown to him in English.

"Direct relation," said Conscience, "is a record of Truth:
Quia antelatae rei est recordatium,
To follow backward and to find the foundation of strength,
And to stand forth strongly in the strength of the foundation,—
As agreement in kind, and case and number.   320
A loyal labourer believes that his master
Will pay him or have pity on him in pure truth—
Pay him for his performance or pity him for his failure,
And leave him for his labour all that truth warrants.
So hope springs from a whole heart; and honest labour
Seeks and pursues its substantive salvation,
Which is God, the ground of all, and a gracious antecedent.
He is in direct relation who is upright and truthful;
He agrees with Christ in kind: *verbum caro factum est;*
In case, *credere in ecclesia,* to believe in Holychurch;   330
In number, to rot and to arise, and to attain remission
And absolution and cleansing of our sins' offences,
With the last clause of our creed: in Christ to eternity.
This is the direct relation, as the right adjective and substantive
Accord in all kinds with their antecedent.
The indirect relation is in him who covets
To know and to acknowledge all natural being

Without agreement in case or a common number,
Though some are good and some not good, without a guide
 for either.
It is not reasonable or right to refuse my sire's surname 340
Since as son and servant I sue for his possession;
But whoever will wed with my worldly daughter
I will endow with a dowery of due and undue earnings.
So the indirect relation is to covet inly
An accordance in all kinds and in case and number
Without the care and the cost of common labour,
Without reason for reward and without recking of others.
The direct relation is a rightful custom,
As the claim of the king to have the commons at his service,
To follow him, to defend him and to find him counsel, 350
That all may love him and loyally accord with him.
So the commons claim of the king three kinds of duty,
Love, law and loyalty, in the lord antecedent,
Both their head and their king, holding with no party,
Standing as a stake sticking in the mire
Between two lands, for a true boundary.
But the most men in the land are in misdirection,
For their wish and will is their own profit,
Though it cost the king and the commune dearly.
Reason reproves such imperfect people, 360
And holds them unsteadfast, for case is wanting.
In these indirect relatives reckoning is careless
Of the course of case, if they catch the silver.
Profits are paid and the parties quarrel—
But if men have meed it makes little matter;
And souls go for shillings as fast as for nobles.
How Mede's clients accord never broke on her slumber.
But adjective and substantive is, as I told you,
A unity and accordance in case, kind and number.
Which means without metaphor no more nor less 370

Than that all manner of men, women and children
Should conform in one kind, believe in Holy Church,
And covet the case when they come to discretion,
Sigh for their sins and suffer hard penance
For that Lord's love who for our love was martyred,
Who so coveted our kind that he was called as we are,
Deus homo,
And betook himself into our number, now and forever,
Qui in caritate manet in deo manet, et deus in eo.
So man and mankind are in the manner of a substantive, 380
As *hic et haec homo,* asking an adjective.
Of three true terminations: *trinitas unus deus,*
Nominativo, pater et filius et spiritus sanctus.

Did you never read *Regum,* recreant lady,
Where vengeance fell on Saul and on his children?
God said to Saul through Samuel the prophet
That Agog of Amalek and all his people
Should die for a deed done by their fathers.
Then Samuel said to Saul, "God himself commands you
To obey his bidding and fulfill his wishes: 390
'Go to Amalek with your host, and what you find—destroy it!
Burn men and beasts, burn them to ashes,
Widows and wives, women and children,
All that moves and is immovable, and all you may find there—
Burn it! Bear nothing off! and you shall speed the better.'"
But because he coveted their goods and granted the king life
And forbore to slay his beasts, as the Bible witnesses,
And opposed the words and warning of the prophet,
God said to Samuel that Saul should perish
And all his seed for one sin have a shameful ending.   400
Meed made the misfortune that Saul suffered,
And made God hate him and his heirs forever after.
I may not mention the moral of this judgement;

I will make no end lest it annoy your subjects.
For as the way of the world is with the powerful
He who tells the truth is blamed the soonest.

I, Conscience, conceive, for Common Wit taught me,
That reason should reign and rule the kingdoms.
And what Agog had shall hap to others.
Samuel shall slay him, and Saul be convicted,   410
And David will be diademed and daunt all.
One Christian king shall keep the earth.

Mede shall no more be master, as at present,
But love and lowliness and loyalty shall together
Be masters of mankind, and maintain truth.

Trespassers against truth shall be taken forcefully,
And loyalty alone read law upon them.
No sergeant in their service shall wear a silk hood,
Nor fix fur on the robes of formal pleading.
The meed of misdoers makes many nobles,   420
And rules the realms and overrules knighthood.

But the love of kind and Conscience shall come together
And make a labourer of law, and love shall arise
And such a peace and perfect truth be with the nations
That Jews will wonder whether finally
Moses or the Messiah has come among them,
And wonder in their hearts how men are so true.

All who bear baselards, broad swords or lances,
Axes or hatchets or any other weapons,
Will be doomed to die unless they smithy them   430
Into sickle or scythe, share or coulter:
Conflabunt gladios suos in vomeres, etc.

Men shall practice ploughing, picking or spading,
Spin or spread dung, or sloth shall destroy them.

Priests and parsons shall take *placebo* for their hunting,
And ding upon David daily till even.
If any one haunt hunting or hawking,
His boasted benefice shall be taken from him.
Neither king nor knight, constable nor mayor
Shall crush the commons or give them court summons,   440
Or put them in panels and pledge them for justice;
One doom shall be dealt after the deed is committed,
With mercy or no mercy, as truth may will it.
The king's court and the common court, the consistory and
    the chapter,
Shall all be one court, and no baron be justice.
Then True-tongue shall come, a trusty man who betrayed me
    never,
Battles shall there be none, and no man bear weapons,
And the smith who smithies one shall be stricken with it:
Non levabit gens contra gentem gladium, etc.
But before this fortune befall men they shall find the worst,
By six suns and a ship and half a sheaf of arrows,   451
And the middle of the moon shall make the Jews Christians,
And Saracens at that sight shall sing *Gloria in excelsis,*
And Mahomet and Mede meet with disaster.
For, *melius est bonum nomen quam divitiae multae.*"

Mede was wrathful as the wind in an instant,
"I cannot talk Latin," she cried, "but you clerks should
    remember
What Solomon says in the Book of Sapience:
They who give gifts get the victory,
And have the worship of others, as Holywrit teaches: 460
Honorem adquiret qui dat munera, etc.

He who gives gifts shall acquire honour."

"I believe, lady," said Conscience, "that the Latin is truthful;
But you are like the lady who read a lesson in her chamber
With *omnia probate*, and that pleased her entirely,
For the line was no longer where the leaf ended.
But if she had looked at the other half on the leaf following
She would have met with more words, and an altered meaning:
Quod bonum est tenete; a text that Truth has written.
And so fared you, Madam. You could read no further   470
Though you looked on Sapience sitting in your study.
That text that you have taken is good for rulers;
But you wanted a cunning clerk who could turn the page.
If you search in Solomon you shall find thereafter
A text that is trying to all who take your presents;
That is, *animam autem aufert accipientium, etc.*
This is the tail of the text that you have taken to witness:
He who wins honour and worship at Mede's giving
Will see to the same measure his soul in bondage."

EASE," said the king, "I will suffer you no longer.
You shall be reconciled strictly and serve me
together.
I command you to kiss her," said the king to
Conscience.

"No, by Christ," said Conscience, "rather dismiss me.
Unless Reason direct me I would rather die."
"I command," said the king to Conscience hastily,
"That you make ready to ride and fetch Reason to London.
Command him to come to my council speedily.
He shall rule my realm and direct me wisely
Regarding Mede and many others and what man should   10
   wed her,
And account with you, Conscience, so Christ help me,
In how you lead the learned and the laity of my nation."

"I am glad of that agreement ," said Conscience quickly,
And he rode straight to Reason and rounded him in his ear,
Gave the king's message, and as quickly left him.
"Rest a while," said Reason, "while I make ready for our
   riding."
He called his knave Cato, courteous in his language,
And also Tom True⸱tongue⸱tell⸱me no⸱stories⸱
Nor⸱lies⸱to⸱laugh⸱at for⸱I⸱loved⸱them⸱never;
"And set my saddle upon Suffer⸱till⸱I⸱know⸱my⸱season; 20
We shall harness him well with Wise⸱word's girdle,
And hang on him the heavy bridle to hold his head lower,
For he will whinny twice ere he come to town."

Then Conscience cantered quickly to London;
And as Reason rode beside him they whispered together
Of the mastery that Mede maintains on earth.
One Waryn Wisdom and Witty his brother

Followed them fast, for they had business
In the exchequer and in chancery where they discharged their
    practice.
They rode fast that Reason might rule in their dealing,   30
And save them for silver from shame and trouble.

Conscience was well acquainted with their covetous natures,
And bad Reason ride faster and reck nothing of them:
"Their words are wily and they dwell with Mede's servants.
Wherever wrath and wrangling are they will win silver;
But wherever love and loyalty are they will keep their distance.
Contritio et infelicitas in viis eorum, etc.
They give not the wing of a goose for God Almighty.
Non est timor Dei ante oculos eorum, etc.
God knows, they would do more for a dozen chickens,   40
Or for as many capons, or for an horse-load of oats,
Than for the love of our Lord and all the saints in heaven!
So Reason, for all their riches, let them ride alone.
Conscience cannot know them, nor Christ, I wager!"
Then Reason rode fast, at a right good gallop,
And Conscience was his guard, till they came to London.

Then the king came courteously to greet Reason.
He sat him between himself and his son on the benches,
And they conversed gravely for a great while together.
Then Peace came to Parliament and proffered his charges. 50
Wrong against his will took his wife from him
And ravished Rose, Reginald's sweetheart,
And Margaret of her maidenhead, without mercy upon them.
"His prowlers prey on pigs and ganders,
I am so filled with fear that fight with him I dare not,
I bear no silver in safety to Saint Giles on-the-Down-Lands.
He watches well when I carry money.
When I am plodding on the path he is prying about it,

Or robs me and rifles me if I ride softly.
He is bold to borrow and a bad payer. 60
He borrowed my bay horse but he never returned her,
Nor a farthing for her, for all my pleading.
He maintains his men in murdering my servants;
He forestalls my fairs; he fights in my markets;
He breaks my barn door; bears off my provisions;
And tenders me but a tally for ten quarter of oats.
More than this, he beats me, and lies with my servant;
And through him I have no hardihood even to look about me."

The king credited his words, for Conscience told him
That Wrong was a wicked man who brought woe to many.

Then Wrong was afraid, and wished Wisdom 71
To make peace with pence, and proffered him freely:
"If I had the love of my lord the king, little would I trouble,
Though Peace and his party complained to him forever."

Then one Wisdom and Sir Waryn the Witty,
Since all Wrong's works were weighed against him,
Warned him well with their wise counsel:
"Whoever is wilful raises wrath often.
I see this in yourself, and you shall find it also.
But if Mede will make up with them your misfortune is over.
Both life and land lie in her favour." 81
Then Wrong wooed Wisdom eagerly,
And bad him make peace with his pence, in privy payments.
Wisdom and Witty next went together
With Mede in the midst to get mercy from the judges.
Peace put forward a pate that was all bloody:
"God knows, I got it without guile or mischief.
Conscience and the Commons can tell you truly."

Wisdom and Witty were still working
To overcome the king with coin, if might be.　　　90
The king swore by Christ and by his crown together
That Wrong should suffer for his shameful practice.
He commanded a constable to cast him in irons:
"He shall not see his feet once for seven years."

"God knows," said Wisdom, "this is not prudent!
If he make amends, Bail must have him,
And be a pledge for his payment, and buy him mercy,
And amend what is misdone—and no more trouble."

Witty said the same, and seconded his measure:
"Better that bail bring baseness to an ending,　　　100
Than baseness be beaten, and bail none the better."
Then Mede remembered him, and asked mercy for him,
And gave Peace a present of pure gold;
"Have this, man, of me," she said, "to amend your trouble.
I will wager it for Wrong that he will harm you no longer."

Then peace piteously prayed to his sovereign
To have mercy on the man who mistreated him so often:
"He has waged me well, as Wisdom taught him;
And I forgive him his guilt with a good charity.
If the king assent, I can speak no further.　　　110
Mede has made me amends, and no more is due me."

"No," cried the king, "so Christ help me,
Wrong shall not get away! I will hear further.
If he leapt off so lightly he would laugh and scorn us,
And be so much the bolder to beat my servants.
Unless Reason have ruth on him, he shall rest in my prison,
And for as long as he lives, unless lowliness bail him."

Some men addressed Reason to have ruth on that villain,
And counselled the king and Conscience also,
Moving that Mede should make pledges.   120
"Address me not," said Reason, "to have ruth on any
Till lords and ladies love truth wholly,
And leave all licence, listening to it or speaking it;
Till the purflings of Pernel are put in her closet;
And cherishing of children is chastizing with branches;
Till hypocrites' holiness is held at nothing;
Till the covetousness of clerks is to clothe and feed poor men;
Till religious roamers *recordare* in their cloisters,
As Saint Benet bad them, and Bernard and Francis;
Till preachers' preaching is proved in their living;   130
Till the king's council is the common profit;
Till the bishop's bay horse buys the beggar's lodging;
Till their hawks and their hounds help religious poor folk;
Till Saint James is sought as I assign it—
In prisons, and poor huts, where the poor are lying—
Till no man go to Galis unless he go forever;
Till no runner to Rome bears, for robbers on the highway,
Silver over seas, with the sign of the kingdom,
Graven or ungraven, gold or silver,
Or forfeit his fee, if they find it at Dover,—   140
Except merchants and their men, or messengers with letters,
Provisors or priests or penitent sinners."
"Now," said Reason, "by the rood, no ruth shall I show you
While Mede has the mastery in the moot hall with us.
I might show examples that I have seen elsewhere,
But I shall speak for myself; if so it happened
That I were king and crowned, and the keeper of a kingdom,
No wrong in the world which I might witness
Should within my power be unpunished, on peril of my
    salvation.
None, so God save me, would get grace by favour,   150

Nor would I have mercy for Mede, unless meekness bad it.
For the man *Nullum Malum* met with *Impunitum*,
And bad *Nullum Bonum* be *Irremuneratum*.

Let your confessor, sir king, construe this without glossing;
And if your works witness it, my ears are my wager
That law shall be a labourer and led afield to dunging,
And love shall lead your land to your best liking."

Clerks who were confessors gathered themselves together
To construe this clause to the king's profit,
And not for the comfort of the commune or the king's   160
    conscience.
Mede winked in the moot hall on men of justice,
And they leapt to her laughing, and many left Reason.

Waryn Wisdom was winking at this lady,
And said, "Madam, I am your man, whatever my mouth
    jangles;
I fall upon florins," he said, "and fail in speaking."

The upright recognized that Reason spoke truly,
And with courteous words Witty commended him.
Most men in the moot hall, and many of the mighty,
Took Meekness for the master and Mede for a traitor.

Love held her lightly, and loyalty at less,   170
And spoke on high so that all the hall heard it:
"If any has her for a wife for her wealth and treasure,
Knock off my nose, if he is not known for a cuckold!"

Then Mede mourned and made herself wretched,
For the most common in that court called her dishonest.
But an assizer and a sompnour sued her closely.

And a sheriff's clerk scorned the assembly:
"For I have often," he said, "helped you on trial,
And you never rewarded me a rush in bribery."

First the king called Conscience and then Reason,   180
And recorded what Reason had rightfully witnessed.
He looked moodily at Mede; he was moved deeply;
And was wrathful at law, for Mede had almost ruined it.
He said, "Through your law, as I believe, I lose many
     payments;
Mede overmasters law, and much truth is thwarted.
But Reason shall reckon with you if I reign longer.
By this day! he shall deal you the doom that you merit.
Mede shall not maintain you, by Mary in heaven!
I will have loyalty in law, and leave your jangling,   189
And as most have well witnessed, Wrong shall be punished."
Then Conscience said to the king, "Unless the commune
     wish it,
By my head, it is hard to have it settled
That all your liege lords shall be led in justice!"

"By him who rose on the rood," said Reason to the sovereign,
"Unless I rule your realm so, rend me to pieces!
If all be obedient, be of my counsel."

"I will assent," said the king, "by Saint Mary, my lady,
When my council is gathered from the clerks and barons.
Reason shall not readily ride from me,
For as long as I live I shall never leave him."   200
"I am ready," said Reason, "to remain with you forever.
If Conscience is of your council I care for no better."

"And I grant," said the king, "and God forbid failure,
That as long as life lasts we shall live together."

D

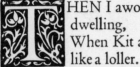 HEN I awoke, God knows, on Cornhill in my
dwelling,
When Kit and I were in a cottage, and I clothed
like a loller.
But I was little loved, believe me truly,
By lollers of London and lewd hermits,
For I wrote of those wretches as Reason taught me.
When I had come upon Conscience, Reason met me,
In a hot harvest when I had good health
And limbs to labour with, but when I loved good living,
And to do nothing but to dine, to drink and to sleep.
So, whole in health and hale in spirit,   10
Reason met me, roaming in memory.

"Can you serve," he said, "or sing in churches,
Or cock hay in my harvest, or handle a hay-fork,
Mow or mound it or make sheaves or bindings,
Reap, or be an head reaper, and rise early,
Or have an horn and be an hayward, and be out till morning,
And keep my corn in my croft from pickers and stealers?
Or make shoes, or sew cloth, or tend sheep or cattle,
Or make hedges, or harrow, or drive geese, or be swineherd?
Or can you work at any craft which the commune calls for,
To be means of livelihood to the bed-ridden?"   21

"Surely," I said, "so God help me,
I am too weak to work with scythe or sickle,
And too tall, trust me, to stoop earthward,
And work for any while at workman's labour."

"Have you lands to live by," said Reason, "or liberal parents
Who find you food? for you seem idle.
Are you a spendthrift who must spend, or a spill-time fellow?

Or do you beg your bread about door yards?
Or feign poverty on Fridays or on feastdays in churches?—30
Which is a loller's life, and little valued
Where righteousness rewards the rights of others.
Reddit unicuique juxta opera sua.
Or are you broken, as may be, in body or in a member?
Or maimed through some mishap, and may so be licensed?"

"When I was young," said I, "many years past,
My father and my friends furnished my schooling,
Till I was trained truly in the doctrine of Scripture,
In what is best for the body, as the Book tells us,
And safest for the soul—in such may I continue!   40
Yet by my faith, I never found, since my friends perished,
Any life that I liked out of these long garments.
If I should live by labour and a livelihood of my making,
I should live by learning, and labour in my calling:
In eadem vocatione in qua vocati estis, manete,
But I live in London and upon London also.
The tools that I have taken to toil for my living
Are my *pater noster* and my primer, *placebo* and *dirige,*
My seven psalms, and sometimes my psalter.
So I sing for the souls of such as help me;   50
And those who furnish my food find me also
A welcome when I come, for a while, monthly,
Now with him and now with her, and so I go begging
Without bag or bottle, but with my belly only.
And also, Sir Reason, it seems to my thinking,
Men should constrain no clerks to common labour.
For by the law of Leviticus, which our Lord established,
Clerks who are crowned should in course of reason
Neither serve, nor sweat, nor swear at inquests,
Nor fight in the van, to the foes grievance: 60
Non reddas malum pro malo.

Those are heirs of heaven who have such a crowning,
And in the church or choir are Christ's ministers.
Dominus pars hereditatis mihi; et alibi: Clementia non constringit.
It becomes clerks to serve Christ only,
And uncrowned knaves to cart and labour.
No clerk should be crowned who comes from other
Than franklins or freemen and folks who are wedded.
Bondmen and bastards and beggars' children
Should live as labourers; and lord's children   70
Serve God and good men as degree commands them.
Some should sing masses; others sit at writing,
Rule and receive what Reason should distribute.
But since boys of bondmen have become bishops,
Since boys of bastards have become archdeacons,
Since soap-makers and their sons have knighthood for silver,
Since lords have become labourers laying lands to mortgage
For the right of the realm, and riding against our enemies,
For the good of the Commons' and the king's honour,   79
Since monks and nuns, who should be mendicants' patrons,
Have raised relatives to knighthood, and received knight-fees:
Popes and patrons decline poor knighthood,
And choose Simon's son for the sanctuary's keeper;
Holy living and loving have been long from them,
And will be, till this is outworn, or otherwise altered.

So do not rebuke me wrongfully, Reason, I pray you,
For I know in my conscience at what Christ would have me
    labour.
Prayer of a perfect man, and penance with discretion,
Is the loyal labour in which our Lord takes pleasure.
Non de solo, I said, for surely *vivit homo*   90
Nec in pane et pabulo, the *pater noster* witnesses.
Fiat voluntas tua furnishes us with all things."

Conscience said, "By Christ, I cannot grant this reason,
For it seems to me to be no perfection to be a city beggar,
Unless you be an obediencer to a priory or to a minster."

"This is certain," I said, "and sadly must I confess it.
I have tost time away and time wasted.
And yet I hope, as he who has often bargained,
And lost and lost, but at last happened
To buy such a bargain that he was blest forever,   100
And held his loss at a leaf beside his latter fortune,
Such wealth had he won through the words of his Master:
Simile est regnum coelorum thesauro abscondito in agro, etc.
Mulier quae invenit dragmam, etc.
So I hope to have from him who is Almighty
A glimpse of his grace, and begin a season
When all times of my time will turn to profit."

"I counsel you," quoth Reason, "to begin quickly
The life which is loyal and lawful in the spirit."
"Yea, and continue it," said Conscience,—And I   110
    came to the church.

I came to the church to do God honour,
Before the cross on my knees I knocked my breast,
Sighing for my sins, saying my *pater noster*,
Weeping and wailing till I went to sleep.

Then I saw much more than I have yet mentioned.
For I saw the field full of folk, which I before witnessed,
And Reason making ready to remonstrate with the people.
He placed his cross before the king, and commenced a sermon.

He proved that the pestilences were for penance only,
And that the southwest wind on a Saturday at even   120

Was plainly to punish the pride of sinners.
Pear trees and plum trees were puffed to splinters,
In meaning, you men, that you must do better;
Beeches and broad oaks were blown to ruin,
Torn and overturned, in token of the terror
Lest deadly sin destroy you at Doomsday wholly.
On such matters I might mumble longer,
But I shall say what I saw, and so God help me:
How plainly Reason preached before the people.
He bad Waster go to work where he was most wanted,   130
And win what he had wasted with honest labour.
He prayed Pernel to put off her finery,
And keep it in a coffer in case of hardship.
He taught Tom Stow to take two cudgels
And fetch Felice home from the woman's penance.
He warned Watt that his wife was guilty,
That her hat was worth half a mark, his hood not worth a
    groat.
He bad one Bet cut boughs aplenty
And beat Betar with them if she would not labour.
And then he charged chapmen to chastize their children,140
To let no wealth weaken them while they were tender,
Nor in the plight of pestilence to please them over-fondly.
My sire said to me and so did my mother,
That the dearer the child the more discipline is needed;
And Solomon, who wrote Sapience, said it also:
Qui parcit virgae, odit filium.
The English of this Latin, for whoever will know it,
Is that he who spares the stick spoils his children.

And then he prayed prelates and priests with them:
"What you preach the people you should prove in your living;
Put it in practice and it will profit you forever.   151
If you live by your lore we shall believe you the better."

Then he reasoned with religious orders that their rules should
    be followed;
"Lest the king and his council cut your allowance,
And be stewards in your stead till you are established justly."
He counselled the king to love the commune dearly,
"They are your treasure in treason and treacle in peril."
And then he prayed the pope to have pity on Holy Church,
And before he gave a grace to govern himself accordingly.
"You who keep laws, covet truth rather   160
Than gold or other gifts, and God will accept you.
God knows not, nor any saint in heaven,
The man who betrays truth, he tells us in the gospel:
Amen dico vobis, nescio vos.
And you who seek Saint James and the saints in Rome,
Seek Saint Truth, who may save all men;
Qui cum patre et filio, may fortune favour
All who assent to my sermon." Thus said Reason.

Then Repentance ran and rehearsed his message;
And Will began to weep and water to flow from him: 170

SUPERBIA
Pernel proud heart fell prone before him,
And lay long ere she looked up, and cried, "Lord, mercy!"
And vowed to the father who fashioned all men
That she would unsew her shift, and with a shirt of horse hair
Enfeeble her flesh that was fierce in sinning.
"No high heart shall bolden me. I shall hold myself humble,
And suffer men to scorn me, and so I did never.
But now I make myself meek. Mercy is my petition.
For all this I have hated in my heart of hearts."

LUXURIA
Then Lechery said, "Alas," and cried to our Lady   180

To put mercy for his misdeeds between his soul and the Father;
And said that on Saturday for seven years after
He should drink only with the duck and dine but once.

INVIDIA

With an heavy heart Envy asked pardon,
And commenced sorrowfully to say *mea culpa*.
He was pale as a pebble, as if palsy shook him,
And clothed in a coarse suit—I cannot describe it,
Short coat and curtle, with a cutlass beside him.
The foresleeves of his frock were of friar's clothing.
His cheeks lowered and looked as foully   190
As a leek that has long lain in sunshine.
His body was bursting with wrath; he bit lips fiercely,
And clenched hands hard, as if he hoped finally
In words or works to wreck his anger.
The words that he wrung forth were tongued as adders,
Backbiting and besmearing, bearing false witness,
Chiding and challenging were his chief diet.
And this was all his courtesy wherever he wandered.

"I would shrive myself," said this shrew, "and for shame I
    dare not.
I would be more glad, by God, that Gyb had misfortune   200
Than to win this week a wey of the cheese of Essex.
I have a neighbour near me whom I annoy often
And belie him to lords to make him lose silver,
And to make his friends foes through my false speaking.
His gain and his good luck grieve me sorely.
Between house and house I sow hatred,
So that life and limb are lost through my whispers.
When I meet at market the man whom I envy
I greet him graciously or with friendly manners
And fear to offend him, for he is the stronger.   210

If I had might and mastery, God knows my wishes!

When I should come before the cross kneeling in the churches,
And pray for the people as the priest teaches,
For pilgrims and for palmers and all people after them—
Then I cry on my knees, "Christ give them sorrow,
Who took off my tankard and tore my linen!"

Then my eyes wander away from the altar
And note how Elene has a new jacket.
I wish it were mine and all its web with it.
I laugh when men lose for it delights my humour;   220
I wail when men win, and weep in misery.
I declare they do ill when I do worse,
And mortally hate the man who reminds me of my offences.
I wish that everyone were my own servant,
For he who has more than I angers me sorely.
So I live without love, like a low mongrel,
And all my body bursts from the bitterness of my anger.

Many years I might not eat as a man normally,
For envy and an evil will sit evilly on the stomach.
May no sugar nor sweet food assuage my swelling,   230
No *diapenidion* disgorge it from me,
Nor shrift, nor shame, without scraping my palate?"

"Yes, readily," said Repentance, and addressed him wisely,
"Sorrow for sin is the soul's salvation."

"I am sorry," he said; "I am seldom otherwise.
And this makes me so meagre, that I miss vengeance!
I have been with burgesses who dwell in London,
And made backbiting a broker to blame merchandise.
When he sold and I not, I was always ready
    D*

To lie and to lower and to libel my neighbours,   240
Their words, their works, and whatever I imagined.
Now conscience grips me that I committed such evil.
Lord, before I leave life, for the love of thyself,
Grant me, good Lord, some grace for amendment!"

IRA

Now Wrath awoke with white eyes staring,
Snivelling through his nose, and with his neck hanging.

"I am Wrath," he said, "I was once a friar,
Grafting and grubbing in the garden of our convent.
Also on lectors and on limitours my lies were grafted;
And bore leaves of lowly speech for lords and ladies;   250
And later blossomed abroad in bowers of confession;
And now the fruit is fallen; and the folk more willing
To show their shrifts to them than to shrive them to their
    parsons.
Now that parsons have perceived that friars part the winnings,
Possessioners preach and deprave the friars,
And friars find them in fault, as the folk witness;
And when both preach to the people in places without
    number,
I, Wrath, walk beside them, and win them with my teaching.
So these spirituals speak, each despising the other,
Until they are both beggars and live by my spirituality,   260
Or else are rich and ride through the country.
I, Wrath, never rest from roving forever
After these false folk, for such is my pleasure.

My aunt is a nun; yea, and an abbess;
She would sooner swoon and die than suffer discomfort.
I have been cook in her kitchen and the convent's servant
Many a long month, and served monks also.

I was pottage maker to the prioress and to other poor ladies;
And made them junkets of jangling that dame Joan
　　was a bastard,
That dame Clarice was a knight's daughter, but her　　270
　　father was a cuckold,
That dame Pernel was a priest's wench,—prioress will she be
　　never,
For she had a child in cherry time; all our chapter knew it.

I, Wrath, made their warts of wicked speeches,
Till "you lie" and "you lie" leapt out together,
And each hit the other under the cheekbone.
Had they knives, by Christ, they would have killed each other!
I am wont to worship with wives and widows,
Imparked in pews; and the parson may tell you
How little I loved Lettice-at-the-Hedge-Row,　　279
For when she had holy bread before me my heart began to alter.

I might go among monks, but many times I shun them,
For they have many sturdy spirits to spy into my doings,
As the prior and the subprior and our own *pater abbas*.
If I tell any tales, they take them to the council,
And make me fast Fridays on bread and water.
I am chastened like a child in the chapter chamber,
And beaten on the bare back and no breech to save me.
So I have no liking to live among them.
I dine there on dry fish and drink ale that is feeble,
And if wine comes once, and I drink wine at even,　　290
I have the flux of a foul mouth five days after.
All the wickedness that I hear of any of our brethren
I carry to our cloister, and all our convent knows it."

"Now repent," said Repentance, "and repeat no longer
Any news that you may know of, naturally or by connivance.

And do not drink over delicately, nor too deep neither,
Lest will and wrath be worse than ever.
Esto sobrius," he said, and assoiled me afterwards,
And bad me weep for my wickedness and wish amendment.

AVARICIA

Next came Covetousness; I cannot describe him,   300
So hungry and so hollow were Sir Harvey's features.
He was beetle browed; his lips bulged also;
He had two bleared eyes, like a blind hag.
His cheeks lolled like a leathern wallet;
The skin sunk below the chin, shivering and aged;
His beard was beslobbered with bacon like a bondman's.
He wore an hood on his head, a lousy hat above it,
And a tawny tabard of twelve years' service,
Tattered and dirty, and full of lice creeping.
Unless a louse were a good leaper   310
He could never have crawled on a cloth so threadbare.
"I have been covetous," said this caitiff, "I confess it freely.
For sometimes I have served Sim-at-the-hedges,
And was plighted his prentice for the profit of his trading.
Leaf by leaf I learned lying,
And wily weighing was my first lesson.
To Wye and Winchester I went in fair-time
With all manner of merchandise, as my master bad me.
Unless the grace of guile had gone with my dealing
The stuff had lain seven years unsold, so God help me!   320

Then I practised my primer in a party of drapers,
And learned to stretch the selvage so that it looked longer.
With striped silks I studied a lesson.
I pierced them with a packneedle and plaited them together,
And put them in a press and pinned them fast,
Till ten yards or twelve told thirteen in the total.

My wife was a webster and wove woollens.
She spoke to the spinners to spin it thinner.
But the pound that she payed by passed by a quarter
My own weight, if you weighed rightly.   330

I bought her barley malt, and she brewed it for the traffic;
Penny ale and pudding ale were poured together
For labourers and poor folk;—she laid that aside.
The best was in the ben or in my bed-chamber;
Whoever took the bung from that, bought it thereafter
A gallon for a groat, God wot, or dearer.
And yet it came out by cup-fulls, craftily measured.
Rose the Retailer was her right name.
She had worked at huckstering all her lifetime.

But I swear now, so may I thrive, to sin no longer,   340
And never to weigh wickedly or use wily practice;
But take the highway to Walsingham and my wife with me,
And bid the rood of Bromeholm bring me from debt."

"Did you ever repent?" asked Repentance, "and make
    restitution?"
"Yes, once I inned," said he, "among an host of tradesmen,
I rose when they were at rest and rifled their bundles."

"That was no restitution," said Repentance, "but robber's
    dealing.
You are the more worthy of an halter for thieving
Than for all the sins which you have confessed already."

"I thought rifling was restitution; I am no reader or scholar;
I know no French, in faith, but from the farthest end of   351
    Norfolk."

"Have you used usury," asked Repentance, "in your lifetime?"
"No, surely," he said, "except that in my boyhood
I learned my lesson in the Lombard Jewry:
To weigh pence and pennies, and pare the heaviest;
To lend it for love of the cross; or to lay a wager and lose it:—
So I worded the deed, if his day should be broken.
I have more manors through arrears than through *miseretur et commodat.*
I have sold my stock to serve lords and ladies,
And been their brokers after, and bought it myself.   360
Mortages and margins are matter for my handicraft.
I lend men who will lose a lip off each noble.
I brought Lombard letters from London to Rome,
Took gold by the tally here, there told them less for it."

"Did you ever lend lords for leave to swindle?"
"Yea, I have lent lords who never loved me after;
And made many a knight a mercer or a draper,
Who never paid for his prenticeship a pair of gauntlets!"

"Have you pitied poor men who needed to borrow?"
"I have as much pity of poor men as a pedlar has of cats.   370
He will kill them if he can, from coveting to skin them."

"Do you deal to neighbours drink and provisions?"
"A cur in the kitchen," said he, "is held courteous as I am.
Among my nearest neighbours my name is the blackest."

"Unless you repent soon," said Repentance, "may you never
   in this world
Have God's grace to spend your goods wisely.
Nor your heirs after you have joy in your treasure,
Nor executors spend wisely the silver that you leave them;
And what was won wrongly be wasted by the wicked!

Were I a friar in the house of good faith and charity,   380
Your gifts would not cope us nor complete our chapel,
Nor add a penny to my pittance, by my soul's safety,—
Not for the best book in our house, though bright gold were
    the pages!
If I saw you certainly to be such as your confession,
Or could hear this honestly by some other practice.
Servus es alterius, cum fercula pinguia quaeris;
Pane tuo potius vescere, liber eris.

You are an unkind creature, I cannot assoil you
Till you make restitution and a reckoning with all men;
Till Reason enroll in the register of heaven   390
That you have made each man good, I may not absolve you.
Non dimittitur peccatum, donec restituatur oblatum.
For all who have your goods, I have God to witness,
Will be held at the high doom to help you to restore them.
Let who sees not that this is so, seek in the psalter,
In *Miserere mei, Deus,* whether my meaning is true:
Ecce enim veritatem dilexisti, etc.
No workman in this world will thrive with your winnings,
Cum sancto sanctus eris—construe me that in English."

The wretch was wild, and would have hung himself,   400
Had not Repentance reasoned with him and reassured him
    mildly:
"Have mercy in your mind, and let your mouth implore it.
For God's mercy is greater than all his other creatures:
Misericordia eius super omnia opera eius, etc.
And all the wickedness of this world, in men's works or
    thinking,
Is no more to God's mercy than a spark in the ocean:
Omnis iniquitas quantum ad misericordiam Dei, est quasi scintilla in
    medio maris.

Keep mercy in your mind and cast merchandise behind you.
You have no good cause to gain a living
Unless with your tongue or with your two hands.   410
All the goods that you have gained began in falsehood;
And as long as you live by them you lend nothing, but borrow.
If you know no man nor any heir to receive it,
Pay it to the bishop and beseech him duly
To possess it himself, as best for your safety.
For he shall answer for you at the high doom;
For you and for many more that man shall give reckoning.
Believe in no other law than in what in Lent he taught you,
And in what he lent you of our Lord's goods to deliver you
    from sin."

GULA

Now Gluttony gets him on his way to confession,   420
And shuffles churchward to show his offences.
But Breton the brewster bad him good morrow,
And asked him with that whither he was going:
"To holy church," said he, "to hear the service,
And so I will be shriven and sin no longer."
"I have good ale, gossip; Glutton, will you try it?"
"What have you?" he asked,—"any hot spices?"
"I have pepper and peonies," she said, "and a pound of garlic,
And a farthing worth of fennel seed for fasting seasons."
Then Gluttony goes in with a great crowd after: 430
Cis the shoemaker sat on the benches,
Watt the warner, and his wife beside him,
Tim the tinker and two of his prentices,
Hick the hackneyman and Hugh the needle-seller,
Clarice of Cockslain and the clerk of the parish,
Daw the ditcher and a dozen others—
Sir Piers of Predie and Pernelle of Flanders,
A ribeck player, a rat catcher, a raker of Cheapside,

A rope maker, a rider, and Rose the dish-seller,
Godfry of Garlickhithe and Griffen the Welshman,   440
And an whole heap of upholsterers, early in the morning,
Gave Glutton good cheer and good ale aplenty.

Clement the cobbler cast off his jacket
And played New Fair, and put it to wager.
Hick the hackneyman threw his hood after it,
And bad Bet the butcher be of his party.
Then venders were found to value the wager,
For he who had the hood should have amends for his jacket.
Two were up in a hurry, whispering together,
And appraising these pennyworths apart in a corner.   450
For Conscience' sake they could not agree peaceably
Till Robin the rope-maker arose for justice
And named himself an umpire, so that no one should quarrel,
And the bargain be tried between the three of them.

Hick the hackneyman had the jacket,
In agreement that Clement should cup him nobly,
And have the hackneyman's hood, and hold himself contented;
He who first repented should rise up afterwards,
And greet Sir Glutton with a gallon of ale.

Then there was laughing and lowering and "let the cup go it,"
And sitting till evensong and singing catches,   461
Till Glutton had gulped a gallon and a gill.
His guts began to grumble like greedy porkers.
He had pissed a pot in a *pater noster* minute,
He blew the round bugle at his ridge bone's bottom,
So that all who heard that horn held their nose after,
And wished it had been wiped with a wisp of rushes.

He could neither step nor stand till a staff held him,

And then began to go like a gleeman's mongrel,
Sometimes aside and sometimes backwards,   470
Like one who lays lures to lime wild-fowl.

As he drew to the door all dimmed before him,
He stumbled on the threshold and was thrown forwards.
Clement the cobbler caught him by the stomach
To lay him on his lap, but he lifted badly;
Glutton, the great churl, was a grim burden,
And coughed up a caudle in Clement's breeches.
There was no hungry hound in Hertford Shire
Durst lap up the leavings, they stank so loudly.

With all the weeping in the world his wife and his daughter
Bore him home to his bed and brought him in it.   481
After all this excess he was attacked with slothfulness,
And slept Saturday and Sunday till the sun was setting.
Then he awoke, and winked, and wiped his eyelids,
And the first word that he uttered was, "where's the bowl?"
Wife and Conscience upbraided him for his wicked living,
The shrew was ashamed, and shrived himself earnestly,
And prayed before Repentance; "Have pity on me, a sinner,
Thou living Lord and life of all things!
To thee, God, I Glutton yield me guilty   490
Of more trespass through tongue than I can tell thee ever.
I have sworn "by thy soul" and "by thy sides" and "so help me
     God Almighty,"
When there was no need, and many times falsely.
I have sat too long at supper and sometimes at breakfast,
Till I, Glutton, gulped it up before I had gone a furlong,
And spilt what might have been spared and spent on the
     hungry.
I have drunk and eaten delicately on days of fasting,
And sat sometimes so long that I have slept and eaten together.

I have sought taverns for love of tales and to drink the longer.
And I have eaten meat before noon on days of fasting."   500

"This showing your shrift," said Repentance, "shall be
   merit for you."
And then Glutton grieved and made a great dolour,
For the loathsome life that he had lived in evil.
He vowed to fast: "Neither thirst nor hunger
Shall make fish on Friday defile my stomach,
Till my aunt Abstinence has given me permission;
And yet I have hated her all my lifetime."

ACCIDIA

Then Sloth came all beslobbered, with slime on his eyelids;
"I must sit," he said, "or else I shall slumber.
I cannot stand or stoop, and want a stool for kneeling.   510
If I were brought to bed, unless my buttocks made me,
No ringing should make me rise till I was ripe for dinner."

He began *benedicite* with a belch, and beat his forehead,
And roared and raved and snored for a conclusion.
"Awake! awake! wretch," cried Repentance, "make ready
   for shriving."
"If I should die to-day I should never do it.
I cannot say *pater noster* perfectly, as the priest sings it.
I know rhymes of Robin Hood and Randolph Earl of Chester,
But of our Lord or of our Lady I have learned nothing.
I have made forty vows and forgotten them on the morrow.
I never performed the penance as the priest commanded,   521
Nor was sorry for my sins as a man should be.
And if I pray at my beads, unless Wrath bids me,
What I tell with my tongue is two miles from my meaning.
I am occupied each day, on holy days and all days,
With idle tales at ale, or at other times in churches.

Rarely do I remember God's pain and passion.

I never visit the feeble nor the fettered men in prison.
I had rather hear ribaldry or a summer game of cobblers,
Or lies to laugh at and belie my neighbour,   530
Than all that the four evangelists have ever written.
Vigils and fasting days slip unheeded.
I lie abed in Lent with my leman beside me,
And when matins and mass are over I go to my friars.
If I arrive at *ite missa est* I have done my duty.
Sometimes I am not shriven, unless sickness force me,
More than twice in two years, and then I do it by guess work.

I have been priest and parson for the past thirty winters,
Yet I know neither the scales nor the singing nor the Saint's
    Legends.
I can find an hare afield or frighten him from his furrow   540
Better than read *beatus vir* or *beati omnes*,
Construe their clauses and instruct my parishioners.
I can hold love-days and hear a reeve's reckoning,
But I cannot construe a line in the Canons or Decretals.

If I beg or borrow and it be not tallied
I forget it as quickly; men can ask me
Six times or seven and I will swear to the falsehood.
So I trouble true men twenty times over.

The salary of my servants is seldom even.
I answer angrily when the accounts are reckoned,   550
And my workman's wages are wrath and cursing.
If any man does me a favour or helps me in trouble,
I answer courtesy with unkindness, and cannot understand it.
I have now and I have ever had a hawk's manners.
I am not lured with love where nothing lies in the fingers.

Sixty times I, Sloth, have since forgotten
The kindness that fellow Christians have granted to me.
Sometimes I spill—in speech or silence—
Both flesh and fish and many other victuals,
Bread and ale, butter milk and cheeses,   560
All slobbered in my service till they may serve no man.

I was a roamer in my youth and reckless in study,
And ever since have been a beggar from foul slothfulness:
Heu mihi! quia sterilem vitam duxi juvenilem!"

"Do you repent," said Repentance,—but the wretch was
    swooning,
Till Vigilate, the watcher, threw water on his forehead,
And flung it in his face, and vehemently addressed him,
And cried, "Beware of Desperation, that betrays many!
Say, 'I am sorry for my sins', say it and believe it.
Beat your breast and beseech Him to have mercy;   570
For there is no guilt so great that His goodness is not greater."

Then Sloth sat up and so crossed himself quickly,
And made a vow before God: "For my foul living
Every Sunday this seven years, unless sickness keep me,
I will go down before day break to the dear chapel,
And hear matins and mass, like a monk in his cloister.
No ale after meat shall hold me absent
Till I have heard evensong, I vow by the rood-tree."

There was a Welshman there wonderfully sorry.
His name was Yuan-Yield-Again-if-I-have-Sufficient.   580
"And now will I yield, if I am able,
All that I have won wickedly since my years of manhood.
And though I lack a livelihood, I shall labour truly
Till each shall have his own ere I go hence.

With the remainder and the remnant, by the Rood of Chester,
I shall seek Truth before I see Rome!"

Robert the robber saw *reddite* in the gospel,
And because his wealth was missing he wept sorely.
Yet this wicked wretch whispered in secret:
"Christ who was crucified on Calvary for sinners,   590
Who when Dismas, my brother, besought thee for mercy
Had mercy upon that man for the sake of *memento*,
So now have ruth upon a robber in whom *reddere* is wanting,
And who will never win it with his own labour!
But for the Might of thy Mercy grant mitigation, I beseech thee,
And damn me not at Doomsday for what I did so evilly!"

What befell this felon I cannot fully tell you;
Yet I know well that he wept and that the water flowed fast.
He acknowledged his guilt to Christ soon after,
Took his pick, *poenitencia*, polished it freshly,   600
And leaped over the land with it all his life after;
For he had lain with *Latro*, Lucifer's aunt.

Then Repentance had pity, and prayed them to kneel
     together:
"For I shall beseech the Saviour's grace for all sinful people
That he amend us of our misdeeds and have mercy upon us."

"Now God," said he, "who in thy goodness created all things,
And made all of nought, and man in thy image,
And after suffered sin, the sickness of all men,
And all in our belief for the best, as the Book tells us:
O *felix culpa! O necessarium peccatum Adae! etc.*   610
For through that sin thy Son was sent to this earth,
Became man through a maid for mankind's salvation,
And made thyself similar to us in soul and body:

Faciamus hominem ad imaginem et similitudinem nostram;
et alibi: qui manet in caritate, in Deo manet, et Deus in eo.
And since with thine own Son in our suit thou diedst,
On a Friday, in man's form, and didst feel our sorrow:
Captivam duxit captivitatem.
The sun in sorrow lost its brightness,
About mid´day, in mid´light, and at the meal time of   620
   thy holy ones;
And thou didst feed with thy fresh blood our fore´
   fathers in darkness:
Populus qui ambulabat in tenebris, vidit lucem magnam.
And through the light that leaped from thee Lucifer was
   blinded,
And all thy blessed blown into the bliss of Paradise;
The third day after thou walkedst in our garment,
And a sinful Mary saw thee ere Saint Mary thy Mother,
And all to solace the sinful thou sufferedst it to be so:
Non veni vocare justos sed peccatores ad poenitentiam.
And all that the four evangelists have ever written
Of thy most doughty deeds done in our armour: 630
Verbum caro factum est, et habitavit in nobis.
By so much, meseemeth, we may safely pray thee,
Bid and beseech, if it be thy purpose,
Who art our father and our brother, to be merciful to us,
And have ruth on these wretches who repent so sorely,
That they ever wrathed thee in this world in word, thought,
   or deed."

Then Hope took an horn of *Deus, tu conversus vivificabis,*
And blew it with *Beati quorum remissae sunt iniquitates,*
And all the saints in heaven sang together:
Homines et jumenta salvabis, quemadmodum multiplicasti   640
   misericordiam tuam.

Then a thousand men thronged together,
Crying upward to Christ and to his clean Mother,
That grace might go with them to seek Truth.

But none was so wise that he knew the way thither.
They blustered as beasts over banks and mountains.
It was late and long when they lighted on a traveller
Apparelled like a pilgrim in pagan clothing.
He bore a staff bound with a broad fillet,
That like a winding weed wound about it.
At his belt he bore a bowl and wallet.   650
An hundred ampules hung at his hatband,
Signs from Sinai and shells from Galice,
Many a cross on his cloak, and keys from Rome,
And the vernicle in front, that friends might find it,
And see by his signs what shrines he had been to.

The folk asked him first from whence he was coming.
"From Sinai," he said, "and from our Lord's sepulchre.
In Bethlehem and Babylon I have been for a season;
In Armenia and Alexandria, in many other places.
You may see by the signs that stick in my hatband   660
How I have walked full wide in wet and dry.
I have sought good saints for my soul's welfare."

"Know you ought of a Saint whom men call Truth?
Can you put us on the path to the place where he is dwelling?"

"No, so God help me!" said this great traveller,
"I never saw a palmer, with pike and wallet,
Ask after him before, till now, at this moment!"

"Peter!" cried a plowman, and put forth his shoulders,
"I know him as closely as clerk knows his lessons.

Conscience and Common Wit directed me to his dwelling,
And made me safely assure them to be his servant forever, 671
To sow and to set so long as I may labour.
I have followed him faithfully for forty winters.
I have sown his seed and served his cattle,
And indoors and outdoors done what profits him.
I ditch and I delve, and do what Truth bids me,
Sometimes a sower, sometimes a thresher,
At tailoring or tinkering, as Truth devises.
I weave and I wind, and do what Truth teaches.
For though I say it myself, I serve him to his pleasure,   680
And have my hire of him well, and often beyond it.
He is the promptest payer that the poor man knows;
He withholds none his hire, that he has it not at even.
He is lowly as a lamb and loveable in speaking.
And if you wish to know the way to his manor,
I shall put you on the path to the place where he is dwelling."

"Yea, Piers," said the pilgrims, and proffered him wages
To take them with him to Truth's dwelling.
"No, by my soul's health!" swore Piers, and spoke earnestly,
"I would not finger a farthing, by Saint Thomas' body! 690
Truth would love me the less a long time after.
But if you wish to go well, this is the way thither.
I shall gladly speak and set you on it.

You must go through meekness, you men and women,
Till you come to Conscience, and till Christ knows surely
That you love our Lord liefest of all things,
And your neighbour next, and in no way hurt him
Otherwise than you would he should do to you.

And so bend by a brook, Be-Obedient-in-Speaking,
Till you find the ford, Do-Your-Fathers-Honour;   700

Honora patrem et matrem.
Wade in that water and wash well in it,
And you shall leap the lighter all your lifetime.
And so you shall see Swear-Not-Unless-it-be-Needful,
And Name-Not-Idly-the-Name-of-God-Almighty.
Then you shall come by a croft, but come not in it;
This croft is Covet-Not-Men's-Cattle-nor-their-Women,
No-nor-their-Servants,-and-Annoy-them-Never.
Look you break no boughs there but what are yours rightly.

Two stocks stand there; but stay not by them: 710
They are Steal-Not and Slay-Not; but strike out boldly.
Leave them on your left hand and look not backward.
Hold your holy day well and honestly till even.

Then bend by a barrow, Bear-No-False-Witness.
It is fenced with florins and fees without number.
Look you pluck no plant there and imperil your salvation.

Then you shall see Say-Truth-Such-as-it-is-Surely,
And-in-no-other-Manner-at-no-Man's-Bidding.

Then you shall come to a court as clear as sunlight.
With a moat of Mercy is that manor encircled.   720
All the walls are of Wit to hold Will from it:
Crenellated with Christendom for mankind's salvation,
And buttressed with Believe-So-or-Thou-Beest-Not-Saved.
All the houses are tiled, halls and chambers,
With no lead but with Love and Low-Speech-of-Brethren.
The bridge is of Bide-Well-and Speed-the-Better.
Each pillar is of Penance and of Prayers of Saints.
Almsdeeds are the hooks that the gates hang on.
In the Tower sits Truth above the sun in heaven.
He may do with the day-star what desire bids him.   730

Death dare not do the deed that Truth denies him.

Grace is the gate-ward, a good man, I may tell you.
His man-servant is Amend-You; many men know him.
Tell him this token that Truth knows honest:
'I performed the penance as the priest enjoined me,
And am sorry for my sins, and so shall I be always
When I think upon them, though I were his Holiness.'

Bid Amend-You be meek in his master's presence,
And waive up the wicket that the woman shut
When Adam and Eve ate unroasted apples.   740
Per Evam cunctis clausa est, et per Mariam virginem patefacta est.
For she has the key and the clicket though the king slumbers.

And if Grace grant you to go in freely,
You shall see in yourself Truth in your heart's chamber,
In a chain of charity and a child's likeness
To suffer and to say nothing against your Sire's wishes.

But beware of Wrath-You, for he is a wicked fellow,
And envies him who is in your heart's chamber,
And puts forth pride to praise your merits.
Then the boldness of your benefit blinds eyesight;   750
Then are you driven forth as dew and the door closed,
Keyed and clicketed to keep you without it,
Perhaps an hundred winters till you enter after.
So you may lose his love from liking yourself better,
And perhaps never enter after unless grace is given you.

But seven sisters serve Truth always,
And are porters of the posterns at which his place is entered.
One is Abstinence, and Humility another;
Charity and Chastity are his chief maidens;

Patience and Peace help people often;   760
Largess is a lady who has let in many,
And helped a thousand out of the devil's pen-fold.
Whoso is kin to these seven, so God help me,
Is wondrously welcome and graciously greeted.
But except you are kin to some of these seven,
It is hard, by my head," said Piers, "for any of you ever
To go in at any gate, unless grace be greater!"

"Now by Christ," said a cut-purse, "I have no kin among
    them!"
"Nor I, "said an ape-ward, "by ought that I can hear of."
"By God," said a baker, "if I believed this truly   770
I should not go a foot further, for any friar's preaching!"

"Yes," said Piers the Plowman, and pricked them all to
    goodness.
"Mercy is a Maiden there with Might above all others.
She is kin to the sinful, and her Son also.
And through help in these two (hope in none other)
You may get grace there if you go early.

"By Saint Paul," said a pardoner, "perhaps I am not known
    there!
I will fetch my box of brevets and a bull with bishop's letters."
"By Christ," said a common woman, "I shall keep you   779
    company!
You shall say I am your sister; I know not where mine have
    gone to."

"THIS is a wild way without a leader
To follow each foot," said the folk together.
But Perkin, the Plowman, answered, "By Saint
Peter,
I have half an acre to harrow by the highway!
Had I harrowed this half acre and sown it after,
I would go with you gladly and guide you thither."

"That will be a long delay," said a lady in a wimple;
"At what shall we women work in the meantime?"
"Some must sew the sack," said Piers, "to keep the seed from
    spilling.
And you lovely ladies with your long fingers,   10
Who have silk and sendal to sow when you are able,
Make chasubles for chaplains and for the church's honour.
Wives and widows, spin wool and linen;
Make cloth, I counsel you, and instruct your daughters.
Note how the needy and the naked are lying.
Get them some clothing, for truth commands it.
I shall lend them a livelihood unless the land fail us,
Both meat and bread for rich and poor folk,
As long as I live, for the Lord's love in heaven.
And let all manner of men whom meat nourishes   20
Help those to work well who win your living!"

"By Christ," quoth a knight, "your command is honest!
But truly no one taught me how a team is driven;
But as I can," quoth he, "by Christ, I will do it!"
"By Saint Paul," said Perkin, "you proffer yourself so fairly,
That I shall serve and sweat and sow for us together,
And labour for your love as long as I am living,
In provision that you protect plowmen and churchmen
From wasters and the wicked by whom this world is ruined.
Go and hunt hardily for hares and foxes,   30

For boars and badgers that break down my hedges.
Find good falcons to fetch wild fowl,
For they come to my croft and crop my harvest."

Then the knight commenced a courteous answer:
"To my power, Piers," he said, "I promise truly
To fulfil this offer though I should fight for you.
For as long as you live let me maintain you."

"Ah, but still a point," said Piers, "I pray you also
To task no tenant unless Truth wills it.
And though you may amerce them, let Mercy be taxer,　　40
And Meekness your master, for all Mede's teaching.
And though poor men proffer you presents and tokens,
Take them not, on adventure that you may not deserve them.
For you shall yield them again when a year is over
In a perilous place, Purgatory, men call it.
If you beat not your bondman it will be the better for you.
Though he be your underling here, it may happen in heaven
That he will be the worthier and with more happiness
Than you, unless you do better and live rightfully.
A*mice, ascende superius.*　　　　　　　　　　　50
In a charnel at church churls are known badly,
Or a knight from a knave; know this in your heart.
Be true of your tongue, and love such tales only
As give wit and wisdom in your workman's service.
Hold with no ribalds nor hear their prating.
Avoid minstrels at meal⁄time, when they are most deceiving;
For they are the devil's tale⁄bearers, I tell you truly."

"I assent, by Saint James," said the knight quickly,
"I shall work as you will have me while life is lasting."
"I shall put on," said Perkin, "a pilgrim's garment,.　　60
And I shall go with you till we find Truth.

I shall put on my apparel that is patched and ragged,
My leggings, and my cuffs against cold in my fingers;
Hang my hopper at my neck instead of a wallet,
And I shall bring a bushel of bread corn in it.
I shall sow it myself, and as soon as I have finished
Go on pilgrimage as a palmer, to get pardon for my offences.
He who helps me to harrow and sow here before that journey
Shall have leave, by our Lord, to glean in harvest,
And make merry in it, whoever may grudge him!   70
I shall find food for all faithful livers,
And for all the kinds of craftsmen who can live in truth.—
But not Jack the juggler, nor Janet the dishonest,
Nor Daniel the dicer, nor Denot the bawd,
Nor the false friar, nor folk of his order,
Nor Robin the ribald with his rusty language.
Truth told me once, and bad me tell it after,
Deleantur de libro viventium, I should not deal with them.
The Church is told to take no tythings from them:
Qui cum justis non scribantur.   80
They have escaped by good fortune; now God amend them."

Piers' wife was called dame Work-while-I-am-Able;
His daughter was Do-this-or-thy-Dame-shall-beat-thee;
His son was Suffer-thy-Sovereigns-to-have-their-Wishes,
Dare-not-Judge-them-for-if-thou-Dost-thou-shalt-Dearly-
   Abide-it.—

"May God be with all, for so his word teaches!
Now that I am old and hoary and have enough to live on,
I shall pass to penance and to pilgrimage with these others.
So I write my will before I wander further.
In *Dei nomine*, Amen: I make it without a lawyer.   90
He shall have my soul who has best deserved it;
And defend it from the fiend, so my faith teaches,

Till I have come to his account, as my *credo* tells me.
And have release and remission of that rental forever.
The Church shall keep my corpse and guard my body;
For he commanded my corn and my cattle in his tything.
I paid it to him promptly on peril of my safety;
And he is beholden, I hope, to have me in his masses
And maintain my memory among all Christians.

My wife shall have what I won honestly,   100
And deal it among my daughters and my dear children.
For though I die to-day my debts are cancelled.
I bore home what I borrowed before I went to sleep.
With the remainder and the remnant, by the Rood of Lucas,
I will worship Truth while I am living,
And be his pilgrim at the plow in poor men's service.
My plow foot shall be my pick-staff and pluck roots asunder,
And help my coulter to cut and clean the furrows."

Now Perkin and his pilgrims were plowing together,
With all who helped to harrow the half acre.   110
Dykers and delvers dug up the ridges.
Perkin was pleased with them and praised them often.
Other workmen there were who worked eagerly,
Each in his own way worked honestly,
And some to please Perkin picked up the weeds.

At the high prime Piers left the plow standing
To oversee them himself; and some who served loyally
He should hire hereafter in the harvest season.

Some were sitting and singing in the ale house,
And helped ear his half acre with *"how trolly lolly!"*   120
"By the safety of my soul," Piers said in anger,
"Unless you get up quickly and go to labour,

No grain that grows shall gladden you in famine,
And though you die for dearth, the devil have who cares!"

False men were afraid and feigned blindness;
Some laid their legs under them, as such liars can do,
And made their moan for mercy to him:
"We have no limbs for labour; Lord we bless thee!
But we pray for you Piers, and for your plow also.
God send his grace that your grain may flourish,   130
And yield you your alms that you yield us,
We cannot ear your acre. Illness grips us."

"If what you say is so," said Piers, "I shall soon know it.
But I know that you are wasters; I have Truth to witness.
I am his old hine. He has me to warn him
Who in this world wrong his workmen.
You waste what men win with toil and travail.
But Truth shall teach you how his team is driven,
Or you shall eat barley bread and have the brook for drinking.
But whoever is blind or broken or bolted with crutches   140
Shall eat wheat bread and drink at my table,
Till God of his goodness grants a remedy.
You can toil as Truth wishes, and take meat and wages
For keeping kine in the field or corn from the cattle.
You might ditch or delve or do hard threshing,
Or help make mortar or bear muck for tillage.
But you live in lying, in lechery and in idleness,
So that God's sufferance only shields you from vengeance.

Hermits and anchorites who eat at noon time
And no more till the morrow, shall have my almsdeeds.   150
My goods shall clothe those who have cloisters and churches.
But Robert Run-About shall have nothing of my giving.

E

Nor any preachers unless they preach and have privilege from
    the bishop.
They shall have bread and broth and be at their pleasure,
For it is an unreasonable religion that grants no certainties."

Then Waster was wrathful and wished to fight,
And flung his great fist in the face of Piers Plowman.
A bragging Breton boasted also,
And bad him pack with his plow for a pinching liar:
"Will you or won't you, we will have our pleasure   160
Of your flour and your flesh and fetch at our liking,
And make ourselves merry, and you may go whistling!"

Then Piers the Plowman complained to the knight
To keep him, as he covenanted, from these cursed villains,
These wolvish wasters who make the world wretched:
"They waste and win nothing; and while this is lasting
No people will have plenty, and my plow will lie idle."

Then the knight spoke kindly, as his nature bad him,
And warned Waster, and wished him to do better,
"Or by the order that I bear, I shall bring you to justice!" 170

"I have never worked," said Waster, "and I will not begin it,"
And made light of his law and less of his knighthood,
And set Piers at a penny and his plow with him,
And menaced Piers' men if they should meet after.
"By the peril of my soul," said Piers, "I shall repay you,"—
And halloed for Hunger, who heard him quickly,
"Wreck me on these wretches," he cried, "who ruin all men!"

Then Hunger in haste caught Waster by the gullet,
And so wrung him by the ribs that his eyes watered.
He buffeted the Bretoner beneath the jaw bone,   180

So that he looked like a lantern all his life after.
He so beat them both he half burst their bellies;
If Piers with a peas-loaf had not prayed for them,
They would both have been buried, believe nothing better!
"Let them live," he said, "let them eat in the swine-yard,
Or else beans and bran baked together,
Or milk and mean ale," so Piers besought him.

False men for fear fled to barn-yards,
Flapped with flails from morning till evening;
For a potfull of peas that Piers prepared   190
Hunger was not so hardy to take hold upon them.
An host of hermits hung at his bidding,
Cut up their copes, made short-coats from them,
Went as workmen with spades and shovels,
And dug and ditched to drive off Hunger.
Blind and bed-rid were bettered by the thousand.
Those who sat to beg silver were soon healthy.
What was baked for horses was help for the hungry.
The beggars craved beans and were obedient to labour.
A poor man was well paid who had peas for wages.   200
They were as swift as a sparrow-hawk to serve Piers' wishes.
Piers was proud of them and put them to service,
And gave them meat as he might and moderate wages.

Piers then had pity, and prayed Hunger
To go home to his own earth and hold him contented.
"I am well avenged of wasters through your power.
But I pray you before you pass," said Piers to Hunger,
"What is best to do with beggars and men who bid falsely?
I know well that when you go they will work badly.
Misfortune for the moment has made them humble.   210
The fear of famine puts the folk at my bidding.

They are my blood brethren," said Piers, "for God bought all
    men.
Once Truth taught me to love them equally,
And to help them in all things as their need demanded.
And now I would know what is needful for them,
And know how I might master them and make them labour."

"Hear then," said Hunger, "and hold it in remembrance,
Let hounds-bread and horse-bread hold up the spirits
Of all bold beggars who should be bound to service.
Bring down their bellies with a bean diet,   220
And if they grumble and grutch, bid them go to labour.
He shall sup the sweeter who has so deserved it.

If you find any of your fellows whom fortune has injured,
Or any victim of false men, find out his sorrows,
And comfort him with your goods, for Christ's love in heaven.
Love him and lend him, as God's law teaches:
Alter alterius onera portare.
Of all manner of men whom ever you discover
In need or having nothing, help them kindly,
Love them and blame them not, lest God take vengeance. 230
Though these do evil, let God be avenged:
Mihi vindictam, et ego retribuam.
If you would be gracious to God, do as the gospel teaches;
Be beloved among the lowly, and let God reward you:
Facite vos amicos de Mammone iniquitatis."
"I would not grieve God," said Piers, "for all the goods about
    me.
Might I be sinless, and do as you say?" said Piers to Hunger.
"Yea, I assure you," said Hunger, "or else the Bible lies.
Go to the giant Genesis and the engendering of all things.
'In *sudore* and sorrow thou shalt earn thy meat,   240
And labour for thy livelihood,' so our Lord commanded.

And Solomon says the same; I saw it in the Bible;
Piger prae frigore, shall not till his acre,
And so he shall bid and beg and none abet his hunger.
Matthew with the man's face maintains this teaching.
For *servus nequam* had a talent and would not trade with it,
And forfeited his lord's favour forever after.
The talent was taken from him, for he had not touched it,
And he took the talent who had ten to loan.
Then Holy Church heard the words of her master: 250
'He who hath shall have, and have help if need be,
And he who hath not shall not have; no man shall help him;
And what he thinks to have I will take from him.'

Common Wit wills that each one labour,
In dyking or delving or travailing in prayers:
Contemplative life or active life are Christ's commandments.
The psalter says in the psalm *Beati omnes*
That he who feeds himself with his faithful labour
Is blessed by the Book in body and in spirit:
Labores manuum tuarum, etc."   260

"Yet I pray you," said Piers, "*par charité*, if you know
Any line of leechcraft, that I may learn it from you.
Some of my servants and I myself often
May not work for an whole week, our stomachs ache so."

"I know well," said Hunger, "what sickness ails you.
You have gorged your stomachs and groan for it.
But I would have you," said Hunger, "if your health is precious,
On no day to drink before you have dined somewhat.
And I ask you to eat not till hunger bids it,
And send you the sauce to savour your dishes.   270
Keep something for supper time, and sit not beyond reason.
Arise before appetite has eaten fully.

Let not Sir Surfeit sit at your table.
Believe him not; for he is lecherous and a loose talker,
And a lover of many meats; and his maw is ravenous.

But if you diet discreetly, I dare wager
That Physic shall want food and sell his furred garments,
And his cloak of Calabre and his golden buttons;
And be fain, by my faith, to leave physic to others,
And learn labour on the land, for livelihood is sweet.   280
Many doctors are murderers, may the Lord amend them;
Men die of their drinks before destiny calls them."

"By Saint Paul," said Piers, "this is profitable language!
Wander where you will, Hunger; may it be well with you ever,
For I like your lesson, and the Lord repay you!"
"So help me," said Hunger, "I will not leave you
Till I have dined this day, and drunk deep."

"I have no penny," said Piers, "to buy pullets,
Nor geese nor pigs, but two green cheeses,
A few curds of cream, a cake of oatmeal,   290
Two loaves of beans and bran, baked for my children;
And, by my soul, I swear I have no salt bacon,
Nor cook to make collops, I take Christ to witness!
But I have parsley and pot herbs and a plenty of cabbages,
And a cow and a calf, and a cart mare
To draw my dung afield till the drought is over.
This is the little we must live on till the Lammas season.
And then I hope to have my harvest in the garner.
And then I may spread your supper to my soul's content."

So all the poor people fetched peascods,   300
And brought him beans and baked apples by the lapful,
Ripe cherries, chervils and many small onions,

And offered Piers the present to please Hunger.

Hunger ate all in haste and asked for more.
Then the poor folk had fear, and fed him quickly
With green potherbs and peas, and would have poisoned him
    gladly.
But now harvest was near. New corn came to market;
And the folk were full of cheer and fed him royally
With the good ale of Glutton, till Hunger was sleepy.

Then Waster would not work, but wandered idly.   310
No beggar ate bread if a bean were in it,
But only cocket or clerematyn bread, or clean white bread.
He asked for no ale to be had for a ha'penny,
But the best and the brownest that the borough offered.
Labourers who had no land to live on but their shovels,
If herbs lay over night, would not eat them.
They were pleased with no penny ale or piece of bacon,
But with fresh flesh or fish, fried or roasted,
And that *chaud* or *plus chaud*, against a cold stomach.

Unless his wages are high he is hot in anger,   320
Or bewails the hour he was ever a workman.
He begins to jangle against the counsel of Cato:
Paupertatis onus patienter ferre memento.
He complains against God and grumbles against Reason,
And curses the king and his council with him,
Who license law for labour's sorrow.
Yet none would complain while Hunger was master,
Nor strive against his statute, so sternly he threatened.

But I warn you workmen, win while you are able,
For Hunger hastens hitherwards quickly.   330
He shall awake with water and wasters be confounded.

Before the finish of the fifth year such famine shall threaten,
That fruits shall fail through floods and through foul weather.
Thus said Saturn, and sent you warning;
When you see the sun awry and two monks' heads,
And a maid have the mastery and multiply by eight,
Then the Death shall withdraw, but Dearth shall be Justice,
And Daw the ditcher die from hunger,
Unless God in his goodness grants us relief."

RUTH heard tell of this and told the Plowman
To take his team and till his acre,
And provide him a pardon, *a poena et a culpa*,
For him and for his heirs forever after.
He bad him hold himself at home and harrow his acre;
And all who helped in harrowing, or in sowing or setting
Or in any other means that might aid their master,
Should have pardon with Piers Plowman, as Truth has granted.
Kings and knights, who keep Holy Church,
And who rule rightfully the realms given them,   10
Have pardon to pass through Purgatory lightly,
And to be fellows in Paradise with patriarchs and prophets.
Bishops who are blessed and who become their calling,
As legislators of both laws for the laity's profit,
Who in as much as they may minister to all sinful,
Are peers with the Apostles, as Piers' pardon shows them,
To be at the Day of Doom on the dais of heaven.
Merchants had long remissions in the margin of this pardon.
But the pope would not provide them *a poena et a culpa*,
For they would hold no holidays as Holy Church teaches, 20
And against a clear conscience in their common barter
They would swear "by my soul," and "so God help me!"
But under his secret seal Truth sent them a letter
That they should buy boldly what they best fancied,
And sell it soon after and save the profits
To help hospitals and the halt and feeble,
Always to be busy at the bad highways,
To build bridges broken in the springtime,
To marry maidens or make them novices,
To find the food for poor prisoners,   30
To send scholars to the schools or to some other business,
To relieve religious orders and remedy their losses:
"And I myself shall send you Saint Michael, my archangel,

E*   89

That you may dread no devil nor be terrified in dying,
And so deliver you from despair, if you do rightly,
And send your souls in safety to my saints in heaven."

He made merchants glad, and many wept blissfully,
And praised Piers the Plowman that he had procured the charter.
Lawyers who pled for meed had least pardon in the charter.
For the psalter saves none of them who seek presents,   40
And notably from the innocent, who know no evil:
Super innocentem munera non accipies.
Pleaders should be at pains to plead for such and help them,
Princes and prelates should pay them for their labour.
A regibus et principibus erit merces eorum.
Many a justice and a juror serves Johan more faithfully
Than *pro Dei pietate*, believe nothing better!
But he who spends his speech in speaking for those poor folk
Who are innocent and needy and do no men damage,
He who covets no gifts, but comforts these in trouble,   50
And shows the law for our Lord's love, as he has learned it
      truly—
He shall be daunted by no devil when his death approaches,
Nor doubt the safety of his soul, as the psalter witnesses:
Domine, quis habitabit in tabernaculo tuo?
Sell no water nor wind nor wit nor fire;
The Father made these four for his folk in common.
These are Truth's treasures for true folk's comfort!
These neither wax nor wane without God's commandment.
Great men in the moot hall who take meed from poor men,
And desire indulgences when death draws near them,   60
Have but a poor pardon at their parting hence.
You lawyers and legislators, believe this truly,
Lo, if I lie, the blame is with Matthew;
For he bad me to write this and told me this proverb:
Quodcunque vultis ut faciant vobis homines, facite eis.

But all labourers alive who live in hardship,
Who take wages truly and are true in labour,
Who live in love and under the law, for their lowly spirits
Shall have the same absolution that was sent to Piers.

Bidders and beggars have no place in this pardon,   70
Unless an honest impulse has induced them to begging.
If one begs and bids and be not needy,
He is as false as a fiend and defrauds the wretched,
And beguiles the giver against his wishes.
If the giver knew he were not needy, he would give another
Who was more needy than he, and so the neediest be succoured.
Cato gives this counsel, with the Clerk of History,
Cui des videto, is Cato's teaching.
And he of the History teaches almsdeed as follows:
Sit elemosina tua in manu tua, donec studes cui des.   80
But Gregory was a good man, and bad us give to all men
Who ask, in His love who lends us all:
*Non eligas cui miserearis, ne forte praetereas illum qui meretur
   accipere. Quia incertum est pro quo Deo magis placeas.*
For who knows who is worthy? but God knows who is needy.
The treachery is with the taker if he takes untruly.
For he who gives yields, and may go to rest.
And he who bids borrows and becomes a debtor.
Beggars are ever borrowers, but God is their surety
To pay those who pay them, and to pay with usury.   90
*Quare non dedisti pecuniam meam ad mensam, ut ego veniam cum
   usuris exigere?*
Never bid, you beggars, but when your need is pressing.
Who has enough to buy his bread, as the Book teaches,
Has enough, for he has bread enough, though he have nothing
   further:
Satis dives est, qui non indiget pane.

The needy are our neighbours, if we note rightly;
As prisoners in cells, or poor folk in hovels,
Charged with children and overcharged by landlords.
What they may spare in spinning they spend on rental,
On milk, or on meal to make porridge   100
To still the sobbing of the children at meal time.
Also they themselves suffer much hunger.
They have woe in winter time, and wake at mid-night
To rise and to rock the cradle at the bedside,
To card and to comb, to darn clouts and to wash them,
To rub and to reel and to put rushes on the paving.
The woe of these women who dwell in hovels
Is too sad to speak of or to say in rhyme.
And many other men have much to suffer   109
From hunger and from thirst; they turn the fair side outward,
For they are abashed to beg, lest it should be acknowledged
At their neighbours what they need at noon and even.
I know all this well; for the world has taught me
What befalls another who has many children,
With no claim but his craft to clothe and feed them,
When the mouths are many and the money scarce.
They have bread and penny ale in place of a pittance,
And cold flesh and cold fish for venison from the butcher.
On Fridays and fast days a farthing-worth of mussels
Would be a feast for such folk, with a few cockles.   120
It were an alms to help all with such burdens,
And to comfort such cottagers and crooked men and blind
    folk.

But beggars with bags, to whom breweries are churches,
Unless they are blind or broken or otherwise enfeebled,—
May they fall on their false faces and famine cling them!
Reck nothing of them, you rich folk, though such wretches
    perish.

All who have their health and their eyes at service,
And limbs with which to labour, and who live as lollers,
Live against God's law and the law of Holy Church.

But there are other beggars, healthy in appearance,   130
Who want their wits—men and women also.
They are lunatic lollers and leapers about the country,
And are mad as the moons grow more or less.
They are careless of winter and careless of summer;
They move with the moon, and are moneyless travellers,
With a good will, but witless, through many wide countries.
So Peter and Paul travelled, except that these preach not
And are no makers of miracles. And many times they happen
To prophesy to the people, in sport, one may imagine.
But to my sight it seems that since God is able   140
To make each one whole, and witty and wealthy,
And suffers such wanderers—it seems to my conscience
That such people are as his apostles, or as his privy disciples;
For he has sent them forth silverless, in a summer garment,
Without bag or bread, as the Book tells us:
Quando misi vos sine pane et pera.
They are barefoot and breadless, and beg of no man;
And though one meets with the mayor in the midst of the city,
He renders him no reverence, no more than to another.
Neminem salutaveris per viam.   150
Such manner of men, Saint Matthew tells us,
We should have in our houses, and help on their journey:
Et egenos vagosque induc in domum tuam.
For they are men of merry mouths, minstrels of heaven,
God's servants and God's jesters, as the Scripture teaches:
Si quis videtur sapiens, fiet stultus ut sit sapiens.
It is right for rich men to receive singers
And all manner of minstrels, and make them at their leisure,
For the lords' and ladies' sakes who live with them.

Men suffer all that they say and set it to merriment,   160
And do much more for these men before their parting—
Give them gifts of gold for great men's tokens.
Much rather, you rich men, should you receive truly,
Welcome and honour and help with your presents,
God's minstrels and his messengers and his merry jesters,
Who are lunatic lollers and leapers about the country;
For under God's secret seal their sins are covered.
They bear no bags and bottles under their clothing,
Nor lead the loller's life, like lewd hermits,
Who look lowly to lift men of their almsdeeds.   170
Such hope to sit at evening by the hot chimney,
To unlock their legs, and lie at their leisure,
Rest and roast and turn a rump to the fire.
They drink the can dry and then down to sleep,
And rise when they are ready; and none can rout them earlier.
When these wretches have risen they roam about corners,
Where refreshment is the readiest—a round of bacon,
Silver or sodden meat, or sometimes both together,
A loaf, or a half a loaf, or lumps from cheeses.
Then they carry it to their cots and get their living   180
By idleness and ease and other's labour.
The wretch of this rout who roams the country
With a bag at his back, in beggar's fashion,
And can work at a craft, in case he wish it,
Through which he could come by corn and ale
And a cloak to cover him and keep him from the weather,
Who still lives like a loller—God's law damns him!
Lollers living in sloth and land roamers
Are not in this pardon," said Piers, "till they practise better,
Nor beggars who beg but are never needy.   190
The Book blames all beggary and bans it thus:
Junior fui, et jam senui et non vidi justum derelictum, nec semen ejus, etc.
For your lives are without love, and without law or reason.

Many of you are unwedded to the women you consort with;
And bring forth bastards and beggars' children;
Or you break the back or a bone in childhood,
And are found begging with your infants forever after.
There are more misshapen among these beggars
Than in all manner of men who move among us.
He who lives their life, at his last hour   200
May wail the hour that ever he was born.

Whoever is old and hoary and helpless and strengthless,
And women with child, who are unfit for working,
The blind and the bed-rid and all with broken members,
And all patient poor folk, lepers and others,
Shall have as perfect a pardon as the Plowman himself.
For love of their lowly hearts our Lord has granted them
Their penance and their purgatory in their present station.

"Piers," said a priest, "give me your pardon quickly.
I shall translate the text and turn it into English."   210

Piers opened his pardon at the priest's bidding.
I was behind them both and beheld all the charter.
All lay in two lines, and not a leaf further.
The witness was Truth; and it was written thus:
Et qui bona egerunt, ibunt in vitam eternam.
Qui vero mala, in ignem eternum.
"Peter," said the priest, "there is no pardon in it,
But Do Well and have well, and God shall have your soul,
And do evil and have evil, and you may hope only
That after your death-day the devil shall take you."   220

Then Piers in pure wrath pulled it to pieces,
And said: "Si ambulavero in medio umbrae mortis, non timebo
mala, quoniam tu mecum es.

I shall stop my sowing," said Piers, "and cease from such hard
    labour,
Nor be so busy now about my comfort.
Prayers and penance shall be my plow hereafter.
I shall weep when I should sleep, though wheat bread fail me.
The prophet ate bread in penance and in sorrow.
The psalter says that so did many others.
He who loves God loyally has livelihood easily.
Fuerunt mihi lacrimae meae panes die ac nocte.   230
And unless Luke lie, birds teach us the lesson
Not to be too busy about the world's pleasures.
N*e soliciti sitis*, he says in the gospel,
And gives us guidance in governing ourselves rightly.
Who finds the fowls their food in winter?
They have no garner to go to, but God provisions them."

"What," said the priest to Perkin, "Peter! bless me,
You are lettered a little; where did you learn reading?"
"Abstinence, the abbess." said Piers, "taught the A.B.C. to me,
And Conscience came forward and declared much further."

"If you were a priest, Piers," he said, "you might   241
    preach at your liking,
And be a doctor in divinity, with D*ixit insipiens.*"
"Rude rogue," said Piers, "you have read little in the Bible.
You have seldom seen Solomon's proverbs:
Eji ce derisores et jurgia cum eis, ne crescant," etc.

The priest and Perkin opposed each other,
And at their wrangling I awoke and saw the world about me,
And the sun sailing in the southern heaven.
Meatless and moneyless on the hills of Malvern
I went on my way, wondering at the vision.   250

Often has this vision forced me to wonder
If what I saw asleep were so indeed.
I pondered pensively on Piers the Plowman;
On what a pardon Piers had for all peoples' comfort,
And how the priest impugned it with two pert words.
I am a doubter of dreams, for they deceive men often.
Cato and the Canonists counsel us never
To seek assurance in dreams, for *sompnia ne cures*.
But a book of the Bible bears witness
How Daniel divined the dreams of a monarch,   260
Nebuchadnezzar, he is named by Clergy.
Daniel said, "Sir King, your dreams betoken
That strange soldiers shall come and spoil your kingdom,
And lower lords be left to rule it."
The deed was done as Daniel told it;
The king lost his lordship, and lower men had it.
Joseph also dreamed marvellously how the moon and sun
And the eleven stars hailed him together.
Then Jacob judged Joseph's vision.
"*Beau fitz*," said his father, "we shall fall in peril,   270
I myself and my sons, and seek your comfort."
It fell as his father said: for under Pharaoh
Joseph was justice of the Egyptian kingdom;
It fell as his father said; for his friends sought him.

And all this makes me meditate on the vision:
How the priest proved no pardon so good as Do Well,
And deemed that Do Well surpassed indulgences,
Biennials and triennials and bishop's letters,
And how at the Day of Doom Do Well is honoured,
And passes all the pardon of Saint Peter's Church.   280

Now the pope has power to grant pardon to the people
To pass without penance through the portal of heaven.

This is our belief as the learned teach us.
Quodcumque ligaveris super terram, erit ligatum et in coelis, etc.
And so I believe loyally, Lord forbid otherwise.
Pardon and penance and prayer are salvation
For souls that have sinned seven times mortally.
But to trust to these triennials, truly I consider
Is not so safe for the soul, surely, as Do Well!

Therefore I warn you rich, who are able in this world   290
On trust of your treasure to have triennials and pardons,
Be never the bolder to break the ten commandments;
And most of all you masters, mayors and judges,
Who have the wealth of this world, and are held wise by your
     neighbours,
You who purchase your pardons and papal charters:
At the dread doom, when the dead shall rise
And all come before Christ, and give full accounting,
When the doom will decide what day by day you practised,
How you led your life and were lawful before him,
Though you have pocketfuls of pardons there or   300
     provincial letters,
Though you be found in the fraternity of all the four orders,
Though you have double indulgences,—unless Do Well
     help you
I set your patents and your pardons at the worth of a peascod!
Therefore I counsel all Christians to cry God mercy,
And Mary his Mother be our mean between him,
That God may give us grace, ere we go hence,
To work with such a will, while we are here,
That after our death day, and at the Day of Doom,
Do Well may declare that we did as he commanded.

PASSUS VIII

THUS robed in russet I roamed the country
All a summer season, seeking for Do Well.
I pressed many people whom I passed on the
    highway
If any could inform me of the inn where he was staying.
Or tell what manner of man he might be truly.

But none knew the nature of Do well
Or put me on the path to the place of his dwelling.
Then it befell on a Friday that two friars met me,
Masters of the Minorites, and men of learning.
I greeted them graciously as custom bad me,   10
And prayed them *par charité* before they passed further
That if they could tell me the country or the coasts about it
Where Do Well dwelt, they would do me that favour.
Of all wanderers in the world these walk the farthest,
Know all kinds and conditions, all countries and nations,
Know prince's palace and poor man's cottage,
And surely where Do Well and Do Evil dwell also.

"This man is among us," said the Minorites together,
"He has ever been, and I hope he ever shall be."

"*Contra*," said I as a clerk, and commenced to argue,   20
And said to him, "Surely *septies in die cadit justus*.
Man sins seven times daily; so says the Bible.
And he who sins," I said, "I hold does evil,
And Do Well and Do Evil may not dwell together.
Ergo he is not always among you friars.—
Sometimes he is elsewhere to instruct the people."

'I shall instruct you, my son," said the friar in answer,

"How the upright sin seven times daily.
A parable will present," said he, "this problem nicely.
Place a man in a boat on a broad river,   30
In a tide and a tempest, with his boat tossing.
Many times the man will be falling and rising.
Stand as stiff as he will, he will still be stumbling.
Yet he is safe and sound, for his sole duty
Is to rise with the rudder and direct the steering,
Lest the wind and the water whirl him over,
And his life be lost through lax self-guidance.

"So it happens," said he, "with all men living.
The water is like the world that wanes and waxes;
Goods of the earthly ground are like the great waters,   40
Weltering in the winds and waves forever.
Then the boat is like our body, that is brittle by nature.
So through the fiend and the flesh and the frailty of mortals
The upright sin seven times daily.

"He does no deadly sin, for Do Well guards him,
Who is Charity, our champion and our chief help against
    Satan.
He strengthens men to stand and steers their passage,
And though the body bow, as a boat in water,
The soul is always safe, unless you seek directly
To do a deadly sin and drown your soul.   50
God will suffer such sin if you yourself seek it.
For he has given you gifts for governing yourself freely;
These are Wit and Free Will; each creature has its portion,
Flying fowls and fish and mammals,
But man has the most, and is the most blameworthy
Unless he does the deeds that Do Well teaches."

"I have no natural knowledge," I said, "to interpret your fable;

But if I am left alive I shall try to learn better."
"I commend you to Christ," he said, "and to the cross forever!"
And I said, "The same save you from misfortune,   60
And give you the grace to be good men always."

I walked far and wide, without a comrade,
Till between a wild waste and a wooded valley
I staid my steps to sweet birds' music;
I leaned on a linden in a lawny meadow,
And listened to the lays of these lovely singers.
Those mirthful mouths made me slumber;
Vision found me; and I think truly
The most marvellous dream that man ever witnessed.
I met a tall man who looked much as I do.   70
He came and called me by my natural name.
"Who are you," I said, "who seem to know me?"
"You know well," he said, "and no one better."
"Do I know you?"—"I am Thought," he answered;
"I have pursued you these seven years; have you not seen me
   often?"
"Are you Thought?" I said. "Then can you tell me
Where Do Well dwells, and do me this favour?"

"Do Well and Do Bet and lastly Do Best," he answered,
"Are three fair virtues, and are not far to come on.
He who is true of his tongue and with his two hands,   80
And whose land or labour wins a livelihood for him,
Whose tally is to be trusted, and who takes but his portion,
Who is neither disdainful nor a drunkard—Do Well
   acknowledges him.

Do Bet does this, but does much more also.
He is as low as a lamb and loveable in speaking,
And helps all men as their need arises.

He has broken the boxes and the bags of silver
That Earl Avarous and his heirs held from their neighbours.
He has taken money of Mammon, made friendships,
Has been received into religion, has rendered the Bible,   90
And preaches to the people Saint Paul's doctrine:
Libenter suffertis insipientes, cum sitis ipsi sapientes.
Suffer the simple folk to live with you,
And do good to them in gladness, for so God wishes.

Do Best is above both, and bears the cross of a bishop,
Hooked on one end to haul men from Satan.
A pike is on the point to pull down the wicked,
Who wait in their wickedness to wrong Do Well.
Do Well and Do Bet have ordained between them
To crown one to be their king and to rule them together.   100
So if Do Well and Do Bet do wrong to Do Best,
A king shall come and cast them in prison,
And unless Do Best bid for them they shall be there forever.

So Do Well and Do Bet and Do Best together
Crowned one to be king and to keep them faithfully,
And to rule the realm by their three counsels,
And never otherwise than as these three assented."

I thanked Thought that he had been my teacher: 108
"Yet I am not satisfied with your speeches, for I seek to learn
What Do Well, Do Bet and Do Best do among the people."

"Unless Wit be your witness where these three are dwelling
I know no man who can, and who is now living."

Thus for three days Thought and I journeyed,
Disputing about Do Well one day after another.
But before we were aware, Wit approached us,

He was long and lean, like no other,
Neither pride nor poverty appeared in his clothing,
He was sad in semblance and softly mannered.
I dared suggest no subject to set him talking
Before I had bad Thought be a mean between us.   120
Then I tendered my topic to test Wit's judgement—
How Do Well differed from Do Bet, and Do Best from either.

Thought was timely and spoke as follows:
"Here is Will would know, if Wit can teach him,
Where are Do Well and Do Bet and Do Best in our country,
What lives they live, what laws they practise;
For his wish is to work as they would have him."

PASSUS IX

"SIR Do Well dwells," said Wit, "not a day's journey
In a castle created by Nature from four kinds in
common,
It is made of earth and air mingled together,
And wondrously enwrought with wind and water.
Yet Nature has knit in them another creature,
A lady whom he loves as he loves himself.
Her name is Anima; Envy hates her,
That proud pricker of France, *princeps huius mundi.*
He would win her away with his wiles if he were able,
But Nature notes him and knows how to keep her,   10
And has decreed to her and Sir Do Well the dukedom of
those marches.
Do Bet is her damosel, Sir Do Well's daughter,
Who serves this lady loyally, late and early.
Do Best is above both and a bishop's equal;
What he bids must be done; he rules all together.
The lady Anima is led by his learning.

But the Constable is Conscience, who keeps watch faithfully.
He has five sons by his first marriage;
Sir Seewell and Saywell, and Hearwell, the courteous,
Sir Work-well-with-your-Hands, a weighty man and   20
powerful,
And Sir Godfrey Gowell—all great champions.
These five are set here to save the lady Anima,
Till Nature send for her to preserve her forever."

"But I need first," said I, "to know what Nature is that you
mention."
"Nature," said Wit, "is the knitter of all natural bodies,
The father and former of all that ever was fashioned.

It is the great God, without beginning or ending,
The Lord of Life and of Light, of bliss and of sorrow.
Angels and all beings are at his disposal.
Man is most like him in members and in countenance,   30
And similar in soul to God, unless sin deform him.

He was singular himself and said *faciamus*,
As one who says: more must work than my word only,
And my might must now be a help to my language.
A lord may wish to write a letter and lack parchment,
Or may be able to write, but have no pencil,
And so the letter of this lord, I believe, will never be written.
Thus it seems with him, as the Bible teaches,
Saying, *dixit, et facta sunt.*
His words and wisdom must work also.   40
And in this manner man was made through might of God
   Almighty,
By his word and workmanship, and with life everlasting.

Thus God gave him the ghostly nature of the godhead of heaven,
And granted him of his grace his great bliss,
Which is the life everlasting to his lineage forever.
This is the castle that God made: *Caro* is its title,
Which is as much as to mean a man who is immortal.
Thus man was made by might and majesty,
And wrought with the word and work of God.
True judgment and all the faculties are found within it,   50
For the love of lady Anima, or life, as she is entitled.
She walks and wanders over the whole of man's body,
But her home is in the heart and her chief abode. ¬
Judgment's home is in the head; he harks to Anima,
Is aware of what she wishes and turns his will accordingly;
For after the grace of God the greatest is judgment.

Much woe to those men who misrule their judgment,
And are graceless gluttons; their God is their belly;
Quorum deus venter est.
They are the servants of Satan, and he shall have them hereafter.
Their lives are sinful, their souls are in his likeness,   61
And all who live good lives are in the likeness of the
    Almighty.
Qui manet in caritate, in Deo manet, etc.
Alas, that drink should undo what God has dearly purchased,
And make God forsake those whom he has made in his image:
*Amen dico vobis, nescio vos. Et alibi; Et dimisi eos secundum desideria
    eorum.*

I find that Holy Church should fend all fatherless children,
And all fools and frantic folk who are in default of judgment,
And widows who have no wealth to win them food,
Madmen, and maidens who are hopeless and helpless;   70
All these lack just judgment and require government.

On this matter I might make a long digression;
For the four doctors write fully upon it,
And you may learn from Luke the lesson that I am teaching.

Godfathers and godmothers who see their godchildren
In mischief and misfortune, and may help to amend them,
Shall have penance in Purgatory, unless they perform their
    duty.
More belongs to the little child before the law is taught him
Than the naming of a name, and he never the wiser!
No Christian creature should cry in a doorway,   80
Nor lack bread and pottage, if prelates were as they should be.
A Jew would not see a Jew in unjust beggary
For all the wealth of the world, if he were able to amend it.

Then the Pouk has power, Sir *Princeps huius mundi*,
Over all manner of men who are masters of themselves;
And over fools and frantic folk the fiend has no mastery,
Nor over the deeds that they do, deserving or evil.
Yet fathers and friends are in fault for their children
Who are not warded from wantonness while they are tender.
If they are too poor and penniless to protect them from evil, 90
Holy Church is assigned to save and guard them,
And fend them from follies till they grow older.
Each one in this world who has his understanding
Is sovereign of himself and his soul's captain,
And must keep it and guard it when it comes to manhood,
And save himself from sin; for such is his duty;
Whether he does well or ill, the wit is his own.
Then Do Well is a dyke that destroys vices,
And saves the soul, so that sin is powerless
To ground or rest or root upon it.   100
This is the dread of God, and Do Well makes it:
The beginning of goodness is to fear God truly.
Solomon has said it as a certain proverb:
Initium sapientiae, timor Domini.

Who dreads God, Does Well; but who dreads him from loving
And not for dread of vengeance Does so much Better;
He Does Best who withdraws in day time and in night time
From spilling any speech or spending time idly.
Qui offendit in uno, in omnibus est reus.
Loss of time, truth knows it surely,   110
Is the most hated on earth by those who are in heaven;
And such is the loss of speech, which is the spy of beatitude,
God's gleeman, and the game of heaven!
No faithful father will have his viol untempered,
Nor his gleeman a gad-about and goer to taverns.
All true toilers who desire to labour

Are loved by our Lord, who lends them always
His grace to go with them and gain them a livelihood.
Inquirentes autem Dominum non minuentur omni bono.

But look you grudge not God th ough he give you little!
Be paid with your portion, poor or bountiful.
So Do Well is to dread, and Do Bet to suffer,
For sovereignty itself ascends from patience.
Qui se humiliat, exaltabitur, etc.
This is the lesson of Luke who never lies.
Thus from fear and its effect follows Do Best,
Which is flower and fruit, fostered of them both.

From a ragged root and rough briar
A rose arises, red and fragrant,
Springs and spreads, and spicers wish it.   130
As the blade grows from the ground and the grain from
    the blade,
So Do Best and Do Well and Do Bet forever
Multiply among men who are meek and in charity.
From the love of their lowliness our Lord grants them
Grace to do his deeds and deal him his recompense.

Those who live truly wedded in this world are Do Well;
For they must work and win and be the world's sustenance.
From this kind come all confessors, as we call them,
Kings and knights, kaisers and labourers,
Maidens and martyrs are one man's progeny.   140
The wife was made the way to help man in working;
And so wedlock was wrought with a mediary person;
First by the Father's will, then by the friend's counsel,
And so by the assent of the two together.
Thus wedlock was wrought, and Christ himself performed it;
Its heaven is upon earth; God himself was the witness.

But false and faithless folk, thieves and liars,
Wasters and wretches, are not from wedlock, I assure you,
But are conceived in an evil time, as Cain on his mother.
The psalter speaks of such sinful offspring: 150
Concepit in dolore, et peperit iniquitatem, etc.
All that come from Cain come to bad endings.
For God sent to Seth and said by an angel:
'I will that your issue be wedded with your issue,
And that your kindred never couple with the kindred of your
    brother!'

Yet sometimes against the sentence of our Saviour in heaven,
Seth's kin and Cain's kin coupled together.
Till God was wrathful at his works, and spoke as follows:
'I made man and mourn for it:'
Poenitet me fecisse hominem. 160
Anon he came to Noah and commanded no shirking:
'Go build a boat of boards and timber!
You yourself and your three sons, and your wives with you,
Build this boat and abide in it
Till forty days are fulfilled and the flood abolish
The cursed kin that Cain engendered.
Beast and bird shall ban the hour
That cursed Cain came among them.
All shall die for his deeds in dale and mountain.
All fowls that fly shall feel this also.— 170
Yet save in your ship a single couple
From all the hosts which haunt the world.'
Then the young atoned their elders' evil;
And the offspring felt their fathers' trespass.

But the gospel to some degree is against this, I discover:
*Filius non portabit iniquitatem patris, et pater non portabit iniquitatem
    filii, etc.*

But I find, if the father be false and cruel,
That sometimes the son shall bear the sire's blemish.
Imp an elder, and if the apple is wholesome
There is much at which to marvel, and much more if a villain
Furnish offspring who fare better.   181
They will have some savour of the sire, as you may see often:
Nunquam colligitur de spinis uva, nec de tribulis ficus.

So care came to earth through Cain and his children,
Because they entered wedlock against the will of heaven.
And all who sowed offspring have woe also.
For some as I see, to speak boldly,
Are wedded for greed of goods and against natural feeling.
And such guilt and grief comes of such marriages
As fell on the folk whom I before mentioned.   190
Good people should wed good people, though goods are
    lacking:
I am *via et veritas*, says Christ, I may advance all men.
It is a misbecoming marriage, in my own thinking,
To give a young wench to a man old and feeble,
Or wed some widow for her wealth only,
Who may bear a child between her arms, but otherwise never.
Many a pair since the pestilence have plighted themselves
    together
And the fruit that they bring forth is foul speaking,
Jealousy and joylessness and jangling in private,
And no children but chastizing and chopping themselves to
    pieces.   200
Though they ride to Dunmow, unless the devil help them
To fetch the flitch, they will fail to get it;
Unless both be foresworn the bacon is another's.

So I counsel all Christians to covet no wedding
From greed of goods or for kindred who are wealthy.

Let maidens and maidens match together,
And widows and widowers wed each other.
Look that you wed for no land, but for love only,
And then have God's grace, and so goods enough to live on.
Every secular man who may not continue chaste,   210
Wed and be wise and beware lechery.

When you are wived, beware, and work in season,
Not as Adam and Eve when Cain was engendered.
And if you lead your life thus, the Lord approves it,
For he made wedlock first and spoke honourably of it:
Bonum est ut unusquisque uxorem suam habeat, propter fornicationem.
Whoever are otherwise begotten are held as vagabonds,
As false folks' foundlings, feigners and liars,
Without grace to get possessions or love of the people.
They wander, and waste whatever they capture.   220
They do evil against Do Well and are the devil's servants.
And after their death/day they shall dwell with him,
Unless God give them here the grace of amendment.

Do Well, my friend, is to do as law teaches;
To love your friend and your foe, believe me, that is Do Bet;
To give and to guard both young and old,
To heal and to help, is Do Best, the greatest.
Thus Do Well is to dread God, and Do Bet to suffer,
And so Do Best comes of both, and brings down the obstinate,
Or the wicked will which ruins the work of many,   230
And drives away Do Well through deadly sinning.

IT had a wife whose name was dame Study,
Who had a long look and a lean body.
She was wondrously wrathful that Wit taught me,
And said sternly, staring at her husband:
"You are a wise man, Wit, to waste your teaching
On flatterers and fools, deficient in understanding."
She blamed him and banned him and bad him be silent,
With his learned language lecturing blockheads;
And said, "*Noli mittere*, man, your pearl Margarites
Before hogs who have their husks at pleasure.   10
They drool and drivel on them, and draff is prized more
Than all the precious pearls that Paradise offers.
I speak only of those," she said, "who show in their actions
That they love better their land and their earthly lordship,
Or riches and rents and to rest at leisure,
Than all the certain saws that Solomon uttered.
Now wisdom and wit are not worth parsley
Unless they are carded with covetousness, as clothiers comb
        woollens.
He who can contrive deceits and conspire evil,
And lead a love-day to license robbers,—   20
His craft and cunning are accounted wisdom,
He leads lords with lies and belies honesty.
Job the gentle has adjudged in his history
That the wicked wield the world's riches,
And that they are lords of each land living lawlessly.
Quare impii vivunt, bene est omnibus qui praevaricantur et inique agunt.
The psalter says the same of such as do evil:
Ecce ipsi peccatores abundantes in saeculo obtinuerunt divitias.
'Lo,' says holy learning, 'how lords are wicked!'
Those whom God gives most give least to others;   30
The most unkind to common folk command most riches:
Quae perfecisti destruxerunt, justus autem quid fecit?

Jesters and jugglers and jangling storytellers,
Ribalds in their ribaldry, revel in their favours.

But he who has Holywrit ever in his speeches,
And can tell of Tobias and of the twelve Apostles,
And preach of the penance that Pilate inflicted
On the gentle Jesus whom Jews tortured,—
Little is he loved with such a lesson to show them,
Or called for or comforted, I take God to witness.   40

But those who feign themselves fools and fetch a living
Against the law of our Lord; who lie against themselves,
Who spit and who spew and speak foul language,
Who drink and drivel and demand attention,
Who ape and abuse those who offer no presents,—
They know no more of minstrelsy or of music to make men
     merry
Than Mund the Miller of *Multa fecit Deus.*
Without their sorry scandals, I swear truly,
No king or knight or canon in London
Would give them a groat for their gift at New Year's.   50
But mirth and minstrelsy among men is nowadays
Lechery and lying and loose stories.
Gluttony and great oaths is the good that they cherish.

If these clerics or commoners take Christ for their topic
At meat and in mirth, when minstrels are silent,
They tell perhaps a tale or two of the Trinity,
Bring forth a bald reason and take Bernard to witness,
And put forth a presumption to prove a verity.
So these men drivel from the dais that the deity is known to
     them,
And gnaw God with their gorge when their gut labours. 60

F

The poor may plead and pray in the doorway;
They may quake for cold and thirst and hunger;
None receives them rightfully and relieves their suffering.
They are hooted at like hounds and ordered off.
Little does he love the Lord, who lent him all these favours,
And who so parts his portion with the poor who are in trouble.
If there were no more mercy among poor than among rich men,
Mendicants might go meatless to slumber.
God is often in the gorge of these great masters,
But among lowly men are his mercy and his works;   70
And so says the psalter, as I have seen it often:
Ecce audivimus eam in Effrata, invenimus eam in campis silvae.
Clerics and other conditions converse of God readily,
And have him much in the mouth, but mean men in their
     hearts.

Friars and false men have found such questions
To please proud men since the pestilence season,
And have so preached at Saint Paul's from pure envy of clerics,
That men are not firm in faith nor free in bounty
Nor sorry for their sins. Pride has so multiplied
In religious orders and in the realm, among rich and poor folk,
That prayers have no power to prevent the pestilence,   81
Yet the wretches of this world are not warned by each other.
The dread of death cannot draw pride from them;
Nor are they plentiful to the poor as plain charity wishes;
But glut themselves with their goods in gaiety and gluttony,
And break no bread with the beggar as the Book teaches:
Frange esurienti panem tuum, etc.
Tobias teaches otherwise; take heed, you rich men,
How that book, the Bible, bears witness:
Si tibi sit copia, abundanter tribue, Si autem exiguum, illud   90
     impertiri stude libenter.
Tobias means that he who has much should spend much also,

And that he who wins little should rule himself accordingly.
For there is no lore of our life to tell how long we shall have it.
Lords should love best to learn this lesson,
And how they may be humane, and help lowly folk,
Not to fare as fiddlers and friars for the sake of feasting,
To be at home in others' houses and to hate their own tables.
Woe is in the hall in all times and seasons
Where neither lord nor lady likes to linger.
Now each rich man has a rule to eat in secret,   100
In a private parlour, for poor folk's comfort,
In a chamber with a chimney, perhaps, and leave the chief
    assembly
Which was made for men to have meat and meals in:—
And all to spare to spend what another will spend afterwards!

I have heard high lords eating at the table
Converse as they were clerics upon Christ and his majesty,
And lay faults upon the Father who fashioned all men,
And complain against the clergy with crabbed language:
'Why would our Saviour suffer such a serpent in his happiness
As that which won the woman and the man after,   110
Through whose wiles and words they went to Satan,
And all their seed suffer the same death for their offences?
Here lies your law,' these lords argue,
'As clerks construe it from Christ in the gospel:
Filius non portabit iniquitatem patris, etc.
Why for the works of Adam should we who are living
Rot and be rent? Reason denies it:
Unusquisque portabit onus suum,' etc.
These are the lessons that men learn from these lords in their
    glory,
Which make men disbelieve if they muse much upon them.
(Imagination shall hereafter answer to the purpose.)   121
Augustine rebukes such arguers in the text where he teaches:

Non plus sapere quam oportet.
Never wish to know why God was willing
To suffer Satan to seduce his people,
But believe loyally in the lore of Holy Church,
And pray him for pardon and penance in your living,
And for the might of his mercy to amend you here.
He is a perverted ribald who pries into God's secrets,
Who would ever know why God was willing   130
To suffer Satan to seduce his people,
Or Judas to betray Jesus to the Jews in the garden.
All was as thou wouldest, O worshipful Father,
And all will be as thou wilt, however we argue.
Those who use these wiles to blind men's eyesight
With how Do Well is not Do Bet, may they be deaf forever,
(Since they will not know what these are together)
Unless they live the life that belongs to Do Well!
For I dare be bold that Do Bet miss them,
Though Do Best draw on them one day after another."   140

When Wit was aware what dame Study taught me,
He became so confused that he could not look upward,
And as dumb as death, and drew backwards.
For no prayer nor petition, nor kneeling painfully before him
Could I get a grain of his great wisdom.
He beamed and bowed and beckoned me toward Study,
With a sign that I should try her and beseech her favour.

When I was aware of his will I went to Study
And bowing: "Mercy, Madam, may I be your servant
As long as I shall live, late and early,   150
To work as you will while life is with me,
If you will teach me truly to tell what is Do Well."
"For your meekness, my man," she said, "and for your mild
    speaking

I shall give you to my cousin, Clergy, men call him.
He has wedded a wife within a six month season,
And she is kin to the Seven Arts; Scripture is her title.
These two as I hope, and in accordance with my teaching,
Will declare to you what is DoWell,—yea, I dare assure you."

Then I was blest as a bird with a bright morning,
And gladder than a gleeman with a golden present.   160
I asked her the way to where Clergy was dwelling.
"Tell me some token," I said, "for it is time that I was going."

"Ask for the highway," she said, "from here to Suffer-
Both-wele-and-woe, if you would know it,
And ride forth by Riches, but rest not near them,
For you will never come to Clergy if you couple with them.
Then leave on your left side a long mile at the shortest
Between the Lawn of Liking, or Lechery, as men call it;
Till you come to the court of Keep-your-tongue-closely-
From-Lying-and-Loose-speaking-and-delectable-drinking.
Then you shall see Sobriety and Simplicity-of-Speaking, 171
That each man be willing to show his wit to you.
And so you shall come to Clergy, who can teach deeply.
Show him this sign: I sent him to study,
And that I wish his wife well, for I wrote her many volumes,
And set her to Solomon and the psalter glosses.
She learned her logic and laws from my teaching,
And all the moods and the measures that music uses.
I first put Plato, the poet, to study.
I taught Aristotle argument, and other men also.   180
I caused men first to give grammars to children,
And to beat them with a broom if they were obstinate in
    learning.
For all kinds of craft I contrived instruments,
For carpenters and carvers, and compasses for masons,

I taught them level and line, though my eyes are dim.

I have threatened Theology a thousand times over,
The more I muse on it the mistier I think it;
And the deeper I dive the darker I find it.
It is no science for subleties, so much I am certain.
I should hold it idleness if love were not in it.   190
But because it holds love best I love it the better.
Where love is the leader, grace is never lacking.
Look that you love loyally if your liking is Do Well.
For Do Bet and Do Best are both of love's kindred.
Other sciences say, as I saw once in Cato:
Qui simulat verbis, nec corde est fidus amicus,
Tu quoque fac simile, sic ars deluditur arte.
'Where false men feign, feign also;
Beguile false folk, and foil the faithless.'
This is the counsel that Cato gives clerks who read him. 200
But Theology holds otherwise, whoever will notice.
He counsels the contrary of Cato's teaching.
He bids us be brethren and pray for our enemies,
And love those who belie us, and lend them when they are
    needy.
God himself commands that men do good for evil:
Dum tempus habemus, operemur bonum ad omnes, maxime autem ad
    domesticos fidei.
Paul's lesson to the people who love perfection
Is to do good for the love of God and give men who ask it,
And specially to such as believe with us.
Our Lord teaches us to love those who blame and libel us, 210
Not to grieve those who grieve us—God himself forebad it:
Mihi vindictam, et ego retribuam.
Therefore look that you love as long as you are living,
No science under the sun is so sovereign for salvation.

But Astronomy is an art hard to come by;
Geometry and Geomancy are guileful practice.
Whoever works with them will be long at labour.
Sorcery is the sovereign book which these sciences acknowledge.
There are contrivances in caskets, a common practice,
And experiments in alchemy to deceive the people.   220
If you hope to Do Well never deal in them.
I myself first subtilized and established these sciences,
Determined and devised them to delude others.
Tell these tokens to Clergy and then to Scripture,
To counsel her the courtesy to instruct you in Do Well."
I said, "Much thanks, Madam," and meekly saluted her,
And went quickly away without further hindrance.
Till I came to Clergy I could never linger.
I greeted the good man as Study taught me,
And afterwards his wife, and honoured them duly,   230
And told them the tokens taught me beforehand.
No one on earth since the world was fashioned
Was more graciously greeted and given his pleasure
Than I myself, surely, as soon as he noted
That I was of Wit's house and with his wife, dame Study.
I told him truly how I was directed thither,
To learn Do Well and Do Bet and Do Best the greatest.

"Do Well is a life," said he, "among unlearned people,
Active life men call it and husbandmen use it.
True tillers on earth, tailors and cobblers,   240
And all the kinds of craftsmen who can win their livelihood,
Who travail truly and toil for food,
Ditchers or delvers—Do Well men call it.
But to break bread with beggars, to cover their backs with
    clothing
To comfort the careworn in castles and in fetters,
To seek out the sick and send them what is needful,

To be obedient as brethren and sisters together;
This Do Bet bids us; as the psalter bears witness:
Ecce quam bonum et quam jocundum, habitare, fratres, in unum.
Sorry with the sad, singing with the mirthful: 250
Gaudere cum gaudentibus, et flere cum flentibus,
Doubtless is Do Bet, Do Best knows it truly.
Sir Do Best has benefices, so he is best of all of them,
By what God in his gospel grants and teaches:
Qui facit et docuerit, magnus vocabitur in regno coelorum.
Therefore Do Best is a bishop's equal,
The prince of God's people, to preach and to chasten.

Then Do Bet is to suffer for the soul's welfare
All that the book bids by the Church's teaching;
Which is, "Man, with all thy might, for Mercy's sake,   260
Look that you weave into your works what your word teaches;
Be shown in the assay what you seem outwardly:
Appare quod es, vel esto quod appares.
Let nobody be beguiled by thy bearing and speaking,
But be such in your soul as you seem to all men."

Then Do Best is to be bold and to blame the guilty,
Since you see yourself in soul honest;
But blame nobody where you are blameworthy:
Si culpare velis, culpabilis esse cavebis;
Dogma tuum sordet, cum te tua culpa remordet.   270
God in the gospel grievously reprimands
All who assail any sin and bear the sin upon them:
Qui consideras festucam in oculo fratris tui, trabem in oculo tuo, etc.
Why is your mind moved for a mote in your brother's eye,
Since a beam in your own blinds you darkly?
Ejice primo trabem in oculo tuo, etc.
This stops your own sight somewhat or wholly.
I advise each blind buzzard to look out for himself.

Abbots and priors and all ranks of prelates,
Parsons and parish priests, who should preach to the people
And amend all men by means of their teaching,   281
This text was taken for you to beware before teaching,
For you must be such as you speak to be the salve for others.
God's word would not be lost, for it is at work always.
If it may not avail the commons, it might avail yourselves.

But it seems now surely, to the sight of the world,
That God's word is working neither on learned nor laymen,
Unless in that manner which Mark mentions in the gospel:
Dum caecus ducit caecum, ambo in foveam cadunt.
The unlearned may make this likeness: that the beam   290
    lies in your eye,
And that the pest has fallen from your defaulting
Among all manner of men, through miserable clerics.
The Bible bears witness that all the folk of Israel
Bitterly bought the sins of two bad prelates,
Ophni and Phinees; from their covetousness
Archa dei was withheld and Ely broke his collar.
You correctors, catch hold of this, correct yourselves for a
    beginning,
And then you may say safely, as David in the psalter:
Existimasti inique quod ero tui similis, arguam te, et statuam contra
    faciem tuam.
Then base clerks shall be abashed to blame or to grieve you,
And carp no more as they carp now and call you dumb hounds:
Canes non valentes latrare.   302
And fear to anger you with a word in injury of your labour,
And be prompter at your bidding than for a pound of nobles.
For your holiness have this in your heart's chamber.

One rule is right for the religious orders.
Gregory, the good pope and great author,

F*

Wrote in his *Morales* the rule of these orders,
And showed in a simile that they should do accordingly.
"When the flood fails the fish perish,   310
They die from drought in the dry stretches.
Religious rovers," said Gregory, "also
Starve and stink and steal lords' bounty,
When the cloister and the convent cannot suffice them."
For if heaven be on this earth or ease in any spirit,
I see by many signs that it is in school or cloister,
For all chaffing and chiding are shunned in the cloister,
All there is books and obedience, reading and learning.
There is no scorning in a school, unless a clerk will not study,
And there is great love there and liking, for each loves the other.
But now religion is a rider and roamer on highways,   321
A leader of love-days and a land buyer,
A pricker on a palfrey from manor to manor,
With the hounds behind him, as if he were a noble.
Unless the knave kneel when his cup is brought him,
He lowers on him and asks him, who taught him courtesy?
There is little reason for lords to take lands from their heirs
To give religious men who are regardless of the rain on parish
    altars.
Their vicars are often found indolent,
With no pity on the poor or pretence of charity.   330
Their own lands are so large that they are lords upon them.

But a king shall come and confess the orders,
And punish you, as the Bible tells, for breaking your
    ordinances,
And amend nunneries, monks and canons,
And put them to their penance, *ad pristinum statum ire;*
And barons and earls beat them through *Beatus vir's* teaching,
Which their children shall claim, and chastize you foully:
Hi in curribus et hi in equis ipsi obligati sunt, etc.

Then friars in their refectory shall find a key
Of Constantine's coffers, in which the gold is lying   340
That Gregory's grandchildren have so evilly expended.
Then the Abbot of Abbington and all his issue forever
Shall have a knock from a king and an incurable injury,
That this will be so, seek it, you who study the Bible:
Quomodo cessavit exactor, quievit tributum, contrivit Dominus baculum
impiorum et virgam dominantium caedentium plaga insanabili.
But before that king come, Cain shall awaken;
But Do Well shall dash him down and destroy his authority."

"Then Do Well and Do Bet," I said, "are *dominus* and
    knighthood."
"I will not speak scornfully," quoth Scripture, "unless   350
    scriveners lie.
Neither kingship nor knighthood, for aught that I can witness,
Nor royalty nor riches nor the regalia of lordship,
Help men to heaven an hair's thickness.
Paul proves it impossible for the rich man to have heaven;
And Solomon says also that silver is the worst affection.
Nihil iniquius quam amare pecuniam.
Cato would have us covet it only as need teaches:
Dilige denarium, sed parce dilige formam.
And patriarchs and prophets and poets also
Write to instruct us to wish no riches,   360
And praise patient poverty; the Apostles bear witness
That these have heritage in heaven as just recompense,
Where rich men may claim no rights but through ruth and
    God's favour."

"*Contra*," said I, "by Christ, for I can refute it,
And prove by Peter and by Paul also
That the baptized must be safe, be they rich or poor men."

"That is *in extremis*," said Scripture, "among Jews and
    Saracens.
They may be saved so; for that is our teaching.
An unchristian man may in that case christen an heathen,
And for his loyal belief, when life leaves him,   370
Have the heritage of heaven as any Christian.
But Christian men with no more may not come to heaven,
For Christ died for Christians and confirmed the law
That whoever wills and wishes to arise with him,
Si cum Christo surrexistis, etc.
Should love and believe and fulfil the law,
Which is: love thy lord God liefest of all things,
And then all Christian creatures in common, each the other.
So it belongs to all to love who believe in their salvation.
Unless we do this, indeed, before the Day of Judgement 380
Our clothes that are kept moth-eaten while we see beggars go
    naked,
Our delight in wine and wild-fowl while we know others
    who are hungry,
And all our storing of silver, will sit sorely against us.

Every Christian creature should be kind to others,
And then an help to the heathen, in hope of their amendment.
God commands the high and the low that no man hurt another,
And says, "Slay none similar to my own likeness,
Unless I send you some token;" and says, "*Non occides*,"
Which means, slay not, but suffer; and all is for the better.
For, *mihi vindictam, et ego retribuam*.   390
I shall punish them in purgatory or in the prison of Satan,
Each man for his misdeeds, unless mercy prevent it."

"This is a long lesson," I said, "and I am little the wiser.
You talk of Do Well and of Do Bet in dark speeches.
You tell many tales that Theology teaches;

That I was made a man, and my name entered
In the Legend of Life long ere my creation,
Or else withdrawn for some wickedness, as Holywrit witnesses:
Nemo ascendit ad coelum, nisi qui de coelo descendit.

By our Lord," said I, "I believe it well, and no learning better.
For God gave the grace of wit and all his goods afterwards 401
To Solomon the sage, the writer of Sapience,
That he might rule his realm and be rich and mighty.
He judged well and wisely, as Holywrit tells us.
Aristotle and he knew men most thoroughly.
Masters who teach men of God's mercy, and preachers,
All quote us their words as wisest in their lifetime,
And all Holy Church holds both in damnation.
If I should work by their works to win heaven,
When for their works and wit they dwell with Satan,   410
I should work unworthily—whatever you may preach me.
I do not wonder that the wise often
Have souls that are unseemly in the sight of God Almighty.
For many men in this world are more devoted
To goods than to God, and thus grace fails them
In their direst danger, when they depart hence.
Solomon and many scholars showed great wisdom;
But their works, as Holywrit says, were always the contrary.
The wise and witty and the well-lettered scholars
Seldom practise what they preach and prove it to others. 420
Super cathedra Moysi, etc.

But I think that it will be with many as in the age of Noah,
When he built his boat of boards and timber.
No wright was saved who worked on it nor any of the labourers
But only the birds and the beasts and the blessed Noah,
His wife and his sons and their wives with them
Of all the wrights who worked on it, not one was delivered.

God forbid masters of the faith to fare likewise!
For Holy Church is the harbour and God's house of safety
To shield us from shame, as the ark did the creatures   430
While the men who made it were drowned amid the waters.
The *culorum* of this parable points to curates,
Who are carpenters of the Church for Christ's own creatures.
Homines et jumenta salvabis, Domine, etc.
On Dooms-day the deluge will be of death and fire together,
Therefore I counsel you clerks, who are the wrights of Holy
     Church,
Work the works that you see written, and be wary that you
     come into it.

On Good Friday I find that a felon was rescued,
Who had lived all his life by lying and thieving,
Because he confessed on the cross and Christ assoiled him 440
He was sooner saved than Saint John the Baptist,
Or Adam or Isaiah or any of the prophets,
Who had lain with Lucifer many long ages.
A robber was ransomed rather than these others,
Without any penance of purgatory, to perpetual bliss.

What woman did worse than Mary Magdalene?
Or who worse than David, who sought the death of Uries?
Or Paul the Apostle, a pitiless ruler,
Who condemned many Christians to a cruel death?
And now these are as sovereigns with saints in heaven,   450
Though their works in the world were the most wicked in
     their lifetime.
Those whose words are wise and who wrote many volumes
Of wit and of wisdom, dwell with the damned ones.
What Solomon said I believe sure and certain for all men:
Sunt justi atque sapientes et opera eorum in manu Dei sunt, etc.

Some are witty and live well, but their works are resting
In the hands of Almighty God, and he knows truly
Who will be allowed there for his love and for his loyal service,
Or else for an evil will and for an envious spirit
Also be allowed there, for by the lawless men know virtue. 460
How would men know what is white if all things were in
    darkness,
Or know who were a good man unless there were also some
    villains?
Let us be still with the bad; I believe few are worthy;
When the word 'must' moves toward us we have no more
    than to suffer;
And the surest word that ever God said was when he said
nemo bonus.

Learning was little commended in the Lord's teaching
When he said to Saint Peter and to such as loved him,
Cum steteritis ante reges et praesides, etc.
'Though you come before kings and clerks of justice,
Be not abashed; I shall be in your speeches,   470
And give you the wit and the will and the cunning to answer
All those who argue against Christendom.'

David makes mention that he spoke among princes.
No king might overcome him in cunning speeches.
But wit and wisdom never won the victory
Where men were in misfortune, without more from God's
    favour.

The most redoubtable doctor and diviner of the Trinity,
The elder Augustine, the highest of the fathers,
Said this in a sermon, as I saw once in writing: 479
Ecce ipsi idiotae irapiunt coelum, ubi nos sapientes in inferno mergimur.
The meaning of this may be given tor Englishmen as follows:

'None are so readily ravished from the right doctrine
As these cunning clerks who construe many volumes.
Nor are any sooner saved or more sober in doctrine
Than plowmen and peasants and poor common labourers.'
Shoemakers and shepherds and such simple peasants
Pierce with a *pater noster* the palace of heaven,
And pass purgatory penniless at their earthly parting,
Go into the bliss of paradise for their pure faith,
Who were imperfect here in knowing and living.   490
There have been countless clerks who have cursed the hour
That they could construe further than *credo in deum patrem.*
Many a person has prized the *pater noster* highest.
I see examples myself, as may many another,
Servants who serve lords seldom fall in arrears,
As do the keepers of their lord's goods, clerks and stewards.
The laity and the unlettered and men of little knowledge
Seldom fall so far in arrears or so far in sinning
As do clerks of Holy Church, who keep Christ's treasure, 499
Or the store of souls for salvation, as God says in the gospel."

HEN Scripture scorned me and spoke her reason,
And blamed me in Latin and esteemed me lightly,
And said, *multi multa sciunt et seipsos nesciunt.*
Then I wept in woe and wrath at her language.
I was furious and frantic and fell into a slumber.
A delightful dream took hold upon me.
I was wafted away; Fortune fetched me
And led me alone into the land of Longing.
Here is the mirror of the Middle-Earth. She made me look in it,
And then she said to me: "Here you may see wonders,　　10
Witness what you wish, and win it, peradventure."

Following Fortune were two fair damsels,
Concupiscencia-Carnis men called the elder maiden,
And Covetousness-of-the-Eyes they called the other.
Pride-of-Perfect-living passed in with them,
And bad me to be self-sufficient and to esteem Clergy lightly.
Concupiscencia-Carnis caressed me about the shoulders,
And said, "You are young and eager and have years aplenty
To live long and to love ladies.
Much that is mirthful may be seen in this mirror,　　20
And lead your will lightly all your lifetime."
The second said the same: "I shall pursue your wishes.
Till you are a lord and have land I shall never leave you,
For I shall follow in your fellowship if Fortune permits me."
"He shall find me his friend," said Fortune after her,
"With me no man ever missed happiness."

There was one named Age, heavy and cheerless;
"Man," he said, "if I meet you, by Mary in heaven,
You shall find Fortune fail you when your need is greatest,
And *Concupiscencia-Carnis* clean forsake you.　　30
You shall bitterly ban both hours and seasons

When Covetousness-of-the-Eyes ever encountered you.
And Pride-of-Perfect-living shall imperil you often."

'Never reck of that," said Recklessness, and strode forth in
    ragged clothing,
"Follow as Fortune wishes; you have far till Age meet you.
A man may stoop sometimes when he shall take the tonsure."
"*Homo proponit,*" said a poet, Plato was his name,
"And *Deus disponit,*" he said, "let God have his wishes.
If Truth will witness that it is well to follow Fortune,
Concupiscencia-Carnis and Covetousness-of-Eyesight   40
Shall not greatly grieve or beguile you, unless you wish it."
"So be it, Sparrow!" said Childishness, and thus seduced me
Till *Concupiscencia-Carnis* governed me wholly.

"Alas," said Age and Holiness together,
"That wit should become so wretched for Will to have his
    liking."

Covetousness-of-the-Eyes comforted me after,
And followed me for forty and for five winters.
I disdained Do Well and Do Bet equally.
I had no liking, believe me, to learn of them.

Covetousness-of-the-Eyes comforted me often,   50
And said, "Have no conscience how you come to riches.
Go and confess to some friar and show him your sinning.
For while Fortune is your friend friars will love you,
And fetch you to their fraternity and find occasion
To ask their prior and their principal for a pardon for you,
And pray for you point by point if you are *pecuniosus.*
Sed poena pecuniaria non sufficit pro spiritualibus delictis."

I took advice of this woman, her words were so pleasant,

Till I had forgotten youth and age overtook me.
Then Fortune became my foe, for all her fair promises,   60
And poverty pursued me and put me to humility,
And I found the friars afraid and sulking
Against my first agreement, when I answered that I would not
Be buried in their house but in the church of my parish.
Once I had heard the witness of Conscience
That it was becoming that a body should be buried where it
      was christened,
That the ground of the grave should be the ground of the parish.
The friars held me a fool for saying this to them,
And loved me less for my loyal speaking.   69
But I cried out to my confessor, who considered himself
      so cunning,
"By my faith, friar," I said, "you fare like those widowers
Who only wed widows to wield their property.
Come now, on the cross, you care nothing
Of where my body is buried, if you bag the silver!
I have marvelled much, as have many others,
Why your convent covets to confess and to bury
Rather than immerse infants who are initiates for the sacrament.
Baptism and burial are both necessary,
But there is more merit, methinks, in baptism.
For a baptized man may, as masters tell us,   80
Come through contrition to the high heaven:
Sola contritio, etc.
And a child without baptism may not be so rescued:
Nisi quis renatus fuerit.
Look well, you lettered men, whether I lie or do not."

Then Loyalty looked on me, and I looked at her lowering.
"Why do you lower," said Loyalty, and looked at me harder.
"I would know if I dare tell," I said, "this dream among the
      people?"

"Yes, by Peter and by Paul," she said, "and take them both to
   witness:
Non oderis fratres secrete in corde tuo, sed publice argue illos."   90
"They will also allege," I said, "and have the gospel to prove it:
Nolite iudicare quemquam."
"Whom does law serve," said Loyalty, "unless someone
   enforce it
On falsehood and on feigning, for the apostle said with reason:
Non oderis fratrem.
Also David in the psalter says as follows:
Existimasti inique quod ero tui similis, etc.
The unlearned are licensed to speak openly
Although the tale were true and it touched evil.
Why should you be wary of what all know already,   100
Or of presenting it in poetry to punish vices?
But never be the first by whom a fault is mentioned.
Though you see evil, speak not at first; be sorry it is not
   amended,
Never publish abroad what is private and secret,
Neither laud it from love nor blame it from envy:
Parum lauda, vitupera parcius."

"He speaks truly," said Scripture, and stepped higher to
   address us.
But the more that unlearned men should meditate her teaching
The less, I believe, would they love and honour it.
This was her topic and her text, for I took good note of it: 110
"*Multi* were summoned to a supper and to sit at table,
But the porter unpinned the gate when all the people were
   gathered
And plucked in *pauci* privily and let the remnant go roaming."

My heart trembled with terror at the text which she had spoken.
My mind was in a maze, and I mused secretly

Whether I was chosen or not chosen; I thought of Holy Church
Who brought me to baptism to be one of God's chosen;
Christ called us all to come if we desired it,
Saracens and schismatics, Jews and all men.
O vos omnes sitientes, venite, etc.   120
He bad them to suck with safety for their sin at his breast,
And to drink help for harm, whoever might deny them.

"Then all Christians may come," I cried, "and claim their
    entrance
By the blood with which he bought us and by our baptism also.
Qui crediderit et baptizatus fuerit, etc.
For although a Christian coveted to renounce his christening,
To renounce it rightfully would be contrary to reason.

No churl may make a charter to sell his possessions
Without the leave of his lord; for no law permits him.
But he may run into arrears and so roam from home,   130
And rove so recklessly as a renegade caitiff,
That Reason shall reckon with him and rebuke him finally,
Conscience account with him and cast him in arrears,
And so put him in a prison or a purgatory to burn him,
And there reward him for his arrears till the Day of Doom,—
Unless Contrition come and cry during his lifetime
From the mouth and from the mind for mercy on his offences."

"That is certain," said Scripture, "and no sin may hinder
That Mercy and her fellow, Meekness, amend all men,
For both, as our books tell us, are above all God's creatures:
Misericordia ejus super omnia opera ejus."   141

"Yea, baw for books!" cried one broken out of hell,
Named Trojanus, who had been a true knight; and took a pope
    to witness

How he was dead and damned and dwelt in sorrow,
As an unchristian creature,—"Clerks know truly
That all the learning under our Lord could not lift me from
   that sorrow,
But only love and loyalty and my lawful judgements.
Gregory knew this well, and wished my spirit
A rescue for the righteousness which my works revealed to him.
And after he wept and wished that I were granted   150
Grace, without bead-bidding the boon was given,
And I saved, as you may see, without the singing of masses.
My love and my learning and my living in truth
Brought me as no prayer might from bitter sorrow."

"Lo you lords, what loyalty did for a Roman emperor,
Who was an unchristian creature, as clerks may tell you.
Not through the prayer of a pope but through his pure truth
Was that Saracen saved, as Saint Gregory witnesses.
You lords who keep the laws should hold this lesson in
   remembrance:
Think on the truth of Trojanus, and be true to the people.   160

This is murky for many, but, you men of Holy Church,
The *Legenda Sanctorum* instructs more spaciously than I can tell
   you.
Thus loyal love and living in truth
Hauled out of hell an heathen Roman!
Blessed be Truth, that so broke hell's portals,
And saved the Saracen from Satan's power,
Which all the laws of learning were listless to accomplish!
Love and loyalty is the lofty science!
For this is the Book blessed with bliss and joyfulness;
God wrought it and wrote it with his own finger,   170
And gave it to Moses on the Mount that all men should learn it.
On law without love," he said, "I would not lay a bean,

Nor on any science under the sun, the Seven Arts nor any other;
Unless they are learned with our Lord's love, all is lost and
    wasted.
They are not clasps to catch silver nor to have men called master,
But are all for the love of our Lord and the better to love the
    people.
For Saint John said it, and his words are sure:
Qui non diligit, manet in morte.
He who loves not, believe me, lives in dying.
Let all manner of men, enemies and brothers,   180
Love each the other, and lend them unselfishly.
Who lends not loves not, God knows it truly,
And commands each creature to conform himself to loving,
And especially poor people, and next our enemies.
Our merit is to love all who are hateful to us,
And to please poor people, and their prayers may help us.
For our joy and for our health Jesus Christ of heaven
In the apparel of a poor man pursues us always,
And looks upon us in their likeness, with a lovely cheer, 189
To know by our kind heart and by the casting of our vision
Whether we love the lords here before our Lord who is blissful.
He excites us by the evangelists that when we make feastings
We should not call our kin nor the kin of rich folk;
'*Cum facitis convivia, nolite invitare amicos,*
But call the careworn, the crooked and the poor folk.
Your friends will feed you and find you requital
For your feasting and your fair gifts, and each befriend the other.
But for the poor I shall pay, and perfectly requite the labour
Of those who give meat or money and lend them for my sake.'
For some of the best are born rich, and some are beggars
    and poor folk.   200
For we are all Christ's creatures, and by his coffer are we
    wealthy,
And brothers of one blood, beggars and nobles.

Christ's blood on Calvary is the spring of Christendom,
And we became blood brethren there, recovered by one body,
As *quasi modo geniti*, and gentle without exception,
None base or a beggar, but when sin cause it.
Qui facit peccatum, servus est peccati.

In the Old Law, as Holywrit tells us,
Men were men's sons, mentioned always
As issue of Adam and of Eve, until the god-man was crucified,
And after his resurrection *Redemptor* was his title,   211
And we his brethren, bought through him, both rich and poor
    men.
Therefore love we as lief brothers, each laughing with the other,
And each give what he can spare as his goods are needed.
Let each man help the other, for we shall all go hence.
Alter alterius onera portate.
Let us be neither unkind with our goods nor with our cunning
    and learning,
For no man knows how near he is to be taken from them.
Therefore let no man be a mocker, though he know more Latin,
Nor correct men coarsely, for our guilt is common.   220
Whatever clerks may argue on Christendom or otherwise,
Christ said to a common woman in a public dinner
That *fides sua* should save her and absolve all her sins.

Then belief is a loyal help, and above law and logic;
Of law or of logic in *Legenda Sanctorum*
Little allowance is made, unless belief help them.
It is long before logic can lay clear a Legend,
And law is loath to love unless he light on silver.
I counsel all Christians not to cleave too closely
Either to law or to logic, where they love no lying.   230
For I find some words written that were faith's teaching,
And which saved sinful men, as Saint John witnesses:

Eadem mensura qua mensi fueritis, remetietur vobis.
Therefore learn we the law of love as our Lord taught it,
And as Saint Gregory has spoken for the soul's wellbeing:
Melius est scrutari scelera nostra, quam naturas rerum.

I move this matter most of all for poor folk,
For in their likeness our Lord often has been discovered.
Witness in the Paschal Week, when he walked to Emmaus.
Cleophas did not recognize Christ before them   240
Through his poor apparel and pilgrim garments,
Till he blessed and broke the bread that they were eating.
They were aware by his works that he was Jesus,
But they could not tell him by his talk and clothing.

All this was in example to us sinful people
That we should all be lowly and loving in our speaking,
And not apparel us over proudly, for we are pilgrims together.
God has many times been met among needy people
In the apparel of a poor man and in a pilgrim's likeness,
But never a soul has seen him in the sect of rich folk.   250

Saint John and other Saints were seen in poor clothing,
And were pilgrims praying for men's almsdeeds.
Jesus alighted upon a Jew's daughter of gentle lineage,
Yet a pure and poor maid, and wedded to a poor man.

Martha moved a complaint against Mary Magdalene
And said such words to our Saviour himself:
Domine, non est tibi curae quod soror mea reliquit me solam ministrare.
God answered hastily that he followed either,
Both Mary's way and Martha's way, as Matthew bears witness,
But God put poverty first and praised it more highly.   260
Maria optimam partem elegit, quae non, etc.
All the wise men that ever were, by aught that I can witness,

Praise poverty as the best life, if patience follow it,
As by far the more blessed and better than riches.
Although it is sour to suffer, sweet comes after,
There is a rough rind around the walnut,
But after that bitter bark has been shelled away
There is a kernel of comfort which conduces health—
So after poverty or penance patiently suffered;
For that makes men mindful of God, and more truly willing
To weep and to pray well, whence mercy arises.   271
And thus Christ is the kernel and comfort of the spirit.
The poor man sleeps more soundly and safely than others.
He dreads death, darkness and robbers
Less than he who is rich, as reason witnesses:
Pauper ego ludo, dum tu dives meditaris.

Although Solomon said, as men see in the Bible,
Divitias nec paupertates, etc.
A wiser than Solomon bore witness and taught us
That perfect poverty is to have no possessions,   280
And is the life that God likes best, as Luke bears witness:
Si vis perfectus esse, vade et vende.
This is to mean to men who live on the mould of earth
That who would be pure and perfect must put possessions
     from him,
Or sell them, as the Book says, take the silver, and distribute
To beggars who go begging and bid goods for God's love.
No man ever lacked meat whom God's mercy tended:
Nihil impossibile volenti.
David says in the psalter to such as are willing
To serve God in godly ways and who grieve him with   290
     no offences
Inquirentes autem Dominum non minuentur omni bono.
They shall lack neither a livelihood nor linen nor woollen.
If priests were perfect they would take no silver

For masses or for matins, nor take meat of usurers,
Nor a curtle nor a coat, though cold should kill them,—
If they did their duty, as David says in the psalter:
Judica me, Deus, et discerne causam meam.

By the growing grain God teaches all men
To meet meekly the misfortunes of this lifetime:
Nisi granum frumenti cadens in terra mortuum fuerit, ipsum   300
   solum manet.
Unless the seed sown in the slough perish
No spur of wheat will spring up, nor spike harden at the ear.
No wheat will rise unless wheat first wither.
Other seeds also have similar courses.
They are laid low in earth and lost within it.
Through the great grace of God grain that is buried
Lances up at last, and we live upon it.
The seeds that are sown and may suffer winters
Are more timely and tougher to do men service
Than seeds that are sown and cannot suffer freezings,   310
Nor the winds and weathering of a winter season.
Lin-seed and leek-seed and lenten sowings
Have not the worth of wheat nor can so well endure
The frost on the fields when it freezes steadily.
And so, surely, those who suffer penances
Will be commended by God as death comes on them,
And praised for their penance and pure martyrdom,
Or recognized confessors who account as rushes
All fear and famine and false men's witness.
An husbandman hopes after an hard winter,   320
If God give him life, to have a good harvest;
So God proves his prophets who are patient in suffering.
Mishaps and misfortunes and many tribulations
Are the true tokens of a time coming
With mirth for their mourning and a much greater garner.

Christ said that his saints who for his sake suffer
Poverty and penance and persecution of the body
Shall have the wages of greater worship and be more worthily
    accounted
Than angels; in their affliction he hailed them as follows:
'*Tristitia vestra vertetur in gaudium.*   330
Your sorrow shall turn to solace in the ending,
And your way is from woe to weal everlasting.'
But read of the rich, and the reverse is written.
God, as the gospel teaches, gives him a foul title,
His ghost shall go and his goods linger.
And God asks him afterwards: 'Who shall have them,
These goods which you keep in coffer and store house?—
And you so loath to leave what you must leave shortly?
O *stulte, ista nocte anima tua egredietur; thesaurizat et ignorat.*
A shiftless servant will spend the remainder,   340
On which many a moth has meanwhile feasted.
Upholsterers on Cornhill shall have it at auction.'

Lo, lords, lo, and ladies! witness
That the sweet liquor lasts but a little season,
Like peapods, and early pears, plums and cherries.
What lances up lightly lasts but a moment,
And what is readiest to ripen rots soonest.
A fat land full of dung breeds foul weeds rankly,
And so are surely all such bishops,
Earls and archdeacons and other rich clerics   350
Who traffic with tradesmen and turn on them if they are beaten,
And have the world at their will to live otherwise.
As weeds run wild on ooze or on the dunghill,
So riches spread upon riches give rise to all vices.
The best wheat is bent before ripening
On land that is overlaid with marle or the dungheap.
And so are surely all such people:

Overplenty feeds the pride which poverty conquers.

The wealth of this world is evil to its keeper,
Howsoever it may be won, unless it be well expended.   360
If he is far from it, he fears often
That false men or felons will fetch away his treasure.
Moreover wealth makes men on many occasions
To sin, and to seek out subtlety and treason,
Or from coveting of goods to kill the keepers.
Thus many have been murdered for their money or riches,
And those who did the deed damned forever,
And he himself, perhaps, in hell for his hard holding;
And greed for goods was the encumbrance of all together.
Pence have often purchased both palaces and terror;   370
Riches are the root of robbery and of murder;
He who so gathers his goods prizes God at little.

Ah! well may it be with poverty, for he may pass untroubled,
And in peace among pillagers if patience follow him!
Our Prince Jesus and his Apostles chose poverty together,
And the longer they lived the less wealth they mastered.
Tanquam nihil habentes, et omnia possidentes.

We hear that Job and Abraham were wondrously wealthy,
With countless goods and costly treasure.
Yet Abraham for all his goods had much sorrow   380
And was put in great poverty; a prince or ruler
Took his wife from him and held her in private.
Abraham was not so hardy as to offer any hindrance,
Nor for all the brightness of her beauty to be known as her
    husband.
Because he suffered and said nothing our Lord sent a token
So that the king cried for Abraham's forgiveness,
And delivered him his wife with a treasure in addition.
What joy had Job the gentle in living?

How bitterly he bought it, as the Book tells us.
Because he sang in his sorrow, 'Si bona accepimus a Domino, 390
O thou good and dear God, give us also mala,'
All his sorrow at that song was changed to solace,
Job became a joyful man; joy revisited him.
So patience relieved the poverty of these patriarchs in sorrow,
And brought them all above, who perished in suffering.
Grain that lies in the ground through grace finally
Springs and spreads aloft. So sped father Abraham,
And Job the gentle. Their joy is without ending.

Do not believe, you lettered men, that I blame riches,
Though I praise poverty and prove it worthier   400
By the words of Holywrit and the wise philosophers.
Both must be good, be certain, I enjoin you,
For they are lives that our Lord loves, and liberal ways to
    heaven.
The patient poor pass purgatory
More readily than the rich, though they run together.

If a merchant and a messenger meet on a journey
And walk one way to where each must harbour
And reckon before Reason a reasonable accounting,
Of what one had and what the other had, and what they had
    jointly,
The merchant must needs be delayed longer than the messenger.
For the particulars of his paper and his private ledgers   411
Will delay him, I believe, a league's travel.
The messenger has no more than with his mouth to utter
His errand and to show his letter, and is at once delivered.
And even though they walk on their way together
The messenger may go through the midst of the wheat field,
And no man will be angry with him or ask a toll fee,
No hayward is so hot-headed as to ask a penny:
Necessitas non habet legem.

But if the merchant make his way over the man's corn field, 420
And the hayward happen to see him coming,
The merchant must offer money from his wallet,
Or his hat or his hood or else his gauntlets—
And yet be delayed, I believe; for the law requires
That merchants in many places must pay toll for their
     merchandise.
If they went on their way to Winchester fair,
The merchant with his merchandise might not go so quickly
As the messenger may, nor with so much readiness.
One bears but a box with a brevet in it,
While the merchant brings a bag with bundles and wares,
And dreads death and that the dark is hiding   431
Robbers who rifle the rich of their treasure.
The messenger is always merry and his mouth full of singing,
He believes that with his letters no man will harm him.
And yet the merchant, through money and many favours,
May have horses and horsemen; and though he met with robbers
None will assail him on account of his followers,
And he be as safe as the messenger and as soon at his hostelry.

You know well, you wise men, what is my meaning.
The meaning of the merchant is that men who are wealthy 440
Are accountable to Christ and to the king of heaven,
And must hold evenly the highway of the commandments,
And love and lend to loyal and disloyal,
Have ruth, and relieve with their great riches
All manner of men in misery and affliction,
Find beggars bread and bring clothes to the frozen.
To pay their tythes truly is a toll, or seems such,
For which our Lord looks from all who live and prosper
Without wiles or wrong or women at the brothels,
And still more, to make peace and to quit men of their burdens,
To save and to spare and to spend upon the needy,   451

As Christ himself commands of all Christian people:
Alter alterius onera portate, etc.
The messengers are mendicants who live by men's almsdeeds.
They are not bound by the two laws as those bind the rich folk,
They neither lend nor learn nor keep lenten fasting,
And other private penances; for the priest knows well
That the law will leave such lowly folk exempted.
They have no tythes to tythe nor clothes to give the naked,
Nor need come to inquests nor be *contumax* if they labour   460
On holiday or on holy eves to win a livelihood.
If one love and believe as the law teaches,
Qui crediderit et baptizatus fuerit, etc.
And tell the Lord his tale as a true messenger,
And show by seal and by letter with what lord he is dwelling,
And acknowledge himself a Christian in the creed of holy
    Church,
There is no law, I believe, that will leave him at the portal,
Where God himself is gate-ward and knows each comer.
The porter in his pity will perform justice,
Since the man wills and wishes to each man as to himself.   470
Will is worth as much in a wretched beggar
As all that the rich reach for and rightfully distribute.
He has as much meed for the mite that he offers
As the rich man for all his money and more, by the gospel:
Amen dico vobis, quia haec vidua paupercula, etc.
Thus patient poverty is the most perfect living,
And all priests who seek perfection should draw towards
    poverty.

Spera in deo is spoken of priests who have no spending of silver;
But if they toil truly and trust in God Almighty
They shall lack no livelihood, nor woollen nor linen.—   480
The title by which you take orders tells your promotion;
You have no need to take silver for the chanting of masses;

God who gave you your title should give you your wages,
Or the bishop who blessed you, if you be worthy of them.—

No king could make a knight without gold at his disposal
To provide for him properly and to repay his service.
Without land or lineage or applause from his master,
He is a sad servant and a sorry king made him.
The same may be said truly of all such preachers
Without training or ties, but the tonsure only,   490
And a title that is a tittle for their trust in a livelihood.
They have more faith, I fancy, to fetch a living
With the tonsure than with training or with truthful conduct.
I wonder often why the bishop
Approves such priests who betray the lowly.

A charter is challengeable to a chief justice.
If false Latin is in the letter or lines omitted,
Or if there is lettering between the lines, the law impugns it.
The man who makes such charters is mocked as a blockhead.
So he is a fool, by my faith, who falters in his gospel,   500
Or in mass or in matins, or who makes an error.
Qui offendit in uno, in omnibus est reus.
So David in the psalter says of abbreviators:
*Psallite Deo nostro, psallite, quoniam rex terrae Deus Israel, psallite
     sapienter.*
The bishop will be blamed before God, in my opinion,
When he crowns as God's knights those who cannot *sapienter*
Sing or read psalms or say the daily masses.
Both the bishops and the chaplain are to blame equally;
For each is indicted of *ignorancia*
Non excusat episcopos nec unlearned clergy.   510

This denouncing of dull priests made me digress from poverty
Which I praise in the patient as more perfect than riches."
     G

One disputed with me in doctrine; I dreamed much further;
I saw all this sleeping. So Nature approached me,
And named me by my name and bad me note all things,
And let the wonders of this world teach wisdom to me.
I was led alone to learn by parables
Unto a mountain named Middle-Earth, as it seemed in my
    vision,
And to love my Creator and his creatures in their kinds and
    species.
I saw the sun and the sea and the sand beside it,   520
And where birds and beasts walked beside their partners,
Wild serpents in the woods and wonderful birds
In feathers flecked with fantastic colours.
Man and his mate moved before me;
Poverty and plenty, peace and battle,
Bliss and bale were both beside me;
I saw man take meed, and mercy neglected.

I saw that Reason was sure in pursuing all animals
In their eating and drinking and engendering of the species.
After the course of conception none cared for the other,   530
As in the rule of rutting time. Directly after
Males drew to males as morning brightened,
And at evening also males left females.
No cow nor creature like her that had conceived would after
Bellow after bulls nor boar after sow.
Neither horses nor hounds nor any others
Would mix with their mates out of season.

I saw bushes where birds build for nesting.
No one has the wit to work so rarely.
I wondered from whom and where the magpie   540
Had learned to lay the sticks on which she lies for breeding.
No carpenter could have constructed that cage for wages.

If a mason should make a mould for it there were much to
    wonder at.

Yet I marvelled more how many wild fowl
Conceal and cover their eggs so closely,
On moors and on marshes, that men may not find them,
And hide their eggs whenever they leave them,
Lest wild animals and hawks should know it.
Some tread their mates and breed in the branches
And bring forth the young birds above all danger;   550
Or the brood is begot at the bill with breathing.
I watched their ways; and how the peacock engenders.
I marvelled much what master taught them,
And who taught them to timber in the trees so boldly,
Where no man nor beast may reach them nesting.

So I saw the sea and the stars afterwards,
And many strange sights that I spare to mention.
I marked the flowers in the field and their fair colours,
And how many hues were in the green meadows.
I thought it strange that some were sweet and some bitter; 560
It would take long to tell their types and colours.
But that which most moved me and made me thoughtful
Was that Reason regarded and ruled all creatures
But man and his mate; many times, I thought,
That Reason ruled neither rich nor poor folk.
Then I rebuked Reason and addressed him boldly:
"I wonder," said I, "why you are held so prudent,
And do not rather rule man than other creatures!
For surely I see none surfeit so often;
They are immoderate with meat and many times in drinking,
In wealth and women and in words also;   571
They are excessive in all things, and so are no others.
Reason rules beasts always and rules man seldom.

I marvel still more that since man by nature
Is most like you, in his wit and actions,
That he should not love your law and live in your teaching."
Then Reason berated me and said: "Never trouble
At what I allow or do not allow; leave that to me!
Amend if you may, for my time is in waiting.
Sufferance is a sovereign virtue and a swift vengeance.   580
Who suffers more than God?" said he; "No soul, I warrant.
He might amend in a minute what is misshapen in nature;
But for the good of some he suffers, and so he profits us."

"Scripture," he said, "shows men what is sufferance:
Propter deum subjecti estote omni creaturae.
Frenchmen and freemen thus tame their children:
Bele vertue est suffrance, mal dire est petyt veniance,
Bien dire et bien soffrir fait lui soffrant à bien venir.
I would have you," he said, "hold your tongue better,
And blame nobody before you are praiseworthy.   590
No creature under Christ can make himself.
And if Christian creatures could make themselves
Everybody would be blameless, believe me surely!
Yet you will find but few who are fain to listen
To their foul faults rehearsed before them.
The wise and the witty wrote thus in the Bible:
De re quae te non molestat, noli certare.
Whether a man is fair or deformed, it is a fault to mock at
The form and figure which God fashioned for him.
All that he did was well done, as Holywrit witnesses: 600
Et vidit Deus cuncta quae fecerat, et erant valde bona.
He called every creature to increase his species,
And to minister to man, who must endure sorrow
While the fiend and the flesh fall upon him.
Man is made of such matter that he may not avoid sometimes
To be forced forward and to follow nature.

Cato grants it, *nemo sine crimine vivit.*"

Then I caught heat quickly and commenced to be ashamed,
And awoke therewith, and thought, "Woe betide me
That I might not have learned more in my long dreaming!
Now methinks I know what Do Well is," I cried,   611
    "by dear God in heaven!"
And as I cast up mine eyes one looked at me and questioned
What was Do Well: "Yea, sire," I answered,
"To see much and to suffer more, surely," I said, "is Do Well!"

"If you had suffered," he said, "as you were sleeping formerly
You should have come at what Clergy knows and conceived
    more through Reason.
Reason would have rehearsed what is recorded by Clergy.
For your own interruptions you are here forsaken.
Philosophus esses, sitacuisses.
Adam while he said nothing had Paradise at pleasure;   620
But when he prated about apples and interrupted to discover
The wisdom and the wit of God, he was barred from happiness.
This drove Reason from you; your rude language
Blamed and praised things beyond your judgement.
Then he had no wish to instruct you further.

"Reason refused you and would not rest with you,
From the pride and presumption of your perfect living.
No challenging and chiding will chasten a man so quickly
As shame that shows his sin and incites him to amendment.
If a drunken fool fall into the gutter,   630
Let him lie as he likes and never look to him.
If Reason rebukes him then, he recks nothing of him;
He accounts the counsel of Clergy as rushes.
To blame or beat him then were but time wasted.
Yet when Need fetches him forth, from fear of starving,

And Shame washes his shins and scrapes his clothing,
Then the drunken fool will know why he is blameworthy."

"You speak well," I said, "I have seen this often.
Nothing strikes so smartly or smells so foully
As Shame when he shows himself, for he is shunned by all men.
You speak thus to me," I said, "because I rebuked Reason."

"Certainly," he said, "that is so," and set off walking.   642
I arose at that and followed after,
And prayed him by his courtesy to tell me his name.

"I AM Imagination," he said, "I am never idle,
Though I hold by myself in health and sickness.
I have followed you faithfully forty-five winters,
And many times told you what Do Well signifies.
I have counselled you for Christ's sake to beguile no one,
Neither to lie nor to blame nor to teach what is forbidden,
Nor to waste words in idle speaking,
Nor to trouble a thing that is true, nor spend time idly,
But to live a lowly life in the law of Holy Church.
Then, doubtless you Do Well—whoever may do better.   10
But you meddle with making poems when you might say
    your psalter,
And pray for them who give you bread; there are books aplenty
To tell men what are Do Well, Do Bet and Do Best,
And preachers to prove it, as many a pair of friars."
I saw that he spoke truth, but said to excuse me:
"Cato counselled his son, clerk though he was primarily,
And thus solaced himself some time as I do with my poetry:
Interpone tuis interdum gaudia curis.
And I have heard," said I, "that the holy in other ages
Practised it to be more perfect in many places.   20
But if there were anyone who would tell me truly
What are Do Well and Do Bet and Do Best the greatest,
I should make a truce with toil and turn to Holy Church,
And, save in eating and sleeping, stay at my beadroll."

"Paul," said he, "in his Epistle proves what is Do Well:
Fides, spes, caritas, et major horum, etc.
Faith, Hope and Charity; all are virtues
And save men surely, but none so soon as charity.
He, doubtless, Does Well who does as loyalty teaches,
Thus if one is a married man, love your helpmate truly,   30
And live as the law wills while you live together;

Or if in an order, never ramble across country
To Rome or to Roquemadour, unless your rule bid you,
But hold yourself in obedience, which is an highway to heaven.
If you are unmarried and a maiden and may continue wisely,
Seek no saint afar for your soul's welfare.
For what made Lucifer lose the high heaven,
Or Samson his strength, or Solomon his wisdom?
Job the gentle Jew bought his joy dearly,
Aristotle and many others, Hippocrates and Virgil.   40
Alexander won all and ended shamefully.
Wealth and native wisdom weighed down all of them.
The fairness of Felice fell all to slander,
And Rosamond ruefully and wretchedly sold herself.
The beauty of her body was bestowed badly.
You may read of many such men and women,
Who show wise words and whose works are evil.
Sunt homines nequam bene de virtute loquentes.
Those who have wealth hoard and gather,
That men whom they most hate may own it after.   50
Because they have seen the suffering of so many needy
And loved them not as our Lord bad, they have lost salvation.
Date et dabitur vobis, etc.
Wisdom, says Holywrit, will swell a man's spirit:
Sapientia inflat, etc.
Riches raise men equally unless the root is honour.
Yet the herb of grace will abate and heal these evils.
But that grass grows alone among the lowly;
Patience and poverty is the place where it is growing,
In men who live in loyalty and whose lives are holy.   60
Through the gift of the Holy Ghost, as the gospel teaches:
Spiritus ubi vult spirat, etc.
So grace without the grace of God and good works
May not be had, be certain, though we pray forever.

"Clergy's knowledge and natural knowledge are known
    through sight and teaching,
As the Book bears witness to people who can read it:
Quod scimus, loquimur; quod vidimus, testamur.
Clergy's knowledge is from *quod scimus*, and can teach of heaven
And natural knowledge from *quod vidimus*, and the
    knowing of many people.
But grace is the gift of God; great love begets it;   70
Neither clerk nor Nature knows its secrets:
Nescit aliquis unde venit, aut quo vadit, etc.
Yet common knowledge and Clergy's knowledge are
    commended highly,
And Clergy especially for Christ's love, the ground of
    such knowledge.
Moses witnessed that God wrote to instruct the people,
In the Old Law or Jewish Law, as God's letter tells us:
A woman taken in adultery, were she in wealth or poverty,
Was stricken with stones till she was stoned to death.
But Christ in his courtesy rescued her by learning:
Through the characters that Christ wrote the accusers   80
    discovered
That they were more guilty before God and in greater
    sinfulness
Than the woman who was there; and were ashamed and
    left them.
And so Christ comforted the woman with Clergy's learning.
Holy Church knows well that in Christ's writing is salvation,
And thus Clergy is the comfort of all Christians in repentance,
And woe to the wicked at their way's ending.

"God's body may not be made from bread without Clergy,
His body is both a bliss to the righteous
And death and damnation to him who does evilly.
Both comfort and condemnation were in Christ's writing, 90

When the Jews judged the woman for whom Jesus sought
    salvation;
So God's body, my brothers, unless it be worthily taken,
Will condemn us at Dooms-day as the writing did the Hebrews.
Therefore I counsel you for Christ's sake to love Clergy dearly.
For Natural Knowledge is his kin and both near cousins
To our Lord, believe me truly; therefore love them, I counsel;
For both must be mirrors to amend our errors
And be leaders for the learned and laity together.

"You will never blame logic nor law nor their habits
Nor ever oppose learning, if you believe me truly.   100
A clerk can see no more without coming first to study
Then a man may see whose eyes are missing.
Although man makes books, God is the master,
And the Holy Spirit the sampler showing what men should
    copy.
And as sight serves a man to see his highway,
True learning leads the laity to Reason.
A man with natural knowledge and no more may never
Come into Christendom and gain salvation;
He is a blind man in a battle who bears a weapon
But has no hope that his axe will hit his enemy.   110
So clerks hold the keys of Christ's treasure,
To unlock it at their liking for unlearned people,
And to give mercy for their misdeeds to men who ask it
Obediently and humbly and pray for it as a grace.
Archa Dei in the Old Law was in the Levites' keeping.
No laymen had leave to lay hands upon it,
But only priests and priests' sons, patriarchs and prophets.

"Saul sacrificed upon it and sorrow befell him,
And his sons also have suffered for that error.
Many other men who were not of Levi   120

Went to *Archa Dei* in worship and in reverence,
Laid hands on it and lifted it up, but lost their lives after.
Therefore I counsel Christians never to condemn Clergy,
Nor to scorn their science, whatsoever they may practise.
Take their words at their worth, for their witness is faithful.
Meddle rarely in these matters and do not move their anger,
Lest struggle breed strife and men strike each other.
Nolite tangere christos meos, etc.

"Clergy is our keeper under Christ in heaven.
There never was a knight unless Clergy made him.   130
Another aristocracy arose from natural knowledge
Of clouds and of customs and contrivances beyond number,
Of birds and beasts, of bliss and sorrow.
Men have marked their ways and mused upon them,
Have seen strange sights and so taught their children,
And held their wisdom as an high science.
But, alas, through this science no soul was delivered,
Nor have their books brought them to bliss and happiness.—
Natural knowledge is but numberless observation.

"Patriarchs and prophets reproved their science,   140
And said their words and their wisdom were in themselves a
    vanity;
To the Clergy of Christ it was accounted a trifle.
Sapientia hujus mundi, stultitia est apud Deum.
For the high and holy Spirit shall cleave heaven asunder,
And love shall leap out after it into the low earth.
Cleanness shall catch it and clerks shall find it;
Pastores loquebantur ad invicem.
The witty and the wealthy were not mentioned in this passage,
Nor lords who are unlettered, but the most learned only.
Ibant magi ab oriente, etc.   150
If any friar were found there, I give you five shillings!

That baby was not born in a beggar's cottage;
The best house of the burgesses in Bethlehem lodged him.
Sed non erat ei locus in diversorio; et pauper non habet diversorium.

"The angel appeared to poets and to pastors,
And bad them go to Bethlehem and do God's honour,
And sang a song of mirth, *Gloria in excelsis Deo.*
The rich were at rest, snoring in their houses,
When there shone before the shepherds God's sign of beatitude.

"Clerks considered it well and came with their presents,   160
And did their homage honourably to him who was Almighty
I have told you this tale for I took good notice
How you contended with Clergy in crabbed language,
That clerks of God and nature among Christian people
And all learned are less readily saved than the unlearned.

"You spoke truly of some, but see in what manner.
Throw two strong men over the Thames embankment,
Each naked as a needle and neither safer than the other.
One is a swift swimmer and a shrewd diver;
The other knows neither art and has no such cunning.   170
Which of the two do you think dreads the Thames more?
He who knows no strokes and never learned diving,
Or the swimmer who is safe if it so please him,
While his fellow floats at the flood's pleasure?"
"He who cannot swim," I said, "it seems in my judgement."
"So," said this man, "it seems in reason
That he who consults Clergy can sooner be rescued
From his sin, and be safe, though he sin often,
If he wishes and wills it, than any of the contumacious.
A good clerk can tell what is sinful,   180
And how contrition without confession comforts the spirit.
In several of the psalms you may see plainly

How contrition is commended as a cure for sinners:
Beati quorum remissae sunt iniquitates, et quorum tecta sunt, etc.
This comforts every clerk and keeps him from despairing,—
That flood in which the fiend fights with man the hardest.
The unlearned man lies still and looks for lenten penance;
He has no contrition before he come to shrift, and then he can
    tell but little,
But trusts his teacher and takes his counsel.—
He is a parish priest or parson and, peradventure,   190
Himself unlearned and a blind leader, as Luke bears witness:
Dum caecus ducit caecum, etc.

"He was marked for woe who must wade with the ignorant.
Well may the lad bless him who sent him to learning! .
The life of learning saved him, life and spirit.
Dominus pars hereditatis meae is a merry versicle
That has taken from Tyborne twenty strong robbers,
When the stupid are strung up—see how it saves them!   198

"The thief had God's grace on Good Friday, as you mention,
Because he believed the Cross of Christ and acknowledged
    himself guilty,
And asked God's grace, who will grant it freely
To all who ask it humbly and intend amendment.
But although the thief had heaven, he had no such happiness
As Saint John and other saints who served God better.
Some men give me meat but leave me unseated;
I have more meat than enough but not so much honour
As those who sit at the side table or with the sovereign of the
    manor.
And I a beggar on the bare ground, by myself and silent!   208
So it fared on Good Friday with the felon who was rescued;
He sits neither with Saint John, nor Saint Jude, nor Simon,
Nor with maidens or martyrs, confessors or widows,

But solitary and aside and served beyond the rushes.
He who is once a thief is always in danger.
His life and limb are at the law's pleasure.
De *peccato propitiato, noli esse sine metu.*
To serve at table such a saint and such a thief together
Has no more right nor reason than to reward them equally:

"Trojanus was a true knight, his tent not so deep in hell
That our Lord could not lift him out; and so I believe the
   thief in heaven:
For he is the lowest in heaven, if our belief is truthful,   220
And he is lolling there loosely, by the law of Holy Church.
Quia reddit unicuique juxta opera sua, etc.
Why one thief on the cross yielded himself a Christian
Rather than the other thief, although you might question
All the clerks in Christendom, none could answer you:
Quare placuit, quia voluit.
And so I say to you who seek the whys and wherefores,
And reason with Reason and rebuke him craftily:
What of the flowers of the field and their fair colours?
Where have they caught colours so clear and shining?   230
Would you know of beasts and birds and their breeding habits
Why some are low and some aloft—would you like such
   knowledge?
Will you study the stones, and the stars in heaven?
How each bird and beast is blessed with instinct?
Clergy nor Natural Knowledge never knew the causes,
But Nature himself knows them and no other creature.
He is the pye's patron and puts it in his head
To build and to breed where the thorn-bush shields him.
Nature bids the peacock to breed in such a manner.
He taught Adam to know his privy members,   240
And Adam and Eve to hide them with leafage.

"Many times unlettered men ask masters boldly
Why Adam did not hide first his mouth that ate the apple.
So these ignorant fellows inquire of scholars!
Nature knows why he did so and no clerk beside him.
People in times past, great poets and teachers,
Made bird and beast bring examples;
As that the fairest fowls are the foulest breeders,
And fly most feebly of all feathered creatures.
These are the peacock and the pea-hen, and mean the   250
    proud and wealthy.
The peacock, when men pursue him, cannot fly to safety.
His tail trails on the ground, and he is taken quickly.
His flesh is a foul flesh, his feet are ugly;
Screaming and screeching is the song of a peacock.

"So the wealth of the wealthy, if they hoard it blindly
And deal it only on their death day, is their tail of sorrow.
As the pens of the peacock pain him in flying,
So the possession of pence is pain and penance
To all who hold them till death plucks their feathers.
And though the rich man repent and rue the hour   260
That he gathered so greedily and gave so little,
Though he cry to Christ with keen desire,
I believe his voice in our Lord's ear is like a pye's chattering.
When his corpse comes in his coffin to burial
I believe it will scent the soil with so pernicious an odour
That all others where he is lying will be envenomed with his
    poison.
By the peacock's feet are understood, as I have learned in
    Avianus,
Executors and false friends who will not fulfil his wishes,
Though written while those are witnesses to work for   269
    their accomplishment.
The poet proves that the peacock is praised only for his feathers,

As the rich is reverenced by reason of his riches.

"The lark is not so large, but is a lovely singer,
And on the wing far and away swifter than the peacock,
And his flesh is far fatter and sweeter.
This lark is a likeness for lowly livers.
Aristotle was a great clerk and told such stories;
And this in his logic is the likeness for the least bird living.

'Whether he be saved or not saved has not been shown to
     Clergy.
No study in Solomon or Socrates can tell us.   279
But God, I hope, is so gracious that since he gave them faculties
To point us out the path (who believe ourselves saved, and
     more surely
To be saved through their books)—we are bound to petition
That God of his grace may give rest to their spirits;
For the learned were unlearned but for the lore in their
     writings."

"All the clerks," quoth I, "who have Christ to witness
Say in their sermons that neither Saracens nor Hebrews
Nor any creature in Christ's likeness can be saved without
     baptism."

"*Contra*," quoth Imagination then, and commenced to frown,
Saying, " '*Salvabitur vix justus in die judicii.*'
Ergo Salvabitur " he said, and spoke no more in Latin.   290
"Trojanus was a true knight and never took baptism,
And he is saved, as the book says, and his soul in heaven.
There is baptism by the font, and baptism in blood-shedding,
And baptism by fire, and this we believe firmly.
Advenit ignis divinus non comburens, sed illuminans, etc.
Truth that never trespassed nor transgressed against his
     commandments,

But lives as his law teaches, and believes there is no better,
But if there were would amend, and with this will dies,—298
The true God would never allow his truth to be dishonoured.
But whether this shall be or shall not be, the true man is strong,
And an hope is with him that he shall have meed for his truth.
For, *Deus dicitur quasi dans vitam aeternam suis, hoc est fidelibus.*
Et alibi; Si ambulavero in medio umbrae mortis.
The gloss grants at this verse a great meed to truth.
Wit and wisdom," said that man, "were once a treasure
With which to keep a kingdom; no gold was held better,
And much mirth and manhood,"—and at that he vanished.

ITH that I awaked; my wits were troubled.
I went forth as a wanderer; I walked freely
In the manner of a mendicant many years after.
Many times I marvelled at my strange vision.
First, how Fortune failed me when my need was greatest;
And how Age menaced me if I might ever meet him;
How the friars followed the folk who had money,
And put a low price on their poor neighbours;
How they would bury no bodies in the church or churchyard
Unless they would give them their goods or quit them of their
    debits;   10
How this covetousness overcame clerks and parsons;
And how the unlearned were led, unless our Lord helped them,
Through ignorant clerics to incurable sorrow;
How the man Imagination met me dreaming
And acquainted me with Nature's cunning and his kindness
    for his creatures,
And how loving he is to all life on land or water,
And leaves no life unheeded, either the least or greatest,
And how he governs the engendering of all creeping things.
I wondered in my heart how Imagination witnessed
That *justus* before Jesus, *in die judicii*   20
N*on salvabitur* unless *vix* aid him;
And when he had spoken so how suddenly he vanished.

I lay down long and thought and at last I slumbered.
And as Christ would there came Conscience to comfort me
And bad me come to his court with Clergy to dinner.
Since Conscience and Clergy bad me I came the readier.
There was a Master of Divinity, but what manner of man I
    know not.
He bowed low and benignly to Scripture.
Conscience knew him well and welcomed him graciously.

They washed and wiped themselves and went to dinner. 30
Patience came as a poor creature and prayed meat for charity,
Like Piers Plowman in palmer's clothing.
He craved meat and cried for it for Christ's love in heaven,
A meal's meat for a poor man, or money, if they had it.

Conscience called him in and courteously said to him:
"Welcome friend; go and wash, and you shall eat shortly."

The great Master was made to sit, for he was the most worthy;
And then Clergy and Conscience, and Patience came
    afterwards.
Patience and I were partners; we were put together
With seats by ourselves at a side table.   40

Clergy called for meat, and then came Scripture,
And served him shortly with separate dishes
Of Augustine and Ambrose and of all the four evangelists:
Edentes et bibentes quae apud eos sunt.
But this Master and his man would eat no moderate cuttings,
But only the more costly meats, as pounded meats and pottages.
What men amassed wrongly made them their comfort.
But their sauce was over-sour and unsavourily grounded
In a mortar, *post mortem*, with many bitter sorrows
Unless they sing for those souls and weep salt tears. 50
*Vos qui peccata hominum comeditis nisi pro eis lacrimas et orationes
effunderitis, ea quae in deliciis comeditis, in tormentis evometis.*
Then Conscience courteously commanded Scripture
To bring bread before Patience and before me who was his
    messmate.
He sat a sour loaf before us and said *"Agite poenitentiam,"*
And then he drew us the drink of *diu perseverans.*
"As long," I cried, "as life and limb endure!"
"Here is proper service," said Patience; "no prince fares
    better."

And then he brought us a mess of meat of *Miserere mei, Deus*
And he brought us *Beati quorum*, as *Beatus vir es* made it, 60
Et quorum tecta sunt peccata in dishes
Of secret shrift, as *Dixi* and *confitebor tibi*.
"Bring Patience some pittance," said Conscience privily;
And then Patience had a pittance of *pro hac orabit ad te omnis sanctus in tempore opportuno*,
And Conscience comforted us and gladdened us with his stories.
Cor contritum et humiliatum Deus non despicies.
Patience himself was proud of such proper service
And made mirth at his meat, but I mourned within me
That the Doctor on the high dais drank wine so madly.
Vae vobis qui potentes estis ad bibendum vinum. 70
He ate many kinds of meat, meat pies and pounded meat,
Belly clouts and wild boars and eggs fried with grease.
Then I said to myself, but so that Patience heard me:
"It is not four days that the Doctor before the Dean in Paul's Churchyard
Preached of the penances that Paul suffered,
In fame et frigore, with flagellations and scourging.
Ter caesus sum, et a Judeis quinquies quadragenas, etc.
But they omit one sentence from all their sermons,
Which Paul in his epistle published to all men:
Periculum est in falsis fratribus. 80
Holywrit bids men beware, but I will not write it
In English on adventure that it would be rehearsed too often,
And grieve good men also; but grammarians may witness:
Unus quisque a fratre se custodiat, quia, ut dicitur, periculum est in falsis fratribus.

"No follower of the friars before the English people
Ever took that for his text and treated it frankly .
They preach the penance that is profitable for the spirit,

And how Christ bore for mankind the great sorrow,
But this glutton of God," said I, "with his great jaw bone
Has no pity on us poor; he practises evil!   90
He does not practise what he preaches!" I said to Patience.
I wished heartily, angrily and eagerly
That this same Doctor would devour dishes and platters,
And they be molten in his mouth, and Mohammed in his belly!
"I'll ask this bottle-bellied bulging jordan
To tell me what penance is, of which he preached so finely."

Patience perceived my thoughts and beckoned me to be silent,
And said, "Soon you shall see, when he may swill no longer,
He will have his penance in his paunch and puff at each
     sentence.
Then his guts will grumble and he will gape afterwards.   100
Now he has drunk so deep that he will divine shortly,
And prove by the Glutton's Apocalypse and by the passion
     of Saint Advisa
That brawn and bacon, boiled meat and pottage
Are neither fish nor flesh but food for a penitent.
Then he will testify of the Trinity and take his friend to witness
What he found at the bottom of a friar's basket.
Unless the first line is a lie, never believe me after.
Then you will have occasion to ask this Doctor
Of Do Well and of Do Bet, and if Do Best is any penance."

I sat still, as Patience said, and shortly this Doctor   110
Grew red as a rose and rubbed his jowls
And hemmed and hawed, and Conscience heard him,
And told him of a Trinity. Then he turned toward us.—
"What is Do Well, Doctor?" I asked. "Is Do Well any
     penance?"
"Do Well," said this Doctor, and took a cup and drained it,
"Is do no harm to your neighbour nor to yourself either;

Then you do wisely and well, and I admit it freely."

"By this day, Doctor," I said, "then you are not Do Well!
For you have harmed two of us, in that you ate the pudding
And your messes of meat and gave no morsel to help us.   120
If you treat your sick friars so, it would seem to me a wonder
If Do Well do not accuse you *in die judicii*.
I permute my penance with yours, for I am at the point to do
    well."

Then Conscience courteously gave me his signal,
And bad Patience to pray me to be silent.
He himself said, "Sir Doctor, be good to tell us
What are Do Well and Do Bet? You divines know them."
"Do Well," said this Doctor, "is do as clerks tell you,
And Do Bet is he who teaches and toils to teach others,
And Do Best shows in himself what he has said in preaching.
Qui facit et docuerit, magnus vocabitur in regno coelorum."   131

"Now then, Clergy," said Conscience, "consider what is Do
    Well."
"I have seven sons," said Clergy, "who serve in a castle,
Where the lord of life gives lessons to them to Do Well.
Till I see those seven, and satisfy myself with them
I am unable," he said, "in any way to prove it.
One Piers the Plowman has impugned all of us,
And set all sciences at a sop save love only,
And he takes no text to maintain his teaching
But *dilige Deum* and *Domine, quis habitabit, etc.*   140
He says that Do Well and Do Bet are two infinities,
Which infinities, with faith, find out Do Best,
Who shall save men's souls. Thus saith Piers Plowman."

"I cannot argue on this," said Conscience, "but I know the
    Plowman.

He will not speak against Holywrit, I can well assure you."

Said Piers the Plowman: "*Patientes vincunt!*
Before the perpetual peace I shall prove my sentence,
And avow before God and never forsake it:
Disce, doce, dilige Deum and thine enemy.
Help him heartily according to thy power;   150
Cast hot coals on his head with kind speeches;
Try with wit and with words to win his affection;
Give him again and yet again, and always when he is needy;
Comfort him with thy goods and with kind speaking;
And lie on him with love till you laugh together.
Unless he bow under this beating may he be blind forever!"—

When he had said these words no one wist surely
What had become of Piers Plowman, so privily he vanished.
Reason ran out after and walked right beside him.
Only Conscience and Clergy kept their stations.   160
But when Piers had passed Patience spoke mildly:

"Natural love needs no goods but speeches,
With half a lamp-line in Latin, *ex vi transitionis.*
I bear about Do Well fast bound within it,
In the sign of Saturday that first set the calendar,
With all the worth of Wednesday of the week following;
The middle of the moon is the might of either,
And I am welcome with this when I have it with me."

"Undo it! Let this Doctor judge if Do Well is in it!
For by him who made me, may no poverty,   170
Misery or misfortune or malicious speaking,
Cold or care or the company of robbers,
No heat nor hail nor hell's goblin,
Nor fire nor flood nor fear of an enemy

Trouble you at any time, if you take it with you.
Caritas nihil timet.

"So, God have my soul, if you seek it truly
There is neither emperor nor empress, earl, king nor baron,
Pope nor patriarch whom plain reason will not warrant
The master of all these men through the might of this riddle!
The king and queen and all the commons after,   181
Not through witchcraft but through wit (if you wish it truly),
Shall give you all that they may give, as their best guardian,
And do as you determine all their days after.
Patientes vincunt."

"This is but a *Dido*," said the Doctor, "a dicer's story,
All the skill under the sun and strong men's efforts
Cannot bring peace between the pope and his enemies,
And two Christian kings cannot be pacified   189
To the profit of either people."—He pushed the table from him
And took Clergy and Conscience into a consultation, as I
     thought it,—
And Patience must pass on, for pilgrims are good liars.
First Conscience cried aloud, but kindly answered:
"Friends, fare you well,"—And finally to Clergy:
"If God will give me grace I will go with this person,
And be a pilgrim with Patience till I have proved men further."

"What," said Clergy to Conscience, "do you covet also
New Year's funds or favours or feel the need for riddles?
I shall bring you a Bible and in a book of the Old Law
Prove at your pleasure the least point of doctrine   200
Which Patience, the pilgrim, never properly mastered."
"No, by Christ," said Conscience to Clergy, "God requite
     you!
Though Patience proffers me much, my pride is humbled.

The will of that wayfarer and the will of folk about me
Have moved my mind to mourn for my sins.
The good will within us was never brought to fullness.
True will is the treasure of all treasures the dearest.
Had not Mary Magdalene more for her ointment
Than Zaccheus when he said *dimidium bonorum meorum do
pauperibus,*
And the poor widow for two pennies   210
Than all those who offered into *gazophilacium* ?"

First Conscience said farewell to the friar courteously,
And he whispered softly in the ear of Clergy:
"I would sooner, by our Saviour, if I should live longer,
Have perfect patience than half your pack of volumes."
Clergy would not give Conscience his greeting,
But said very soberly, "You will see the season
When you will be weary of walking and will wish my counsel."

"That is certain," said Conscience, "so God help me!
But if Patience is our partner and privy between us,   220
There is no woe in the world that we shall not remedy,
And make kings and all countries conform to peace.
Saracens and Syrians, Jews and heathen
Will turn into the true faith and into one covenant."
"That is so," said Clergy; "I see your meaning.
I shall dwell here and do my duty, as I should do it always,
I shall defend infants and the folk who are learned,
Till Patience has proved you and perfected your training."

Then Conscience passed out with Patience, pilgrims together.
Patience, after the use of pilgrims, had a pocket of victuals;
Sobriety and simple speaking and steadfast believing   231
Should comfort him and Conscience if they came to places
Where unkindness and covetousness are, for they are hungry
countries.

As they went on their way, talking of Do Well,
They met with a man, a minstrel I thought him.
Patience approached and prayed him kindly
To tell Conscience what his craft was and to what country he
    was travelling.
"I am a minstrel," said that man, "my name is *Activa Vita*.
I hate all idleness, for my name is from activity.
I am a wafer-seller, if you would know, and wait on   240
    many nobles,
But I find few robes or furred garments.
Could I lie to make men laugh I should lightly capture
Money or a mantle among lords and ladies.
But I know neither tabor nor trump nor how to tell stories,
Nor to blow my fife nor to fiddle at feasts, nor harping,
Nor joking nor juggling nor gentle piping,
No, nor to tumble, or dance nor to sing with the gittern.
I have no good gifts from these great nobles
For any bread that I bring them, except a blessing on Sunday,
When the priest bids the people to offer *pater noster*   250
For Piers the Plowman and those who serve his profit.
And such am I, Active, who hate idleness;
From Michaelmas to Michaelmas I find wafers
For all the true toilers and tillers among us.

"False men and friars and folk with broad tonsures,
Beggars and bidders crave bread from me.
I find bread for the pope and provender for his palfrey.
I never had from him, I have God to witness,
Either prebend or parsonage from the pope's favour,
Except a pardon with a piece of lead and two polls in the
    middle!   260
Had I a clerk who could write, I would give a petition
That he send me under his seal a salve for the pestilence,
And bring down boils with his bulls and blessings:

In nomine meo daemonia ejicient, et super aegros manus imponent, et
bene habebunt.

I should be prepared to make pasty for the people
And be blithe and busy about bread and drinking
For him and for all his, if I found that his pardon
Might medicine a man, as my faith is it should do.
Since the pope has the power that Peter himself had
He has the pot with the salve, assuredly, to my thinking: 270
Argentum et aurum non est mihi; quod autem habeo tibi do; in nomine
Domini surge et ambula.
If his power of miracle is missing it is because men are unworthy
To have the grace of God, and not from a guilty pontiff.
No blessing may medicine us unless we amend truly;
No man's mass can make peace among Christians
Till pride is purged wholly, through pestilence and famine.

"Before my bread is meal I must sweat often.
Before the commune have corn enough I have many a cold
    morning.
Before my cakes are cooked I have much care and trouble.

"All Londoners, I believe, like my wafers,   280
And lower if they lack them. Not long passed
There was a careworn commune. No cart came to London
With baked bread from Stratford. Then beggars were weeping
And labourers believed that it would be long remembered.
In the date of the deity, in a dry April
A thousand and three hundred and twice thirty and ten
My wafers were scarce when Chichester was mayor."

I gave good heed, by Christ, and Conscience also,
To Haukyn the Active Man, and what clothes he had on him.
He had a coat of Christendom as Holy Church teaches,   290
But it was marked in many places with many patches,

A patch there from pride, and there a patch of mad speaking,
Of scorning and of scoffing and of unschooled arrogance,
As pride among people in apparel and bearing.
He is willing that all men should hold him what he is not.
He shows himself otherwise than his heart warrants.
Therefore he boasts and brags with bold swearing.
He dislikes to be blamed by any living creature.
He is singular to himself in the sight of all people.
There is none such as himself nor so pope-holy.   300
He is in the habit of an hermit in an order of his making,
A religion without rule or reasonable obedience.
He blames the learned and the unlearned equally,
Praises the loyal life and is a liar in his conscience.
His observation and reflection, study and fancy
Are what is best for the body and bad for his name.
He interferes everywhere where he has no business,
And wishes that all men thought his wit the shrewdest,
Thought him a clever craftsman or a clerk unequalled,
Or strongest on a steed or stoutest under the girdle,   310
And loveliest to look on and most loyal in action,
And none so holy as he nor of such honest living,
Nor fairer in features in form or in stature,
Or a subtler singer or with slyer fingers,
Both liberal in lending and lax in taking;
(If he gives to poor creatures he tells what he deals them)
Poor in possessions, in purse and in coffer,
With a look like a lion and lordly in speaking;
The boldest of beggars; a boaster who has nothing;
A teller of tales in town and taverns;   320
He says what he never saw and swears to his honesty;
He devises deeds that were done by no man,
Or is the witness of his well doing, and will say sometimes:
"Look! If you believe me not, or think I lie basely
Ask him or ask him, and he can tell you

What I suffered and saw and owned sometimes,
Of what kin I am come, and what I could do or teach."
He wished men aware of all his words and actions
Which might please the people and be praise to himself.
Si hominibus placerem, Christi servus non essem. Et alibi: 330
Nemo potest duobus dominis servire.

"By Christ," said Conscience, "your best coat, Haukyn,
Has many spots and mendings and must be well washed."
"Yes, if you will take heed," said Haukyn, "in all parts of it,
By the back and by the belly and by the sides also,
You will find many folds and foul patches."
Then he turned about quickly and I took good heed
That it was a far fouler coat than I had first thought it.
It was running with wrath and a wretched wilfulness,
With envy and evil speaking and inciting contention,   340
Lying and laughing and loose chiding.
He told all that he heard of evil in any,
And blamed men behind their backs and prayed for their
    misfortune.
What he heard of Will he told to Watkin,
And what Watkin heard Will heard after.
He made friends foes by his false talking.
"Treachery of tongue or the brawn of others
Has avenged me often, or I have fretted inwardly
Like the shears of a seamstress, and beshrewed my fellow 349
    Christians.
Cujus maledictione os plenum est et amaritudine, sub lingua ejus labor
    et dolor. Et alibi: Filii hominum, dentes eorum arma et sagittae, et
    lingua eorum gladius acutus.

"I love no man long; nothing lasts with me.
For the tales that I tell I am trusted nowhere.
And when I may not have the mastery the melancholy takes me.

On some days I catch the cramp and the cardiacle on others,
Or an ague in anger. Sometimes a fever
Will take me an whole twelve-month, till I despise wholly
The leachcraft of our Lord and believe in witches,
And claim that no clerk nor Christ can cure me   360
As the shoemaker of Southwark or the Shoreditch dame
    Emma.
I claim that God's word never gave me assistance,
But that I chanced upon a charm, and that chiefly cured me."

I saw the cloak more closely and the discolourings on it
From a liking for lechery, from looks and glances
At each maid whom he met, and from making motions
Seemingly sinward, and sometimes he tasted
About the mouth and the breast and began to fumble
Till wills were keen and the work hastened,
Both on fasting days and Fridays and forbidden evenings, 370
As well in Lent as out of Lent, and all times equally.
Such works with them were never out of season,
Till they might command them no more, and then to merry
    stories
Of how the lecherous love; with laughter and jesting,
Age relates the ribaldry and riots of manhood.

Then Patience perceived that patches on his jacket
Were grimy from covetousness and unkind desires.
This creature loved God less than goods and chattels,
And imagined how he might have them easily
With meting out false measures and with false witness;   380
He lent for love of interest and was loath to do honestly.
He lay in wait warily on ways of deception.
He manipulated his merchandise and made a good muster,
"The worst lay within; and I held that witty.
If my neighbour had an hine or any creature

More profitable than mine, I managed shrewdly
With as much wit as I had how I might get it.
If I could have it no other way at last I stole it,
Or shook his purse privily, or picked his latches.
So I gather by guile the goods that I covet,   390
By day and by night, busy everywhere.

"If I plant or plow I pinch so narrowly
That I fetch a furrow or a foot's swathing
From my next neighbour, and gnaw his half acre.
If I reap I over-reach, or tell the reaper privately
To seize for me with his sickle what was sown by another.

"Whoever borrowed from me bought it dearly
With privy presents or paid for it openly.
So whatever he won I won always;
All my kith and my kin have grieved at my unkindness. 400

"I quarrelled with each customer who criticised my bargains;
He must proffer to pay me a penny or twopence
More than it was worth, or I would swear boldly
That it cost me much more than his miserable pittance.

"On holy days at Holy Church when I heard masses
I never had the will honestly to petition
Mercy for my misdeeds; but I mourned rather
For the loss of goods, believe me, than for a life of wickedness.
If I had done a deadly sin I dreaded it not so sorely
As when I had lent and believed it lost or long in payment.
If I had spent my silver to serve my fellow Christians,   411
My heart was wrung with cruel torment.
If I had sent my servants over seas to Brugge,
Or my prentice into Prussia to protect my interests,
To buy money and merchandise and make exchanges,

Neither mass nor matins nor any manner of diversion
Might give me comfort in the cruel interval.
I never performed penance nor said a *pater noster*
When my mind was not more on my fear of losses
Than on the grace of God and his great mercy.   420
U*bi thesaurus tuus, ibi cor tuum.*"

Also this Glutton had stained his cloak with great swearing,
And soiled it and beslobbered it with speaking falsely.
When there was no need he used God's name idly,
And swore so swiftly that he sweat through his jacket.
He ate more meat and drank more than Nature may warrant,
"I was sometimes sick and have surfeited often.
And then I dreaded to die in deadly sin."
Then despair would take him, and doubt of his salvation,
Which is so sorry a sloth that no skill may cure it,   430
Nor any mercy amend the man who dies in it.

What are the branches that bring men to slothfulness?
They are when a man does not mourn for his misdeeds and
    vices;
When he performs the penance badly which the priest has set
    him;
When he does no almsdeeds and dreads no sinning;
When he lives against our belief and is lawless and reckless;
When each day is for him an holiday or a high fair.
If he wishes to hear anything it is the harping of ribaldry.
When men consider Christ and cleanness of spirit
He is wrathful and will only hear words of merriment.   440
As for penance and poor men and the passion of God's holy
    ones,
He hates to hear of it and all who speak it.—
Beware, for these are the branches that bring men to despairing.
You lords and ladies and legates of Holy Church,

Who feed your wise fools and flatterers and liars,
Who have a liking to listen to those who set you laughing,
Vae vobis qui ridetis, etc.
Who give meat and meed to them and maltreat poor men,
In the day of your death I dread sorely
Lest these three modes of minstrelsy bring you to much
  sorrow.
Consentientes et agentes pari poena punientur.   451
Patriarchs and prophets and preachers of God's teaching
Save men's souls from hell by sermons and discourses.
So fools and flatterers are the fiend's disciples,
Enticing men by their tales to sin and ribaldry.
Clerks who know God's teaching should acquaint rulers
With what David says of such men, as his psalter tells us:
*Non habitabit in medio domus meae, qui facit superbiam, et qui loquitur
  iniqua.*
Such men should have no audience in hall or chamber
Where wise men are, as God's word witnesses,   460
Nor proud pretenders be admitted among nobility.

Clerks and knights welcome king's minstrels,
And for the love of our Lord listen to them at feastings.
Much more, methinks, should men often
Have beggars before them, for they are God's minstrels,
As he has said himself, with Saint John to witness:
Qui vos spernit, me spernit.
Therefore I advise you wealthy, when you have revels,
For the solace of your souls have such minstrels.
Have the poor for your fool at the high table,   470
As a learned man to lesson you in what our Lord suffered,
To save your soul from Satan your enemy,
And fiddle you without flattery the Good Friday story;
A blind man or a bed´rid woman be your bourdier and your
  jester,

H

To cry your goodness before God and pray God to give you his
   largess.
These three manner of minstrels make a man merry,
And in the day of his death do him kind service,
If in his life he has listened to them and loved their voices.
These solace his soul, till he himself enter
Into good hope, for his works are with those of sainthood. 480
But flatterers and fools with their foul speaking
Lead those who love them to Lucifer's banquet,
With *turpiloquio*, a lay of sorrow, Lucifer's own fiddling.—

So Haukyn the Active Man had soiled his garment
Till Conscience inquired in a courteous manner
Why he had not washed it and wiped it with a brush.

"I HAVE but one whole suit," said Haukyn; "I
am the less blameworthy
If it is soiled and seldom clean; I sleep in it also.
I have an housewife, hinds and children,
Uxorem duxi, et ideo non possum venire.
Who will spot it sometimes in spite of my efforts.
I have washed it in Lent and out of Lent often
With the wondrous soap of sickness that sinks so deeply;
And after the loss of goods I have been loath to injure
God or any good man, by ought that I could know of.   9
I shrived myself to the priest, who gave me against my sinning
The penance of patience and to give poor men nourishment;
And so for the sake of my Christianity to keep it cleanly.
But I could never, by Christ, keep it an hour
Without soiling it with some sight or with some idle speaking.
Either through words or works or the will within me
I slobbered and stained it from sunrise to even."

"I shall tell you," quoth Conscience, "how contrition is
   possible,
And that will card your coat of all kinds of filthiness.
Cordis contritio, etc.
Do Well will wash it and wring it through a wise confessor, 20
Oris confessio, etc.
Do Bet will cleanse it and beat it as bright as any scarlet,
And dye it in the grain with good will and with God's grace for
   amendment,
And so send you to satisfaction, and sew the pieces together,
Satisfactio, Do Best.
No mist will mar nor any moth corrupt it,
Nor any fiend or false man defile it in your lifetime;
No herald or harper will have a fairer garment
Than Haukyn the Active Man if you act by my teaching.

No minstrel will be more worthy among rich and poor folk 30
Than the wife of Haukyn the waferer with his *Activa Vita*."

"I shall procure you a paste," said Patience, "though no plow
　　is stirring,
And feed the folk with that flour which is best for the spirit,
Though no grain grow from the ground nor any grape on the
　　vineyard.
I shall find a livelihood for all living creatures.
None will fail to have enough of what he needs truly.
We should not be too busy about our livelihood:
Ne solliciti sitis, etc. Volucres coeli Deus pascit, etc. Patientes vincunt."

Then Haukyn laughed a little, and swore lightly: 　　　　39
"Whoever believes you, by our Lord, I believe will be
　　unhappy!"
"No," said Patience patiently, and pulled from his wallet
Victuals of strange virtue for all manner of creatures,
And said: "Lo, here is livelihood if our belief is true.
Life was never lent unless means were given
To sustain and succour whatsoever is living.

"The wild worm is under the wet earth,
Fish live by the flood and the fire is for the cricket,
The curlew lives on air, and has the cleanest bird's flesh,
Beasts live by grass and by grain and by green saplings,
Meaning that all men may in like manner 　　　　50
Live through loyal faith and love, as God witnesses.
Quodcunque petieritis a patre in nomine meo, etc. Et alibi:
Non in solo pane vivit homo, sed in omni verbo quod procedit de ore Dei."

I looked at what livelihood it was that Patience praised so
　　highly
And found it a piece of the *pater noster; fiat voluntas tua.*

"Have it, Haukyn," said Patience, "and eat when you are
   hungry,
Or when you grow numb from cold or cling from thirst.
No gyves will grieve you nor great lords anger you,
Nor imprisonment pain you, for *patientes vincunt.*
If so that you are sober in sight and talking,   60
In eating and in handling and in all your five senses,
You will never care for corn nor linen cloth nor woollen,
Nor for drink, nor dread death, but die when God wishes,
Either by hunger or by heat; it is as he wills it.
If you live by his lore, the shorter life the better.
Si quis amat Christum, mundum non diligit istum.
For through his breath beasts grow and go abroad roaming,
Dixit, et facta sunt.
Ergo through his breath may beasts and men continue,
As Holywrit witnesses when men say their graces: 70
Aperis tu manum tuam, et imples omne animal benedictione.
It is found that for forty winters folk lived without tilling.
From the flint sprang the flood which folk and beasts drank.
And in Elias' time the heavens were closed together,
So that no rain ran forth. Men read elsewhere
That men lived many winters without meat or tillage.
Seven men slept, says the book, seven hundred winters,
And lived without livelihood, and were at last awakened.
If men lived in moderation there would be no more famine
Among Christian creatures, if Christ is truthful.   80
Over-plenty begets pride among poor and wealthy,
And dearth creates unkindness among Christian people.
But moderation is the mean and may not be too precious.
For the misery and misfortune among the men of Sodom
Grew through abundance of bread and plain slothfulness.
Otiositas et abundantia panis peccatum turpissimum nutrivit.
Because these men were immoderate in meat and drinking
And did deadly sin to the devil's liking,

Vengeance fell upon them for their vile living,
And their cities sank through the sea to hell.   90
Therefore let us measure ourselves well and make our faith our
    shelter;
Contrition comes through faith, as Conscience knows surely,
And this drives away deadly sin, and decreases it to venial.
Although a man may not speak contrition may save him,
And bring his soul to bliss, if faith bear witness
That he believed while he lived in the lore of Holy Church.
Ergo, contrition, faith and conscience are clearly Do Well,
And surgeons for deadly sin, where shrift of mouth is wanting.

"But shrift of mouth is worth more if men are contrite inwardly.
For shrift of mouth slays sin, be it ever so deadly.   100
Per confessionem to a priest *peccata occiduntur*,
Where contrition drives it down till it becomes venial;
As David says in his psalter: *et quorum tecta sunt peccata*.
But satisfaction seeks out the root, slays it and voids it;
It is unseen and sore no longer, but seems a wound healed."

"Where does Charity live?" asked Haukyn, "for I never
    heard of
A man who has spoken with him, as widely as I have
    wandered."

"Where perfect truth and a poor heart and a patient tongue are
Charity is the chief Chamberlain for God himself."

"Is patient poverty," asked Haukyn, "more pleasant to   110
    our Maker
Than riches rightfully won and reasonably expended?"
"Yea, *quis est ille*," said Patience, "that *laudabimus eum*."
Though men read of wealth till the world's ending
I never heard of a wealthy man who at the last reckoning

When his death day drew near did not dread death sorely,
And fell in arrears at that reckoning rather than out of debt.
Then the poor man may plead with plain reason
For an allowance from his Lord, and claim rightfully
Of the just judge the joy that is wanting.
He shall say: 'Lo, birds and beasts, without bliss forever, 120
The wild worms in the woods, have thy winter grievings,
That make them almost meek and mild from famine,
And after thou sendest them summer which is their chief
   happiness,
The bliss of beasts, both wild and common.'
Then may beggars as beasts await bliss hopefully,
Who have lived all their lives in languishing and famine.
Unless God send them some time some manner of happiness,
Either here or elsewhere, Nature speaks falsely.
For wretched is he who will never be joyful.
Angels who are in hell now had joy sometime, 130
And Dives lived on dainties and in *douce vye*.
So reason shows that such men as are wealthy,
And their women with them, are mirthful livers.
God is wondrously willing, as all will witness,
To pay many a man his recompense before he deserve it.
God so rewards some rich men that it is rueful to think on;
For they have their hire here, as it were their heaven,
And a delightful life without labour for the body.
And when they die they are disavowed, as David says in the
   psalter:
Dormierunt, et nihil invenerunt. 140
And in another passage also:
Velut somnium surgentium, Domine, in civitate tua, et ad nihilum
   rediges, etc.
Alas that riches should ravish and rob a man's soul
From the love of our Lord at the last breathing!
Servants who have hire in advance are always needy.

He seldom dies out of debt who dines before he deserve it,
Or before he has done his duty and his day's labour.
When a workman has finished one may witness justly
What his work is worth and what he has merited.
He will filch at nothing before from fear of denial. 150
So I say to you rich men, it seems that you may not
Have heaven while you are here and heaven hereafter.
The workman who had his wages before and wished more after,
As if he had had none already, had no hire at even.
It may not be, you rich men, or Matthew is a liar:
V*ae! deliciis ad delicias difficile est transire.*

'Bu t if you rich show ruth and reward poor folk,
And live as the law teaches and act loyally with all men,
Christ in his courtesy will comfort you in the ending,
And reward all double riches who have rueful hearts. 160
As the hine who had his hire ere he began to labour,
And when he had worked well won a bounty also,
And had a cottage that was not agreed on, so Christ gives
heaven
To men who are poor and not poor, but who show pity in their
lifetime.
All who have done their duty will have double pay for their
labour,
The forgiveness of sins and the life everlasting.

"In the histories of holy saints it is hard to witness
That God rewards double rest to any rich person.
There is much mirth among the rich with meat and fine
clothing,
And there is much mirth in May among wild creatures, 170
And so long as summer lasts they live happily.

But beggars about midsummer go breadless to supper,
And winter is yet worse, for they are wetᐟshod wanderers,
Frozen and famished and foully challenged
And berated by rich men so that it is rueful to listen.
Now Lord, send them summer or some manner of happiness
After their going hence for what they have here suffered.
For thou mightest have made us equal, none meaner than
    another,
With equal wit and wisdom, if such had been thy wishes.
Have ruth on these rich men who reward not thy prisoners;
Many are *ingrati* of the good that thou hast given them.   181
But God, in thy goodness, grant them grace of amendment.
For they dread no dearth nor drought nor freshets,
Nor heat nor hail, if they have their comfort.
Nothing is wanting to them here of what they wish and will.

"But poor people, thy prisoners, Lord, in the pit of misery,
Comfort thy creatures who have such care to suffer
Through dearth, through drought, all their days here.
Woe in winter for want of clothing!
Who seldom in summerᐟtime sup fully!   190
Comfort thy careworn, Christ, in thy riches,
For how thou comfortest all creatures clerks bear witness:
Convertimini ad me, et salvi eritis.
This, *in genere,* of his gentleness, Jesus Christ uttered
To robbers and ravishers, to rich and poor men.
He taught them to take their baptism in the Trinity,
And to be clean through that christening from all kinds of evil
If it befalls that through folly we fall into sin after,
Confession, and acknowledgement and craving his mercy
Will amend us as many times as a man desires.   200
If the Prince of Hell plead against it and punish us in
    conscience,
Christ will take him the acquittal and quickly overcome him:
    H*

Pateat, etc. per passionem Domini.
And so put that Prince from us and prove us under his pledges.
But poverty should be the parchment upon which the patent is
    written,
With pure patience and a perfect faith.
This parchment will slip from the proud and pompous
But is the prize of all people who are poor in heart;
Else all is idle that ever was written,
Pater noster and penances and pilgrimages to Rome.   210
Unless our expense and our spending spring from a true
    purpose
All our labour is lost: lo, how men are writing
For the friars' windows: falsehood is the foundation.
Therefore Christians should be rich in common, and none
    covetous for his person.

"There are seven sins that assail us always;
The fiend follows them all to furnish assistance;
Yet that wretch wins us with wealth the soonest.
Wherever riches reign reverence follows,
Which is pleasant to pride in poor or rich men.
The rich is reverenced by reason of his riches   220
When the poor is put behind, though perhaps more gifted
With wit and with wisdom, which are far and away better
Than rule or than riches, and heard more readily in heaven.
The wealthy are weighed down and walk slowly;
The highway to heaven is often closed against them.
Ita impossibile diviti, etc.
The poor presses before the rich with a pack at his shoulder,
And is bold and importunate, in beggar's fashion.
He asks perpetual bliss for his poverty and patience.
Pride reigns in riches more readily than in poverty,   230
And has his mansion in the master before the man is taken.
But in poverty where there is patience pride is strengthless,

There none of the seven sins may establish themselves firmly,
Nor have power over poverty, if patience follow it.
The poor man is always pressed to please the wealthy.
He is obedient to their bidding for his best advantage.
And boasting and obedience are always conflicting.
Each hates the other and all his ways.

"If Wrath wrestle with the poor he gets the worst of it;
And if both complain the poor is feeble.   240
Quarrelling and contention get him into trouble.
He who must ask his meat and money from another,
Must have lowly looks and the language of humility.

"If Gluttony grieve Poverty his gain is little,
For Poverty has a poor income to buy a rich diet;
Though there is gluttony in good ale, he goes to cold bedding;
His head is uncovered, uncomfortable and uneasy,
And the straw must be his sheet if he stretch beyond the blanket
His great sloth and his gluttony bring him grievous penance,
He is in woe when he wakes, and weeps for cold,   250
And sometimes for his sin; so he has no revel
Without misery and mourning mingled with it.

"Covetousness may not come too close to Poverty,
Especially they may not hang with arms about their shoulders.
Many can tell how Covetousness has keen desire,
With hands and arms that reach widely.
But poverty is a tiny thing, no taller than his waist-band,
And there is no love nor liking between long and short.

"If Avarice would anger the poor he has small foothold.
Poverty has only pockets in which to put his money,   260
But Avarice has armouries and iron bound coffers.
And which is more easily emptied and less heard in breaking,

A beggar's bag or an iron bound coffer?

"Lechery loves him not, for he gives little money,
And never dines him delicately nor drinks wine often.
A straw for the stews; they would not stand, I assure you,
If they had nothing but from poor men, and the tiles were off
   their houses.

"If Sloth pursues Poverty and slights God's service,
Misfortune is his master and makes him consider
How God and no other creature is his greatest helper,   270
And his servant, as he says, and in the suit of his body.
Where he is and where he is not his emblem is poverty,
For in that sect our Saviour saved all mortals.
So each poor man who is patient may boldly ask for
His heavenly bliss after his earthly parting.
Much more hardily might he ask it who might have his pleasure
In lands and in lordship and delights of the body,
And who leaves all for God's love and lives a beggar.
A maiden who loves a man and leaves her mother,
Her father and all her friends, and follows her husband,   280
Is more to be loved by the man whom she chooses
Than a maid who is married in mere brokerage,
With the assent of the several parties and some money in
   addition,
And more from a coveting of goods than for common affection.
Such a preference belongs to all people who leave possessions
   freely
And betake themselves to Patience and choose Poverty in
   marriage,
For she is kin to God himself and to the glory of his holy ones."

"I have God to witness," said Haukyn, "you have praised
   Poverty boldly.

What is patient poverty," he asked, "in its proper meaning?"
"*Paupertas*," said Patience, "*est odibile bonum, remotio curarum,*
   possessio sine calumnia, donum Dei, sanitatis mater, absque sol-
   licitudine semita, sapientiae temperatrix, negotium sine damno,
   incerta fortuna, absque sollicitudine felicitas."   290
"I cannot understand all this," said Haukyn, "you must
   explain it in English."
"It will be hard," he answered, "to explain it in English,
But I shall paraphrase it in part, provided you understand it.
(1) In the first place Pride hates Poverty above all others,
And clearly all is good that gives Pride discomfort.
Contrition is a comfort, as Conscience is aware,
A sorrow for self and a solace to the spirit:
Poverty, joy and penance are plainly to be considered
Pure spiritual health in man's body.
Ergo paupertas est odibile bonum.   300
And Contrition is comfort and *cura animarum.*
(2) Poverty is seldom selected to show evidence,
And never enjoined as a justice to judge his fellows,
Nor to be a manager or a mayor or a minister of the kingdom.
The poor are seldom compelled to punish others.
Remotio curarum.
Ergo Poverty and poor men perform the commandment,
Nolite judicare quemquam. Thirdly:
(3) The poor man rarely becomes rich unless by rightful
   heritage;
He wins nothing with false weights and unsealed measures,
Nor borrows from his neighbours unless he can pay easily:
Possessio sine calumnia."   312
(4) The fourth is a good fortune by which the soul flourishes
With sobriety from all sin; and still further
It frightens the flesh from many follies,
Christ's own gift, and one comfort further:
Donum Dei.

(5) The fifth is mother of health, a friend in all trials,
The medicine of all men and Mistress of all cleanness:
Sanitatis mater.   320
(6) The sixth is a path of peace, yea through the pass of Altoun
Poverty might pass without peril from robbers!
For where poverty passes peace follows,
And he who has least has the hardiest spirit.
Hence Seneca says: *paupertas est absque solicitudine semita,*
And of an hardy heart among an host of robbers.
Cantabit pauper coram latrone viator.
(7) The seventh is well of wisdom; he has few words to offer
For lords give him little praise and listen rarely to his reasons.
He tempers his tongue to truth and desires no treasure.   330
Sapientiae temperatrix.
(8) The eighth is a loyal labourer who is loath to be given
More than he may deserve in summer or in winter.
He acknowledges no loss in his accounts if he may have charity:
Negotium sine damno.
(9) The ninth is so sweet to the soul that no sugar is sweeter;
For patience is the bread that Poverty lives on,
And sobriety is a sweet drink and a good physician.—
For the love of our Lord the learned Augustine
Taught me that poverty and patience is the lowly living   340
Of a blessed life, with no business but the soul's salvation.
Absque sollicitudine felicitas.
Now God who gives all goodness grant rest to his spirit
Who first wrote thus to advise men of the meaning of poverty!"

"Alas!" cried Haukyn the Active Man, "that after my
      christening
I had been dead and dug into earth for the sake of Do Well!
It is so hard," said Haukyn, "to live sinless!
Sin follows us always," he said. Sorrow shook him,
His eyes were weeping and he bewailed the hour

That he ever did a deed to the dear God's displeasure.   350
He sobbed and swooned and sighed continually
That he ever had land or lordship, the least or the greatest,
Or any mastery over any man more than himself.
"I am not worthy, God wot," said Haukyn, "to wear any
   clothing,
Neither shirt nor shoes, but what shame bids me
To cover my nakedness," quoth he, and cried hard for mercy
And wept and wailed;—and with that I awoke.

PASSUS XV

AFTER my waking a vast while followed
Before I knew inwardly the nature of Do Well.
My wits waxed and waned till I was a fool in
Some blamed my life and few liked it.   [earnest.
They held me an abandoned wretch unwilling to reverence
Lords or ladies or any living being,
As persons in fur apparel with pendants of silver.
I never said to sergeants in law or to such people,
"God save you, sirs," and suavely bowed to them.
Such men maintained me a fool, yea, mad in folly.   10
But Reason had ruth on me and rocked me to slumber,
Till I saw as by sorcery a subtle creature
Without tongue or teeth, who told me my destiny
And whence I came and of what kind. I conjured him finally
If he were a Christian creature for Christ's love to tell me.

'I am a Christian creature," he said, "and christened often,
Well known in Christ's court, and of his kin also.
Neither Peter the porter nor Paul with his falchion
Will deny me the door, though I ding on it at midnight.
At midnight and at midday my voice is so known there   20
That each creature in his court welcomes me fairly."

"What are you called," I asked, "in that court by Christian
    people?"
"While I am quick in the body," quoth he, "I am called
    Anima;
And when I wish and will Animus is my title.
For my knowledge and capacity I am called Mens.
When I complain to God I am called Memory.
When I decide and determine to do as Truth tells me

My right name is Ratio, or Reason in English.
When I feel what the folk talk of, my first name is Sensus,
Which is wit and wisdom and the well of all handicraft.   30
When I bid or do not bid, buy or do not buy,
I am called Conscience, God's clerk and notary.
And when I love loyally our Lord and all men
Leal love is my name, in Latin *Amor*.
When I flee from the flesh and forsake the body
I am speechless spirit, and Spiritus is my epithet.
Augustine and Isidore have each wisely
Enumerated my names and you may choose freely,
Now that you know my names, by what name you will call me."

"You must be a bishop," said I, playing with his discourse, 40
"For our blessed bishops have many titles,
Praesul and *pontifex* and *metropolitanus*,
And an host of other names, as *episcopus* and *pastor*."

"That is so," he said, "and now I see your purpose.
You would know and consider the cause of all their titles,
And of mine if you might, my man!" he answered.

"Yes, sire," I said, "so long as I hurt no one
I should like to learn and lightly master
All the sciences under the sun and all their subtle handiwork."

"Then you are imperfect," he said, "and one of Pride's   50
    champions.
Such a lust and liking threw Lucifer from heaven.
Ponam pedem meum in acquilone, et similis ero altissimo.
It is against Nature," quoth he, "and against all common reason
That any creature but Christ should have complete knowledge.
Solomon speaks against such, and despises their judgments:
Sicut qui mel comedit multum, non est ei bonum;

sic qui scrutator est majestatis, opprimitur a gloria.
This means to men who speak English and understand it
That the man who eats much honey will have his mouth glued
together,
And that the more good matter that a man hears spoken
Will do him double injury unless his deeds accord with it. 60
Beatus est, says Saint Bernard, *qui Scripturas legit*
Et verba vertit in opera as fully as he is able.
Adam and Eve were put out of Paradise
For searching sciences and seeking knowledge.
Scientiae appetitus hominem inmortalitatis gloria spoliavit.
Honey is hard to digest and holds the mouth prisoner.
So God withholds grace from any creature who ventures
To reason into the root of his greatness and his nature.
The lust of pride and a bodily liking lies in such motion
Against the counsel of Christ and all clerks' teaching, 70
Which is, *Non plus sapere quam oportet sapere.*
You friars and you masters who preach among the people,
You teach the Trinity and doctrines without number,
So that the belief of the learned and of the unlearned wavers.
It were better if many doctors would abandon such teaching,
And tell men of the ten commandments and touch the seven
sins
And the branches that burgeon from them and bring men to
Satan,
How folly leads the folk to use five wits evilly,
And how friars and other folk are foolish spenders
In exhibiting their erudition, in housing and in clothing, 80
Rather for pomp than for plain charity. The people know truly
That I lie not, to please lords and ladies,
Or reverence the rich more readily than poor men.
Confundantur omnes qui adorant sculptilia. Et alibi: Ut quid diligitis
vanitatem, et quaeritis mendacium.
Go to the comment on that verse, you great scholars.

If my unlearned wit lies, lead me to burning!
It seems that you forswear no man's almsdeed,
Usurers nor whores nor avarous tradesmen,
And leer upon lords who may lend you nobles,
Against your rule and religion. My record is Jesus   90
Who said to his disciples, *ne sitis personarum acceptores*.

"Of this matter I might make a long story,
And of the curators of Christian souls, as clerks bear witness.
I shall tell it for Truth's sake, and he take heed who cares.
As holiness and honesty come out of Holy Church,
Through the lives of holy men who teach the law of heaven,
So all evils come out of Holy Church,
Where priesthood is imperfect in preaching and teaching.
You may see an example in the summer branches.
Some limbs have leaves and other limbs are naked,   100
And the root is rotten where the tree is withered.
So parsons and priests and preachers of Holy Church
Are the root of the right faith to rule the people.
But where the root is rotten Reason tells us
That no flower nor fruit nor fair leaves flourish.

"If you lettered would leave your delightful clothing
And be kind as befits clerks and courteous with Christ's
    treasure,
True of your tongue and of your tally also,
Hate to hear ribaldry and never receive further
The tythes of untruth from tillage or traffic,   110
The unlearned would be loath to hold your lore lightly,
And would amend their misdeeds the more by our examples
Than by our unproved preaching, that is hypocrisy to their
    seeming.
Hypocrisy is likened in Latin to a dunghill
Beneath a shroud of snow, and snakes within it;

Or to a white limed wall with foul contents.
Many priests and preachers, prelates and others
Are blanched with *bele paroles* and beautiful clothing,
But their works and their words under them are full of
   unloveliness.
Johannes Chrysostom speaks so of clerks and parsons.   120
Sicut de templo omne bonum progreditur, sic de templo omne malum
   procedit. Si sacerdotium integrum fuerit, tota floret ecclesia; si autem
   corruptum fuerit, omnis fides marcida est. Si sacerdotium fuerit in
   peccatis, totus populus convertitur ad peccandum. Sicut cum videris
   arborem pallidam et marcidam, intelligis quod vitium habet in radice.
   Ita cum videris populum indisciplinatum et irreligiosum, sine dubio
   sacerdotium ejus non est sanum."

"If an unlearned man might know the meaning of this Latin
And who was my authority, it were a great wonder,
Unless many a priest should bear for his broadsword   130
   and brooches
A band of beads in his hands and a book at his elbow.
Sir John and Sir Geoffrey have a girdle of silver,
A broad sword and a ballock´knife and painted buttons;
A breviary should be their plow to say *placebo*;
But unless their service saves them silver they say it unwillingly.

"Alas, you unlearned men, you lose much through the
   priesthood!
But the wise God wills that the wicked should treasure
What is won wickedly with wiles and falsehood.
These wicked are imperfect priests and preachers for silver,
Executors and subdeans, sompnours and their sweethearts.
What was got with guile is ungraciously expended,   141
Whores and harlots have their property,
And good folk for wanting it fare ill and perish.

"Curators of Holy Church and clerks who are avaricious
Leave their property a prize to profligate livers,
Or die intestate and then the bishop enters
And makes merry with it and his men also.
They cry: 'He was a niggard and had no goods to offer
To friend or to foreigner; the fiend take him
For the wretched house that he kept all his lifetime!   150
We shall spend in sport what he spared and closeted.'
So go the goods when the ghost is parted
Of the learned and unlearned who are loath in spending.
But God knows that for good men men make great sorrow,
And bear in mind good meat givers and bemoan them
    often
In prayers and in penances and in perfect charity."

"What is Charity?" I asked then. "A childish thing," he
    answered.
Nisi efficiamini parvuli, non intrabitis in regnum coelorum.
A frank and a free spirit without folly or childishness."
"Where may men find such a friend with so free an heart? 160
I have lived long in the land; Long Will men call me,
But I never found full charity before or after,
Men are merciful to mendicants and poor folk,
But will lend where they believe to be loyally refunded.
As for the charity that Paul praises as most pleasant to our
    Saviour,
As, *Non inflatur, non est ambitiosa, non quaerit quae sua sunt, etc.*
I never saw such a man, so God help me!
But he would ask after his own and at other times covet
Things which he did not need and take them if possible.
Christ according to the clerks is in all places,   170
But I have only seen him certainly in myself as a in a mirror:
In aenigmate tunc facie ad faciem.
And I trust truly by what men tell of charity

That it is neither the traffic of tradesmen nor the tourneys of
  knighthood."

"Charity," quoth he, "has no claims, nor craves nor bargains.
He is as proud of a penny as of a pound of silver,
And as glad in a garment of grey homespun
As in a tunic of Tartary or in true scarlet.
He is glad with the glad and good to all the wicked,
And believes and loves all that our Lord has fashioned. 180
He curses no creature nor can ever be angry;
Nor has any liking for a lie, nor for laughing scornfully.
What men tell him he holds true and takes all cheerfully,
And bears all manner of misfortune in mildness and quiet.
He covets no earthly good, but the happiness of heaven."

"Has he any rents or riches or any rich comrades?"
"He is reckless of riches and of rents always,
For a friend provides for him and never fails him in trouble.
Fiat voluntas tua provides for him forever.
If he sups he eats but a sop of *spera in* Deo. 190
He can beautify the *pater noster* and paint it with *aves*.
And at other times he is accustomed to walk in pilgrimage
Where poor men lie in prison and have pardon from them.
Though he bear them no bread he bears sweeter viands.
He loves them as our Lord bids and looks upon them.

"When he is weary of that work he will go sometimes
To labour in a laundry as long as a mile's walking.
Then he hastens unto youth and earnestly seeks for
Pride and all its appurtenances and packs them together
And presses them to his breast and beats them clean, 200
And lays on long with *laboravi-in-gemitu-meo*,
And washes them with the warm water of his eyes after.
Sometimes he sings at this labour and sometimes he says
  weeping:

Cor contritum et humiliatum, Deus non despicies."

"By Christ, I would know him," cried I, "no creature dearer!"
"Without help of Piers Plowman," said he, "you will never
 see this person."
"Do clerks know him," quoth I, "who keep Holy Church?"
"Clerks have no knowledge," said he, "except by words and
 actions.
But Piers the Plowman perceives more deeply
Into the means and motives that many tolerate: 210
Et vidit Deus cogitationes eorum.
Many proud-hearted men are patient in speaking,
And obedient in bearing to burgesses and masters,
But to the poor people have pepper in their nostrils
And lower as a lion when men blame their conduct.

"There are beggars and bidders who seem beadsmen outwardly,
Who look like lambs and seem to live in sanctity.
But this poverty is less for penance and perfect living
Than to have a measure of meat with more leisure.
You can never know them by their colours, nor by 220
 clergy and learning,
Nor through words and works, but through the will alone.
That no clerk nor earthly creature can ever tell you,
But only Piers the Plowman, *Petrus, id est, Christus.*
He is not in lollers nor in land-leaping hermits,
Nor at the hampers of anchorites, nor with any such feigners.
Fie upon false men and *in fautores suos!*
Charity is God's champion, like a child that is gentle,
And the merriest of mouth at meat and at table.
For the love that lies in his heart makes him lightsome in
 language,
And he is companionable and cheerful as Christ bids him. 230
Nolite fieri sicut hypocritae tristes, etc.

I have seen him in silk and sometimes in russet,
In grey and in furred gowns and in gilt armour;
And he gave them as gladly to any creature who needed them.
Edmund and Edward were each kings
And considered saints when Charity followed them.
I have seen Charity also singing and reading,
Riding, and running in ragged clothing;
But among bidders and beggars I beheld him never.
In rich robes he is most rarely witnessed,   240
With a cap or a crown glistening and shaven,
Or in cleanly clothes of gauze or Tartary.
In a friar's frock he was found once,
But that was afar back in Saint Francis's lifetime;
In that sect since he has been too seldom witnessed.
He receives the robes of the rich, and praises
All who lead their lives without deception.
Beatus est dives qui, etc.
He comes often in the king's court where the council is honest,
But if Covetousness is of the council he will not come into it.
He comes but seldom in court with jesters,   251
Because of brawling and backbiting and bearing false witness.
He comes but rarely to the consistory where the commissary is
    seated,
For their lawsuits are over long unless they are lifted by silver,
And they make and unmake matrimony for money.
Whom Conscience and Christ have combined firmly
They undo unworthily, these Doctors of Justice.
His ways were once among the clergy,
With archbishops and bishops and prelates of Holy Church,
To apportion Christ's patrimony to the poor and needy. 260
But now Avarice keeps the keys and gives to his kinsmen,
To his executors and his servants and sometimes to his children.

"I blame no man living; but Lord amend us

And give us all grace, good God, to follow Charity!
Though he mistrusts such manners in all men who meet him,
He neither blames nor bans nor boasts nor praises,
Nor lowers nor lauds nor looks sternly,
Nor craves nor covets nor cries after more.
In pace in idipsum dormiam, etc.
The chief livelihood that he lives by is love in God's passion.
He neither bids nor begs nor borrows to render.   271
He misuses no man and his mouth hurts no one.

"Among Christian men this mildness should be lasting;
Have this in heart in all times of anger:
That though they suffered all this, God suffered for us more,
In example that we should do so and take no vengeance
On the falseness of our foes; these are our Father's wishes.
Everyone may know well that if God had wished it himself
Neither Judas nor any Jew would have hung Jesus on the
    roodtree,
Nor have martyred Peter and Paul and put them in prison. 280
But he suffered in example that we should suffer also,
And said to such as would suffer that *Patientes vincunt*.
Verbi gratia," said he, "for many true examples,
Look in *Legenda Sanctorum* and in the lives of the holy ones,
At the penance and poverty and the passion which they
    suffered,
In hunger and heat, and all manner of afflictions.
Antony and Egidie and other holy fathers
Had homes in the wilderness with the wild creatures,
Monks and mendicants were men of solitude
In caves and caverns and conversed rarely.   290
Neither Antony nor Egidie nor any hermit of those ages
Took livelihood from leopards, lions or tigers,
But ate the flesh of fowls, as we find in their Legends.

"Yet once Egidie called an hind to him,
And the milk of that mild creature maintained him thereafter.
Yet he did not have her daily to decrease his hunger,
But seldom and at special hours, as the story teaches.

"Each day Antony at about noon time
Had a bird that brought him the bread he lived on.
Though this good man had a guest, God kept them equally.

"Paul, the *primus heremita*, had imparked his body   301
Where no man might see him for moss and branches.
The fowls fed him for many winters,
Till he founded the friars of the Augustine order.
After his preaching Paul made panniers and baskets,
And won with his hands what hunger demanded.
Peter fished for his food in fellowship with Andrew.
They sold some and cooked some and so they lived together.

"Magdalene drank the dew and took roots against hunger,
But lived mostly through devotion and remembering   310
    God Almighty.
I should not in seven days say through all of them
Who lived thus for our Lord's love long years together.
There was neither lion nor leopard on the lawns about them,
Nor bear nor boar nor any beast of the wilderness,
That would not fall at their feet and fawn with his tail.
If these could have conversed with them, by Christ, I imagine,
They would have fed that folk before the wild fowls.
They were as courteous and caressing as such creatures can be,
And serviceable and submissive when they stalked through the
    forest.
God sent them food by fowl and by no fierce creature   320
Meaning that the meek should by the mild be succoured;
As one should say that just men should support the religious,

And lawful men bring livelihood to all whose lives are holy.

"Great lords and ladies would be loath to injure
Or to take more from a tenant than truth warrants,
If they found that friars would forgo their almsdeeds
And bid them bear it where they borrowed it unjustly.
We are but God's song birds and abide patiently
Till birds bring us the food we live by.
If you had bread and pottage and penny ale for drinking 330
And made your mess of them in moderate fashion,
You would have enough, you religious, as your rule tells me.
*Nunquam, dicit Job, rugit onager cum herbam habuerit, aut mugiet
bos cum ante plenum praesepe steterit. Brutorum animalium
natura te condemnat, quia cum eis pabulum commune sufficiat, ex
adipe prodiit iniquitas tua.*
If the unlearned knew this Latin they would look well whom
they favoured,
And advise themselves before hand, five days or six,
Ere they made over their mortgages to monks and canons.
Alas, lords and ladies, you are led ignorantly   340
To bereave your heirs of what your ancestors left you
And to give for the intercessions of such as are wealthy
And enfeoffed and founded to pray for others.
Who performs this prophecy among the people nowadays;
Dispersit, dedit pauperibus.
If any people practise it they are these poor friars.
What they beg about the country they build into chapels
And spend something on themselves and something on their
labourers.
They take from those who have and give to those who have
nothing.

"But clerks and knights and commoners who are wealthy 350
Often act, methinks, as if I owned a forest

That was full of fair trees; and I figured and fancied
How I might set out more among their company.
You robe those who are rich, you rich patrons,
And help those who help you, and give where none are needy
Like one who filled a tun in a fresh river,
And marched forth with it to moisten the Thames.
You robe and feed the rich, you rich patrons,
And you put at their pleasure priests as rich as you are.

"But religious men who are rich should rather feed beggars
Than burgesses who buy houses, as the book teaches: 361
Quia sacrilegium est res pauperum non pauperibus dare. Item; Pec-
catoribus dare, est daemonibus immolare. Item; Monache, si indiges
et accipis, potius das quam accipis; si autem non eges et accipis, rapis.
Porro non indiget monachus, si habeat quod naturae sufficit.

"Therefore I counsel all Christians to conform to charity,
For charity without challenging discharges our burden
And his prayers save many people from the prison of purgatory.
The folk who keep the faith default grievously,
And so the folk is feeble and infirm in believing.   370
There is an alloy in a lushborgh though it looks like a sterling;
The mark of that money is good but the metal is counterfeit.
So it fares with some folk who are fair speakers,
And have the crown and christening of the king of heaven;
But the metal, which is man's soul, is so alloyed with
    wickedness
That it seems that no soul loves our Saviour or his neighbour.
Through war and rapine and wicked living
No prayer, it appears, can make peace between enemies.
The unlearned have lost their faith and the lettered are erring.
Neither the sea nor the sand nor the seed is yielding   380
As it once would. In whom is the error?
Not in God, for he is good and the ground of all things.

The sea and the seed, the sun and the moon
Do their tasks day and night, and if we did likewise
There would be perpetual peace and plenty forever.
Weather-wise shipmen and other cunning people
Have lost assurance in the sky and in the polar star.
Each day the art of the astronomers fails them,
Though they were once warned of what should happen after.
Shepherds and shipmen with their sheep and vessels   390
Saw by the sky what should follow.
They warned men of winds and weathers often.
Tillers who tilled the earth told their masters
By the seed that they sowed what they should harvest,
And what to lend and what to live by; the land was so faithful.
But now the folk fail on the flood and in the valleys—
Shipmen and shepherds, sowers and reapers—
And no creature can tell one course before another.
Astronomers also are at their wits' end.
They calculate the elements but the contrary confronts them.
Grammar, the ground of all, misguides children,   401
For none of these new clerics, if you note them closely,
Can write verse correctly or compose a letter.
No, not one among an hundred can interpret an author,
And read a letter in any language unless in Latin or English.
Go now into any degree and unless Guile be the master,
And Flatterer his fellow in the forms beneath him,
Among all men, I think, it would be much of a wonder.
Doctors of decrees and Masters of Divinity,
Who should command and contemplate all kinds of   410
   knowledge,
And answer to arguments and to any questionings,
(I dare not say it for shame) if such were examined
Would fail in their philosophy and in their physics also.
Therefore I am in fear that the folk of Holy Church
Pass over as others do their hours and offices.

But if they pass over, as I hope not, our belief suffices.
Clerks on Corpus Christi day sing and read
That *sola fides sufficit* to save the unlearned.

"Thus Saracens may be saved, and Scribes and Hebrews.
Alas then, that our leaders should not live as they teach us, 420
That by their living the unlearned might be more loath to offend
   heaven.
The Saracens have something similar to our faith.
For they love and believe in one Person Almighty,
And we, learned and unlearned, believe God in unity.
But one man, Mohammed, a misbeliever,
Betrayed the Saracens of Syria, and see in what manner.
Mohammed was a christened man, and since he might not be
   pontiff
He sought a home in Syria and with his subtle knowledge
Tamed a dove by daily feeding.
Whatever corn she cropped he concealed in his ear.   430
When he preached among the people or appeared openly
This culver would come to this clerk's ear
To peck at the bread which the priest had hidden.
The folk fell to their knees, for he had already taught them
That the culver came from God in heaven,
A messenger to Mohammed to minister to the people.
Thus by wit and wile and a white culver
Mohammed brought men and women to heresy,
And there the learned and unlearned live in his teaching.
So our Saviour suffered the Saracens to be cheated   440
By a Christian clerk and cursed traitor.
But on dread of death I dare not tell you
How English clerks feed a culver, Covetousness, men call him,
And after the manner of Mohammed, so that no man is honest.

"Anchorites and hermits and monks and friars

Are peers with the Apostles through their perfect living.
The faithful Father would never have his ministers
Take any of their treasure from tyrants who wrong true folk,
But have them do as Antony did, or Dominic and Francis,
Benet and Bernard, who first taught them   450
To live humbly in low houses by loyal almsdeeds.
Grace should grow and be green through their good living,
And the folk should find themselves, when they fall ill,
The better for those prayers in body and in spirit.
Their prayers and their penances should purify all men.
There would be no more debate if beadsmen were faithful.
Petite et accipietis, etc.
Salt saves cattle, say these women:
Vos estis sal terrae, etc.
The heads of Holy Church in holy living   460
Christ calls the salt for Christian people.
Et si sal evanuerit in quo salietur, etc.
Fresh flesh or fish when salt fails them
Are assuredly unsavoury, seethed or roasted,
And so are men's souls who see no good examples
In those of Holy Church, who should know the way and
    show it,
And should be guides to go before, as good banner bearers,
And hearten all who are behind, and yield them good evidence.

"Eleven holy men brought all the world over
Into a firm faith, and far more easily   470
Should all manner of men—we have so many scholars,
Priests and preachers and a pope above them,
Who should be God's salt and save all people.

"All were once heathen in Wales and England
Till Gregory sent clerks to come here as preachers.
Augustine christened the king at Canterbury.

Miracles, as men read, made that march loyal
To Christ and to Christendom and to the cross of glory.
He baptised the people and made them believers
More through miracles than overmuch preaching, 480
As well through works as through holy speeches,
And taught them what baptism and belief signify.

"Cloth that comes from the weaver is not good for wearing
Until it is trod under foot or taken in the stretcher,
Washed well with water, wiped with teasels,
Tucked, and given to the tenter hooks, and to the tailor's
    finishing.
The same belongs to the babe born of woman.
Till it is christened in Christ's name and confirmed by the
    bishop
It is an heathen towards heaven, and helpless in the spirit.

"Heathen is derived from heath, or the untilled barren. 490
So in the wild wilderness the wild creatures
Are rude and unreasoning and run without harness.

"Remember how Matthew writes that a man gave a dinner,
And fed upon no venison nor pheasants from the oven,
But on fowls that never feared him and followed his whistling.
Ecce altilia mea, et omnia parata sunt.
He fed with calves' flesh the folk whom he loved.
The calf stands for cleanness in those who keep statutes.
As the cow's milk nourishes calves till they grow to oxen,
Love and loyalty sustain leal Christians, 500
And maidens and mild men who seek mercy ardently.
Just as the calf comes to the cow for a sweet supper
So do just men seek truth and mercy.
The hand-fed fowls figure his people
Who are loath to love without lessons and parables.

Call the poultry in the courtyard, and they come at a whistle,
For they always look for food and follow men's whistling.
Rude men who have little reason are ruled easily
To love and to believe as the lettered lead them,
And to think and thrive by their words and actions.   510
As those fowls would find their food at that whistling,
So these hope to have heaven through their whistling.
The man who made the feast is the Majesty of the Father,
That is God, who of his grace gives all men heaven.
He warns us as a whistler with his wonders and tempests,
And shall feed us and feast us for evermore together.

"But who are they who excuse themselves? They are priests and
     parsons,
Heads of Holy Church, who have all their wishes.
They have tythes without the toil, for which true men are
     sweating,
And will be angry that I write thus, but my witnesses are many,
Matthew and Mark and *Memento-Domini-David*:   521
Ecce audivimus eam in Effrata, etc.
What pope or prelate now performs what Christ bids him:
Ite in universum mundum et praedicate, etc.

"Alas, that men should believe so long in Mohammed,
When the pope makes prelates to preach among them,
In Nazareth and Nineveh, in Nepthali and Damascus.
Why not go as Christ wills, since they wish their titles,
And be pastors and preach the passion of Jesus,
And do and die as God demands of them: 530
Bonus pastor animam suam ponit, etc.
And speak for the salvation of Saracens and heathens?
Christ commanded his preachers to Christians and heathens;
Ite vos in vineam meam, etc.
Since these Saracens, scribes and Hebrews

I

Have a slip of our belief, the more lightly, I imagine,
Men should turn to that toil and teach them of the Trinity:
Quaerite et invenietis, etc.

"It is rueful to read how righteous men suffered,
Defiled their flesh and forsook their own wishes,   540
Far from kith and kin, and clothed evilly,
Badly bedded, and no book but Conscience,
Nor any riches but the Rood to rejoice their souls.
Absit nobis gloriari nisi in cruce Domini nostri, etc.

"Then there was peace and plenty among poor and rich men.
Now it is rueful to read how the red noble
Is reverenced above the Rood and regarded as more worthy
Than Christ's cross that overcame death and evil.
Now there is war and woe and if you ask the reason—
It is covetousness of the gold cross with the crown upon it. 550
Both rich and religious hold that rood in honour
Which is engraved on groats and gold nobles.
For covetousness of that cross the men of Holy Church
Shall turn as the Templars did in the time approaching.
Do you not know, you historians, how those men honoured
Their treasure more than truth? I dare not tell that story.
Reason and a righteous judgement judged their religion.
So for the covetousness of you clerks they will come presently
To condemn dos ecclesiae and depose you from your prowess.
Deposuit potentes de sede, etc.   560
If Conscience and the Commune and Common Sense and
    Knighthood
Loved each other loyally, believe well, you bishops,
You would lose the lordship of your lands forever,
And live as Levitici, as our Lord teaches:
Per primitias et decimas, etc.

"When the kindness of Constantine gave Holy Church
    endowments
In lands and leases, lordships and servants,
The Romans heard an angel cry on high above them:
'This day *dos ecclesiae* has drunk venom
And all who have Peter's power are poisoned forever.'   570
But a medicine may be given to amend prelates
Who should pray for the peace and whose possessions
    prevent them.
Take their lands, you lords, and let them live by tithing!
If possession is poison and makes imperfect orders,
It were good to dislodge them for the Church's profit,
And purge them of that poison before the peril is greater.

"If priesthood were perfect all the people would be converted
Who are contrary to Christ's law and who hold Christendom
    in dishonour.
All pagans pray and believe rightly
In the great and holy God, and ask his grace to aid them.   580
Their mediator is Mohammed to move their petition.
Thus the folk live in a faith but with a false advocate,
Which is rueful for righteous men in the realms of Christendom,
And a peril to the pope and to the prelates of his creation
Who bear the names of the bishops of Bethlehem and Babylon.

"When the high king of heaven sent his son among us
He performed many miracles to turn men towards him,
In example that they should see by solemn reason
That men might be saved only through the mercy and grace of
    heaven,
And through pain and penance and perfect believing.   590
He became man of a maid and *metropolitanus*,
With the blood of his body he baptised and confirmed
All whom an inward wish willed to believe in him.

Many saints since have suffered martyrdom
To confirm that faith, and have fallen in many countries,
In India and in Alexandria, in Armenia and in Hispania,
And died dolefully for their faith's sake.
In service of that faith Saint Thomas was martyred.
Unnatural Christians killed him; for Christ's love he perished,
And all for the right of this realm and all realms in　　600
　　Christendom.
Holy Church is honoured highly through his dying;
He is patron for all bishops and a bright mirror,
And especially to such as hold the Syrian episcopate,
And hop about England to hallow men's altars
And creep among curates to confess unlawfully:
Nolite mittere falcem in messem alienam, etc.
Many men who loved Christ were martyred in Italy
Before Christianity came there or any cross was honoured.

"Every bishop who bears the cross is thereby commanded
To pass through his province, to bring the people to him,
To tell them of the Trinity, to teach them faithfully,　　611
To feed them with holy food, and to help folk who are needy.
Isaiah and Hosea hold equally
That no man should be a bishop without bearing to the people
Bodily food and holy food, furnishing each as is needed:
In domo mea non est panis neque vestimentum, et ideo nolite constituere
　　me regem.
Hosea says of such as are sick and feeble:
Inferte omnes decimas in horreum meum, ut sit cibus in domo mea.
But we Christian creatures have the cross in honour,
Are firm in the faith, God forbid otherwise,　　620
And have clerks to keep us so and those who will come after us.

"The Jews live in the law that our Lord wrote himself
In stone, for it was steadfast and should stand forever:

Love God and love thy neighbour is the law of the Hebrews.
He took it to Moses, its teacher till the coming of the Messiah.
And they live still in that law and believe it the best.

"They acknowledge Christ, who taught Christendom to them
As a true prophet who preserved many
From evil wounds, as they witnessed often.
He wrought miracles and marvels and gave the   630
    multitude a banquet;
Two fishes and five loaves feasted five thousand.
Men might see by that that he was Messiah, or like him.
He lifted Lazarus who had lain buried
Under a stone and stank. He said loudly:
Lazare, veni foras.
He bad him arise and walk before the people.
They said and swore that sorcery did it,
And strove to stone him and to destroy themselves.
But his patience brought their power to nothing.
Patientes vincunt.   640
Daniel had divined their undoing in his prophecy:
Cum sanctus sanctorum veniat, cessabit unctio vestra.
And those wretches regard him as though he were *pseudo-*
    propheta
And hold his lore a lie and blame it boldly,
And expect that he shall come who shall at last relieve them,
Moses again or Messiah, as their masters still prophesy.
But Pharisees and Saracens, Scribes and Greeks
Are folk of one faith and hold the Father in honour.
And since the Saracens as well as the Hebrews
Know the first clause of our creed, *Credo in Deum*   650
    patrem omnipotentem,
Prelates of Christian provinces if possible should teach them
Little by little *et in Jesum Christum filium,*
Till they can speak and spell *et in Spiritum Sanctum,*

And render it and remember it, with *remissionem peccatorum,
Carnis resurrectionem et vitam eternam. Amen.*"

PASSUS XVI

"NOW fair fortune to you," I said, "for your fair
teaching,
For the love of Haukyn the Active Man I shall
always love you.
And yet I wonder still what is the meaning of Charity."

"Then to tell you truly, it is a fair tree," he answered.
"Mercy is the main root of it and the mid-stock is pity,
The leaves are loyal words and the law of Holy Church,
The blossoms are obedient speech and a benign bearing,
The tree is plainly called patience and simplicity of living;
And so through God and through good men groweth the
fruit, charity."
"I would travel," said I, "to see this tree twenty hundred miles,
And to have my fill of that fruit forsake all other.   11
Lord, what person," said I, "can point me to the place where
it is growing?"

"It grows," said he, "in a garden of God's making;
The shoot is from that stock and shelters in man's body,
And the heart is the home wherein it rises.
Liberum Arbitrium has the land in rental,
And hoes it and weeds it under Piers the Plowman."
"Piers the Plowman," I cried, and for the pure pleasure
That I had in hearing his name I was at once unconscious.
I lay long in a lonely dream, and at last imagined   20
That Piers the Plowman showed me the place fully
And counselled me to gaze on it from crop to bottom.
It was propped with three piles, as I perceived quickly.
"Piers," I said, "I pray you, for what are these piles erected?"
"To ward it, if you would know," he said, "from winds and
tempests:

Cum ceciderit justus, non collidetur, quia Dominus supponit manum suam

Which nip the buds in blossom-time unless the piles save them.
The World is a wicked wind to all who seek Truth.
Covetousness comes on that wind and creeps among the
    branches
And freezes the fruit with fair seeming.   30
Then I put him off with the first pile, *Potentia-Dei-Patris*.
But the flesh is a foul wind, and in flowering season,
Through lust and through liking, blows loud in the branches,
Or feeds foolish visions and fair speeches;
His wicked words are worms of sinning
That bite the petals to the bare leafage.
Then I seize the second pile, *Sapientia-Dei-Patris*,
Which is the passion and the power of our Prince Jesus.
I save it till I see it ripen, and sometimes fruitful
Through prayer and penance and God's passion remembered.
When the fiend sees this fruit he is furious to destroy it,   41
And shakes the stem with all his sleights and cunning.
He casts against the crop unkind neighbours,
Bold men and backbiters, brawlers and chiders,
And lays a ladder against it with liars for the foot rests,
And fetches away my fruit before my own eyes.
But *Liberum Arbitrium* hinders him sometimes;
He is my lieutenant to look to it and has leave to watch it.
Videatis qui peccat in spiritum sanctum nunquam remittetur, etc.
Hoc est idem, qui peccat per liberum arbitrium non repurgatur.   50
When the World, the Flesh and the Fiend come forth together,
Moving behind me and menacing my harvest,
Liberum Arbitrium lashes with the pile remaining
And beats down the Pouk by the pure grace of heaven,
And by the help of the Holy Ghost, and thus I have the
    mastery!"

"Now fair fortune to you, Piers," I said, "so fairly have you
    told me
The power of these piles and their proper uses!
But I have a sheaf-full of fancies for these three stanchions,
About the wood where they were taken and the earth they
    come from.
For all are of equal length, none less than another,   60
And truly to my thinking one tree has grown them;
The grain of each seems green; and they are equal all ways."

"That is certain," said Piers, "and so be it,
I shall tell you truly what the tree figures.
The ground where it grew is called Goodness.—
I have told you what that tree is; Trinity is its meaning."
Then he looked at me angrily, and I spared further
To ask him of that tree; but again bad him
To describe this fruit so fair upon the branches.
This grew in three kinds; I thought it a great wonder,   70
And asked him if it were all of one grafting?

"Yes, certainly," he said, "be sure to believe it.
It is all of one grafting, as I shall tell you truly.
But some are sweeter than others and will soon wither.
Men may see in many apple trees
That apples of one kind are not of equal plumpness,
Nor of the same sweetness, nor smaller by gradation.
For those upon the sunny side are soonest to ripen,
And sweeter and more savoury and also larger
Than those that seldom have the sun and swing on the   80
    north branches.
And so it is surely, my son, with our nature.
Adam was a tree and we are his apples,
Some of us steadfast and some variable,
Some lesser and some larger, like apples of the orchard.

I*

But wedded men and widows and worthy maidens
Who seek the Holy Spirit, the sun of all heaven,
Which comforts these contemplatives who live in continence,
As most of all monks and men of Holy Church,—
These have heat from the Holy Ghost, as the tree top has
    sunshine.
Widows and widowers who have left their own wishes   90
And lead a chaste life are the life of contemplation
And more beloved by our Lord than those who live in Nature
And who follow as the flesh leads and have fruit accordingly,
Which lettered men in their language call *Activa Vita*."

"Yea, sire," I said, "but since there are but two lives
Allowed by our Lord, as the learned teach us,
Activa Vita and *Vita Contemplativa*,
Why grows the fruit in three kinds?" "For a good reason," he
    answered.
"And now I may take from beneath, if the need arises,
Matrimony, a moist fruit, which multiplies the people.   100
Then above is a better fruit, though both are pleasant,
Widowhood, held worthier than wedlock in heaven.
But virginity is more virtuous and the fairest thing in heaven,
For that is equal with the angels and the angels' peer.
It is the first fruit that the Father blest in heaven.
He bad it be a piece of earth, a man of a maiden,
Meaning that the fairest should have the first in honour,
And that the cleanest creature first know his creator.
In a king's court the cleanest and the fairest
Shall serve the lord himself, and so with God Almighty. 110
Maidens and martyrs ministered to him in the body,
And are nearest to him in heaven and rightly next him,
As they were the fairest fruit before him among mortals,
Sweet without swelling, never sour or unsavoury."

"This is a proper plant," I said, "and blossoms secretly,
And brings forth fair fruit among the folk of all nations."
I prayed Piers to pull down an apple, if he were willing,
And let me taste of that tree and test its savour.
Piers cast against the crop, and then it commenced to whimper;
Next he flung at widowhood, and it wept sorely;   120
And finally he flung at matrimony, which made a foul outcry.
I was sorry that Piers shook it, it sighed so ruefully.
Ever as they dropped down the devil was ready
And gathered them all together, the great and the lesser,
Adam and Abraham and Isaiah the prophet,
Samson and Samuel and Saint John the Baptist;
He bore them forth boldly with nobody to stop him,
And made an hell hoard of the holy in *limbo inferni*,
Where there is darkness and dread, and the devil as master.
Then Piers in pure pity took a pile himself   130
And hit after him, hap as it might hap.
Filius at the Father's will, befriended with *Spiritus Sanctus*,
Went to rob that wretch and rescue the fruit from him.

Then *Spiritus Sanctus* spoke through Gabriel
To a maid named Mary, a meek creature,
Said that Jesus, a justice' son, must sleep in her chamber,
Till *plenitudo temporis* were fulfilled truly:
And that Piers' fruit should flower and fall from its station
When Jesus should joust for the judgement of knighthood
On who should harvest that fruit, the fiend or the Plowman.
The maid assented mildly to the messenger of heaven   141
And addressed him humbly, "Lo, here, his handmaid,
To work his will without pollution:
Ecce ancilla Domini, fiat mihi," etc.
He was forty weeks in the womb of Mary,
And became an infant of her flesh, and might have fought early
That fight with the fiend, before the hour was ready.

But Piers the Plowman proved all things.
He learned leachcraft for his life's safety,
And how to heal his wounds if he were hurt in battle.   150
Then he assayed his surgery on sick people
Till his practice was perfect, whatever peril beset him.
He sought out sick and sinful wretches
And healed sick and sinful, blind and crooked.
He turned common women to good and granted them his
     mercy:
Non est sanis opus medicinae, sed in, etc.
He held it no art to heal dumb men
Or the lepers or the lame or the lax and bloody.
But not lightly did he raise Lazarus who had lain in burial
Quatriduanus dead; and delivered him openly.   160
Before he manifested that miracle *moestus cepit esse*,
And his eyes wept water in the witness of many.
Some who saw that sight said boldly
That he was the leach of life and the Lord of high heaven.
The Jews chattered against it and judged by their statutes
That he worked by witchcraft and with hell's assistance:
Daemonium habet, etc.
"You are churls," said Jesus, "and your children like you,
And Satan your Saviour as yourselves witness!
I have saved you," said Christ, "and your sons after you,   170
Your bodies, your beasts and your blind beggars.
I have fed you with fishes and with five loaves of bread,
And you bore in baskets-full the broken remnants!"
He rated those men manfully, menaced them to beat them,
And cut them with a cord, and cast down the tables
Of men who bought and bargained and bickered in the temple.
Then he said in the sight of all and so that all heard him:
"I shall overturn this temple and destroy it utterly,
And three days after I shall again rear it
And build it as great or greater and more glorious than ever,

As lofty and as large, as long and as spacious.   181
And accordingly I command you to call this temple
The place of perfection and prayer and purity:
Domus mea domus orationis vocabitur."
Envy and an evil will were among the people.
They conspired and agreed to kill him secretly,
And day by day delayed and waited.
The Thursday before Easter, when he made his maundy,
Seated at supper he spoke as follows:
"I am sold through one of you; but he shall regret that ever 190
He sold his Saviour for a silver reckoning."

Judas chattered against him, but Jesus answered
That it was assuredly he himself, and said, "*Tu dicis.*"
Then that evil man went forth and met with Jews
And told them of a token to know Jesus,
A token that to this day is too much practised—
Kissing with a fair countenance and unkind wishes.
And so it was with Judas when Jesus was taken.
"*Ave raby,*" cried that wretch, and ran towards him,
And kissed him that he should be captured and killed   200
    by his enemies.
Then Jesus spoke to Judas and to the Jews before him:
"I find falsehood in your fair speaking,
Guile is in thy glad cheer and gall in thy laughing;
Thou shalt be a mirror to men that many are deceivers.
But the worst of your wickedness shall be wrecked upon
    yourself:
*Necesse est ut veniant scandala: Vae homini illi per quem scandalum
    venit!*
Though I am taken by treason and at your own desire,
Leave my Apostles in peace; let them depart peacefully."
On the evening of Thursday he was thus taken,
Through Judas and through Jews, and his name was Jesus.

But on the Friday that followed for man's salvation   211
He jousted in Jerusalem to the joy of all men;
On the cross upon Calvary he gave battle
To death and to the devil and destroyed both,
Died and overcame death and made day of night.—

With that I awoke and wiped my eyelids
And pried where Piers the Plowman vanished.
I wandered into the east and into the west country,
And hurried forth as an idiot in hope of finding
Piers the Plowman in the places that I visited.   220
Then I met with a man on a mid⁄lenten Sunday
As hoar as an hawthorne, and Abraham men called him.
First I asked him fairly from whence he journeyed
And who he was and whither he was going.

"I am Faith," said that father, "for I shall not deceive you,
And am an herald of arms in Abraham's household.
I seek for some one whom I have seen formerly
As a bold beginner in arms; I knew him by his blazon."
"What blazon does he bear?" I said, "so bliss betide you."
"Three persons in one body, separable from each other,   230
Of one size and strength, stature and likeness,
What one does all do, and each does separately.
The first has might and majesty and is Maker of all things;
Pater is his proper name, one person without complement.
The second is the son of that sire, *Filius*,
The warden of the wisdom that is without beginning.
The third is the Holy Ghost, an inseparable person,
The light of all who have life in land or water,
Comforter of all creatures and ground of blessedness.
So three belong to one Lord with lordship divisible   240
Into Might and into a Mean to know this Might

Both in himself and in his Servant, and what they suffer
   together.
So God, who had no beginning but at his good pleasure,
Sent forth his son, a Servant for a season,
To engage himself here till issue had arisen,
Which were the children of Charity, and Holy Church their
   mother.
Patriarchs and prophets and apostles were of their number,
And Christ and Christendom and all Christian people.
Thus man must believe in One God Almighty,
Who wheresoever he wills is witnessed in three persons. 250

"One God Almighty made man and fashioned him
Similar to himself before sin entered.
He is three wheresoever he is and has to witness
The works that he has wrought, and this world among them.
That he is three separable persons in one being only,
Is evident in our essence, if all men are of Adam.
Eve was of Adam, drawn out of his body,
And Abel was their issue; all three are one manhood.
Wedlock without offspring is worth but little;
The Bible bears witness in a book of the old covenant   260
Which curses all couples in whom increase is wanting:
Maledictus sit homo qui non reliquit semen in Israel.
And a man without a mate may never multiply;
Such seed must have a sower, as we see in Nature.
Now if we go to the Godhead in God the Father
We find the Son within himself, to speak in simile,
As Eve was in Adam when God had her from him.
Abel, the offspring of Eve and Adam,
Sprang forth and spoke as a scion of either.
So from the Sire and the Son springs the Holy Spirit,   270
Which is and was and will be forever.

"As these three persons were properly but one manhood,—
Man, and his mate, and the mother's issue,—
So God is God's son in the three persons of the Trinity.
There were three in that marriage, and one man was their
     origin;
There are three in Godhead, and one God is their foundation.
Lo, three encounters three," he said, "in Godhead and in
     manhood."

"Have you ever seen," I said, "all three in unity?"

"I saw him one summer," he said, "as I sat in my doorway.
God came as three persons to the gate beside me.   280
Tres vidit et unum adoravit.
I arose and reverenced God and greeted him fairly,
And washed their feet and wiped them. They ate afterwards
Calves' flesh and cake bread, and could tell what I was
     thinking.
These were the true tokens which they took as witness.
First he found if I loved better
Him or Isaac, my heir, whom he bad me murder.
He knew my will through him, and he commended me for it.
My soul is safer and my son's also.
I circumcised my son for his sake afterwards.   290
Myself and my men and all males with me
Bled blood for that Lord's love and for the bliss of heaven.
My faith and my fidelity are firm in his teaching.
He has promised to me and to my issue after
Land and lordship and life everlasting.
And yet more, he granted to me and to my issue
Mercy for our misdeeds, as many times as we ask it.
Quam olim Abrahae promisisti et semini ejus.
He has sent since to tell me that I should do him sacrifice,
And worship him with bread and with wine together.   300

He has called me the foundation of his faith for his folk's
   salvation,
And has given the folk who believe in me a defence from Satan.
Thus I have been his herald here and in limbo
And have comforted the cares of many who wait his coming.
And now I seek him," he said, "for I have heard lately
Of a bold man who baptised him, and John Baptist was his
   title.
He came to patriarchs and to prophets and to other people in
   darkness
Saying that he had seen him who should save us.
Ecce agnus Dei," *etc.*

I wondered at his words and at his long garments,   310
For he bore in his bosom a thing that he blessed continually.
I looked into his lap, and lo, a leper lay there,
Complaining among the patriarchs and prophets in limbo.
"What do you wait for?" he asked, "and what are you
   seeking?"
"I would know," I answered, "what is in your bosom."
"Look," he said, and let me see. "Lord of mercy!" I uttered,
"Is this a present of great price, that a prince should wear it?"
"It is a precious present," he said, "and the Prince of Hell has it
And me with it," said that man; "and no pledge may quit us,
Nor any be our bail and bring us from this danger;   320
No fund may fetch us from the fiend's penfold
Till he come of whom I have spoken, and Christ is his name.
He will some day deliver us from the devil's clutches,
And bring us a better bail than any merit,
Which is life for life—or lying thus forever.
Lolling in my lap till such a Lord take us."

"Alas," I said, "that sin should so hinder
The might of God's mercy that can amend all men!"

So I wept at his words; but with that I saw another
Who was running rapidly on the road that we had taken. 330
First I asked him fairly from whence he journeyed,
And who he was, and whither he went; and he answered
    quickly.

"I AM SPES," he said, "a scout and spier for a champion
Who took from me a commandment upon the Mount of Sinai
To rule all realms; I bear the writ with me."
"Is it sealed?" I said, "May men see your letters?"
"No," he said, "I seek him who has the seal in keeping;
Which is the Cross of Christendom with Christ hanging upon it.
And when it is sealed so, I know surely
That Lucifer's lordship will last no longer."

"Let us see your letters," I said; "the law may be known to us."
Then he plucked forth his patent upon a piece of granite, 10
On which two words were written expounded as follows:
Dilige Deum et proximum tuum.
This was the true text, for I took good heed of it.
There was a glorious comment in gilt letters:
In his duobus mandatis tota lex pendet et prophetia.
"Are these all your Lord's laws?" I asked, "Yes, believe me," he answered.
"The devil will never daunt nor death frighten
Whoever works accordingly, I dare well wager.
Though I say it myself I have saved with this magic
Men and women by many score thousand." 20
"He speaks well," said the herald, "for I have found it often.
Look here in my lap on those who believe it truly,
On Joshua and Judith and Judas Maccabeus,
Yea, sixty thousand beside who are not seen with us."
"Your words are wonderful," I said; "but which of you is wiser
And the better to believe for body and for spirit?
Abraham says that he has seen the whole Trinity,
Three persons separable in three parts from each other,

227

And all three one God, so Abraham has taught me.

He has saved those who believed so and are sorry for   30
   their offences.

He cannot count the number that have come into his bosom.

Then why is it now needful to make a new covenant,

Since the first suffices for salvation and happiness?

And now Spes comes and speaks as one who has seen the
   covenant,

And tells no tale of the Trinity in his letters,

But, 'First believe and love one Lord Almighty,

And, second, as thou lovest thyself so love all people.'

He who walks with one staff appears hardier

Than he who walks with two staffs, to all who pass them.

It is simpler to show plain men a single lesson   40

Than to teach them two—and too dull to learn the simplest.

To believe in Abraham is hard for any man,

But alas, it is harder yet to love a villain!

It is far easier to have faith in three fair persons

Than to believe and to love alike the honest and the dishonest.

Go your gait," quoth I to Spes; "So God help me,

Those who learn your law will little use it."

As we went on the way talking together

We saw a Samaritan sitting in his saddle,

Riding rapidly on the road that we had taken,   50

Coming from a country that men call Jericho,

And hastening on his way to a joust in Jerusalem.

He overtook the herald and Hope together,

Where a man was wounded and waylaid by robbers.

He could neither stand nor stir nor signal for assistance,

Nor in any way save himself, and seemed half perished,—

Naked as a needle and no help about him.

Faith had first sight of him, but veered around him,

And would not come near him by nine furrows.

Hope came hastening after. He had already boasted   60
How he had helped many men with Moses' covenant.
But when he saw that sight he stepped sidewise
As much in dread, by this day, as a duck of a falcon!

But as soon as the Samaritan saw the sick man
He alighted from his horse and led him by the bridle
And went to that wanderer, found his wounds open,
And perceived by his pulse that he was at the point of dying;
That unless a saviour came speedily he should not rise living.
He unbuckled his two bottles and poured both together,
He washed his wounds with wine and oil,   70
Anointed him and bound his head and carried him carefully
And held him upon his horse till they arrived at *Lex Christi*,
An inn six or seven miles this side the New Market.
He harboured him in the hostelry and called the host to him
And said: "Here, keep this man till I come from the jousting.
Look, here is silver," he said, "for salve for his injuries."
He provided two pennies to pay for his nourishment,
And said: "If he spends further, I shall make good hereafter
For I may not stay," he said; and bestrode his charger,
And so rode rapidly on the highroad to Jerusalem.   80

Faith followed him fast, and would fain have reached him,
And Spes was speedy and sped after,
To overtake him and talk with him before they came to town.
When I saw this I stayed no longer but commenced running,
And pursued that Samaritan who was so full of pity,
And gave myself as his groom. "Gramercy," he answered,
"And you will find me a fellow and a friend in danger."
I thanked him then; and next I told him
How Faith and his fellow fled together

From the sight of one in sorrow, half slain by robbers.   90
"Let them be excused," he said, "for they could help little.
No medicine may heal that man of his afflictions,
Neither Faith nor fair Hope, his wounds so fester,
Without the blood of a babe born of a maiden.
But if he is bathed with that blood and baptised in it,
And then plastered with the penance and passion of that baby,
He may step and stand; but he shall never be stalwart
Till he has eaten his body and drunk his blood.
No one in this world went through that wilderness
Unrobbed and unrifled, riding or walking,   100
Except myself and Faith and Spes, his fellow,
And yourself now and such as see and do likewise.
Outlaws are in the woods and hide under the hollow.
They may see each man and mark easily
Who are behind and who before and who pass on horseback.
And they are harder on those on horseback than on those who
    go walking.
Their chief saw me, who am a Samaritan, pursue Faith and
    his fellow
On *Caro*, my courser, which mankind supplied me.
He was a coward, that caitiff, and got him *in inferno*.
But three days from to‑day I dare wager   110
That that felon will be fettered fast in irons,
And grieve no creature who goes along this highway.
O *mors, ero mors tua, etc.*
Then Faith will be forester here and have the fields in keeping
And call forth countrymen who can tell the roadways
And which and wherefore was my way to Jerusalem.
Hope will keep the hostelry here where the man lies healing.
All the faint and the feeble whom Faith may not tutor,
Hope will lead forth with love, as his license bids him,
   And give them hostelry and healing in Holy Church's   120
     doctrine,

Till I have salve for all the sick; and then I shall return
And come again into this country and give help to all sick folk
Who crave it and covet it, and cry for it faithfully.
For a babe was born in Bethlehem whose blood shall rescue
All who live with Faith and follow his friend's teaching."

"Ah, sweet Sir," I said, "how shall I believe truly
As Faith and his fellow have informed me already?
There are three separate persons, and yet in perpetuity
All three are but one God—so Abraham taught me.
And afterwards came Hope who bad me love   130
One God with all my mind, and all men after,
Love them as myself, and our Lord above all things."
"Set fast your faith," he said, "and your firm believing
According to Abraham, my herald in armour.
And as Hope has bidden you I have bidden you also;
Love your fellows forever as you love yourselves.
If Conscience or Common Reason carp against it,
Or if heretics argue—hold your hand towards them;
For God is fashioned after your hand. Now hear and know it.

"The Father was first like a fist with fingers folded,   140
Till at his love and liking he unloosed his fingers
And proffered his palm to the place that he favoured.
That palm is plainly the hand which proffers the fingers
To make and to minister what the might of the hand wishes.
And truly it betokens, as you may tell at pleasure,
The Holy Ghost of heaven; he is the palm.
The fingers that are free to fold and fashion
Signify the Son, who was sent among us.
The palm taught him to touch and try his mother,
The maiden, Saint Mary, and snatch man's salvation.   150
Qui conceptus est de Spiritu sancto, etc.
The Father is a fist with fingers for handling,

Quia omnia traham ad meipsum, etc.
Whatever the palm perceives profitable to deal with.
They are all one, in a hand's likeness,
Which may be seen as single or in three separate natures.
Since the palm puts forth to us both fist and fingers,
We see how reason will readily recognize it,
And the Sire and the Son show it to be the Spirit.

"The hand holds hard all that is within it,   160
Through four fingers and the thumb and the force of the palm.
So the Sire and the Son and *Spiritus Sanctus*
Hold the whole wide world within them,
Air and wind and earth and water,
Heaven and hell and all that is within them.

"So no man needs another figure
To show how three persons belong to our Lord in heaven,
Sole and separate and yet never asunder,
No more than my hand may move without my fingers.
As my fist is a full hand folded together,   170
So the Father is the full Deity, the former and creator,
And his Might makes all that is made ever.

"The full hand is formed with fingers; for painting and
    drawing
Carving and cutting are all crafts of the fingers.
And so is the Son the science of the Father,
A full Deity as the Father, neither feebler nor stronger.

"The palm is properly the hand, and has powers independent
Of the firm fist and the fingers' workmanship.
The palm has power to place joints outward
And to fold and unfold the fist, for this is its function.   180
It may receive or refuse what is reached it by the fingers

After it has felt what the fist and the fingers give it.
So God the Holy Ghost is neither greater nor lesser
Than the Sire or the Son, but has the same power:
And all but one God, as my hand and fingers,
Folded or unfolded, fist or palmwise,—
All is but one hand, however I turn it.

"He who is hurt in the hand, or especially in the heart of it,
Holds nothing surely, as one sees often.
The pain in the palm prevents grasping,   190
Or folding the fingers and making the fist rigid.
If the middle of my hand were maimed or injured
I could retain nothing rightly that I might reach easily.
If my thumb and my fingers both pained me
And the middle of my hand remained uninjured,
I might still help myself in many actions,
And move and mend, though my fingers were aching.
And so, to my seeming, I see an evidence
That he who sins against the Holy Spirit may be assoiled
    nowhere,
Neither here nor elsewhere, as I have heard it mentioned: 200
Qui peccat in Spiritu sancto, etc.
For he pricks God in the palm who *peccat in Spiritu sancto.*
God the Father is a fist and the Son the fingers;
The Holy Ghost of Heaven is in a palm's likeness.
He who sins against the Spirit seems to injure
God where he grips, and would quench grace wholly.

"So the Trinity is like a torch or a taper burning;
As though the wax and the wick were wound together,
And then a fire flamed forth from either.
As the wax and the wick and the hot fire together   210
Foster their flame to fire the brushwood,
So Sire and Son and *Spiritus Sanctus*

Foster among the folk faith and affection,
And cleanse sin in all the kinds and Christian orders.
As you see sometimes a sudden torchlight
Blaze and blow out, but still the wick is burning,
Without the flame and flare that springs from firebrands,
So the Holy Ghost is God and grace without mercy
To all unkind creatures who covet to injure
The loyal love and life which our Lord created.   220
As the glowing coals gladden not the workmen
Who wake to work on winter evenings,
So much as an hemlock or a candle that catches fire and blazes,
No more do Sire and Son and Holy Spirit together
Grant us any grace or forgiveness for our offences
Till the Holy Ghost begin to glow and flicker.
But the Holy Ghost glows as a coal only
Till loyal love blows upon him.
Then he flares into a fire upon Father and *Filius*,
And melts their Might into Mercy, as men see in winter   230
How icicles on the eaves in the heat of sunshine
Melt in a moment to mist and water.
So the Grace of the Holy Ghost against the great Might of the
    Trinity
Melts Power into Mercy, towards the merciful, and towards
    no others.
Wax with nothing more upon a warm coal
Will burn and blaze if they are both together,
And solace men who would see and who sit in darkness.
So the Father will forgive folk of a mild spirit
Who are rueful and repent and who make restitution,
And in as much as they may amend and remedy.   240
If those have insufficient assets who die in such a purpose,
Mercy will for their meekness make good the remainder.
As the wick and flame make a warm fire
For the mirth of men who are in murky houses,

So will Christ of his courtesy, if men cry him mercy,
Both forgive and forget and pray for us
To the Father of heaven to forgive us our sins.

"Strike fire at a flint four hundred winters,
Unless you have tow to take it, or tinder or brushwood,
All your long labour is lost wholly.   250
For no flame will make a fire where men fail to catch it.
Thus the Holy Ghost is God and grace without mercy
To all unkind Christians, as Christ himself witnesses:
Amen dico vobis, nescio vos, etc.

"Be unkind to your fellow Christians, and all that you can
     petition,
Deal in alms or do in penance day and night forever,—
Though you purchase all the pardons of Pompeluna and Italy,
And indulgences without number—be *ingratus* to your brother,
And the Holy Ghost may neither hear nor help you, be certain!
Unkindness so quenches him that he can shine no longer,
Nor burn nor blaze clear, from that blowing of unkindness.
Paul the Apostle proves whether I am lying: 262
Si linguis hominum loquar, etc.
Therefore beware, you wise men who have the world at plea-
     sure,
Who are rich and who have reason, rule well your spirits!
Be not unkind, I counsel you, to your fellow Christians.
For many of you rich men, by my soul I tell you,
Burn but never blaze, and are like blind beacons:
Non omnis qui dicit Domine! Domine! intrabit, etc.
Dives died and was damned for unkindness,   270
For he dealt no meat nor money to men who were needy.
I advise each rich man to have him in memory,
And to give his goods unto God, whom grace comes from.
He who is unkind to his servants may expect no better

Than to dwell where Dives is days without ending.
Unkindness is a contrary and quickly quenches
The grace of the Holy Ghost and God's own kindness.
Unkindness slays what kindness wins, as cursed robbers,
Unkind Christians, covetous and envious,
Murder a man for his money with mouth or cudgel.   280
The Holy Ghost has in keeping what the heartless ravish,
The life and the love which is the light of a man's body.
For every kind of good man may be compared in simile
To a torch or a taper to reverence the Trinity.
He who murders a good man, methinks, by my conscience,
Blows out the loveliest light to our Lord's honour.
Though in many more ways men offend the Holy Spirit,
The worst way that anyone may ever
Sin against the Holy Spirit is to assent to extinguish,
From coveting the good of nature, what Christ bought dearly.
How may he ask mercy, or how may mercy help him,   291
Who wilfully and wickedly withstands mercy?
Innocence is next to God, and day and night protesting:
'Vengeance! Vengeance! Never forgive him
Who slew us and shed our blood, and destroyed our nature.'
Vindica sanguinem justorum.
Very Charity cries, 'Vengeance, vengeance upon them!'
And since Holy Church and Charity urge it so strictly,
I hold that our Lord will never love those who lack Charity,
Nor have pity for any prayer or complaint that they may utter."

"I suppose that I have sinned so and should now perish,   301
And am sorry that I did so and sinned against Holy Spirit.
I confess and cry grace of God who made all things,
And ask his mercy mildly.—Might I not be saved?"
"Yes," said the Samaritan, "if you were also repentant,
So that righteousness through repentance might have ruth and
    mercy.

But it is seldom seen where there is sound witness
That any creature culpable before a king's justice
Is ransomed by his repentance where all reason damns him.
A party pursues him and the appeal is so urgent   310
That the king may grant no mercy till both men are accorded,
And each have equity, as Holywrit teaches:
Nunquam dimittitur peccatum, etc.
So it fares with the folk who are false in their lifetime,
Who live evilly and never slacken till life is over.
Then dread and despair drive grace from them,
And mercy may not fall upon their minds in dying.
Good hope, that should help them, is at the last despairing.
Not that God has no power or that he is not able
To amend all that is amiss, and that his mercy is not greater
Than all our wicked works, as Holywrit teaches: 321
Misericordia ejus super omnia opera ejus.
But some restitution is required before righteousness becomes
    merciful;
Sorrow is satisfaction for him who can pay nothing.

"There are three things that make man forcefully
To flee from his own house, as Holywrit shows us.
One is a wicked wife, who will not be chastened;
Her man flees from her from fear of her revilings.
If his house become uncovered and it rain on his pallet,
He seeks and seeks till he can sleep dry.   330
And when smoke and smother strike his eyesight,
It is worse than his wife or a wet blanket.
For smoke and smother smite his eyeballs
Till he is bleared and blind and hoarse and weeping,
And coughs and curses that Christ give them sorrow
Who should bring in better wood or blow it into burning!

'These three things that I tell you are interpreted as follows.

The wife is our wicked flesh that will not be chastened;
For nature cleaves to us continually and is contrary to the spirit.
When it falls it finds excuses that its frailty is inherent,   340
And for that is lightly forgiven and the evil forgotten,
Where man ask mercy and purpose amendment.
The rain that rains on restless evenings,
Is the sickness and the sorrow that we suffer often,
As Paul the Apostle preaches to the people:
Virtus infirmitate perficitur, etc.
But though men make great misery of their afflictions,
And are impatient in their pain, plain reason grants them
That they have cause for their contrariness because of sickness;
Our Lord forgives them lightly at their lives' ending;   350
He has mercy on these men impatient in suffering.
But the smoke and the smother that smite our eyeballs
Are covetousness and unkindness that quench God's mercy.
But unkindness is contrary to all common reason.
For no one is so sick or so sad or so far wretched
That he may not like and love and lend heartily
A good will and a good word and wish and pray
All manner of men mercy and forgiveness,
And love them as he loves himself and give his life amendment.
I may delay no longer," he said, and pricked his charger, 360
And went away like the wind; and with that I awoke.

IN WOOLLEN CLOTHES and wet-shod I
walked forth afterwards,
As a reckless wretch who reckons no suffering.
I went forth like a vagrant for all my lifetime,
Till I grew weary of this world and wished to sleep.
I was listless in Lent, and had a long slumber;
I swooned and slept heavily from the song *ramis palmarum;*
I dreamed Christ's passion and penance and of the people who
felt it,
How the children chanted *gloria laus* to Jesus,
And how old folk sang hosanna with the organ playing.
One similar to the Samaritan and sometimes to Piers the   10
Plowman
Came barefoot on an ass's back, bootless yet pricking.
He had no spurs nor spear, but was sprightly in bearing,
Like a squire speeding to the ceremony of knighthood
To get his gilt spurs and cut goloshes.
Then Faith cried from his window, "A, *fili David!*"
As an herald in arms when adventurers come to jousting.
Old Jews in Jerusalem joyously chorused:
Benedictus qui venit in nomine Domini.

Then I asked Faith aside what affair was stirring,
And who should joust in Jerusalem. "Jesus," he answered,   20
"And fetch from the fiend the fruit of Piers Plowman."
"Is Piers in this place?" I said; and his eyes pried through me:
"This gentle Jesus will joust in Piers' armour,
In his helm and harbergin, *humana natura;*
And Christ be so concealed, for *consummatus deus.*
This pricker is in the plate-armour of Piers the Plowman,
And no dart may daunt him, *in deitate patris.*"
"Who will joust with Jesus?" I said; "Jews or Scribes?"
"Nay," he said, "the foul Fiend, Falsehood and Death.
Death says that he shall daunt him and destroy forever   30

All that live or lie in land or water.
Life says that he lies and lays his life in wager
That for all death can do, within three days after
He shall fetch from the Fiend the fruit of Piers Plowman,
Bring it where he pleases, put Lucifer in bondage,
And beat and bring down bale and death forever!
O *mors, ero mors tua.*"
Then came Pilatus with many people, *sedens pro tribunali,*
To see what Death could dare, and decide the battle.
The Jews and the Justices were Jesus' enemies,   40
And their court cried aloud, "*Crucifige! Crucifige!*"
They put him in a pillory before Pilate and shouted:
"This Jesus has jested of our Jewish temple
That he will destroy it in one day and three days after
Build it again anew—here he stands who said it—
Yea build it great or greater and more glorious than ever,
As lofty and as large, as long and as spacious."
"*Crucifige!*" cried a corporal, "I count him a sorcerer."
"*Tolle! tolle!*" cried another, and took a keen thorn stem
And began to make a crown and a keen garland,   50
And crushed it on his head cruelly and cried mocking:
"*Ave Raby!*" cried that ribald and threw reeds at him.
They nailed him with three nails naked on the rood-tree;
They put their poison on a pole and raised it
And bad him drink his death drink, for his days were ended.
"If you are wise now, now help yourself!
If you are Christ the king's son, come down from the
     roodtree!
Then we shall believe that life loves you, and will not let you
     perish."
"*Consummatum est,*" cried Christ, and began swooning,
As piteous and as pale as a prisoner dying.   60
The Lord of Life and of Light then laid his eyes together.
Day withdrew in dread, and the sun darkened in heaven.

The wall quivered and clove, and the ground quaked beneath
   it.
At that din the dead came from deep burial,
And told why that tempest was so long time raging.
"There is a bitter battle," the dead body murmured,
"Life and Death are in this darkness and each despoils the
   other.
No one can well discover who will have the mastery
Till Sunday at sun-rise,"—and sank again to burial.
Some said that he was God's son who so marvellously   70
   perished.
Vere filius Dei erat iste.
And some said that he was a sorcerer; "and so let us discover
Whether he be dead or not dead before we take him down."

On that day two thieves suffered death also
Upon crosses beside Christ, by the common justice.
A sergeant strode forth and smote both their shin bones,
And afterwards broke the arms of each of these robbers.
But no brigand was so bold as to break God's body,
For he was a knight and a king's son, and it was granted by
   nature
That no hangman was so hardy as to lay hand upon him.   80
But with a keen grounded spear a knight came forward
Named Longeus, as his Legend tells, and who had long lost
   his eyesight.
He stood with Pilate and the people in a place of vantage.
For all his bitter vows they finally forced him
To take the spear in his hand and joust with Jesus.
None who waited on horse or foot were sufficiently hardy
To touch him or try him or take him from the rood-tree.
But this blind bachelor-at-arms pierced him through the
   heart.
The blood sprang down from the spear and unsealed his vision

K

Then he fell before him and cried for mercy.   90
"It was against my will to wound you so sorely."
He sighed and said: "I am sad and sorry
For the deed that I have done, and I deliver me to thy mercy!
Have ruth on me, righteous Lord!"—and he wept suddenly.

Then Faith defied those false traitors,
And called them caitiffs and accursed forever
For this foul villainy: "Vengeance on all of you!
To make the blind beat the bound was a boy's counsel!
Accursed caitiffs, common knighthood denies you
To defile a dead body in day or night time.   100
And yet the honour is his, although his hurts are bloody.
For the champion of your chivalry and the chief knight
     among you
Yields him loser in the lists and lies before Jesus.
When this darkness is ended his death will be answered
And you, lordlings, have lost, for Life shall have the victory!
And your franchise among the free has fallen into thralldom,
And you churls and your children shall never thrive after,
Nor have lordship in the land or land in tillage,
But all shall be barren and live by usury,
Which is the life that our Lord in all his laws holds cursed.   110
Now your good days are done, as Daniel prophesied
That when Christ came the crown of their kingdom should
     be broken.
Cum veniat sanctus sanctorum, cessabit unctio vestra."

For fear of this vision and of the false traitors
I drew away from that darkness to descendit ad inferna.
And there I saw surely, secundum scripturas,
A woman as I thought in the western region
Walking on her way with her eyes toward hell.
Mercy was that maiden, mild and comely,

Beautiful in bearing and benign in speech.   120
Her sister, as she seemed, came softly walking,
Afar from the east with her face westward,
A wondrous woman; her name was Truth;
The virtue that followed her made her fearless always.

When the two maidens met, Mercy and Truth,
Each asked the other of this great wonder,
Of the din and of the darkness and how the day was dawning,
And what a light and a gleam lay at hell's portal.
Truth said: "In faith, I am startled with these strange
   happenings;
And I am here to witness what this wonder betokens."   130
"Do not marvel," said Mercy, "for mirth is its meaning!
Mary, a maiden and a mother without knowledge
Of any carnal creature has conceived through the language
And grace of the Holy Ghost, and grown great for
   childbirth,
And thas brought her babe blamelessly to being.
And that my tale is true I take God to witness.
Since this babe was born there have passed thirty winters;
And he has died and suffered death to-day about mid-day.
And this is the cause of this eclipse which has closed the sun in
   heaven,
Meaning that men shall be removed from darkness,   140
While this light and this gleam blind Lucifer.
Patriarchs and prophets have preached often
How man shall save man through a maid's assistance.
That what was lost through a tree a tree shall recover,
And death deliver what death has vanquished."

"Your talk," said Truth, "is but a tale of Waltrot!
As for Adam and Eve, Abraham and all other
Patriarchs and prophets in pain and darkness,—

Never believe that yonder light can lift them higher,
Nor have them out of hell! Hold your tongue, Mercy!   150
You tell but a trifle! I, Truth, know certainly
That who is once in hell will never be rescued.
Job, the patriarch and prophet, reproves your evidence:
Quia in inferno nulla est redemptio."

With her mild mouth Mercy answered:
"Then through experience I hope," she said, "that these will
   be rescued.
Poison kills poison, as we approve it often.
For of all venoms the fiercest flows from the scorpion.
No balm may better the place that he pierces;
Yet dead and drawn toward it he destroys the poisoning   160
Of the first venom through the venom in his body.
So shall death destroy, I dare lay my life on it,
All that death first destroyed through the devil's tempting.
As guile beguiled man in the beginning,
So shall the beginning of grace make a good deception.
Ars ut artem falleret."

"Let us stay," said Truth, "for I see, or am mistaken,
Where out of the nip of the north not far from us
Righteousness comes running; let us rest meanwhile,
She will know more than we, for she is our elder."   170
"That is so," said Mercy, "and I see to the southward
Where Peace comes pleading, clothed in patience.
Love has sought her long; and I believe truly
That he has sent her some message of what this light betokens
That hovers here over hell. She will tell us."

When Peace, clad in Patience, approached nearer
Righteousness reverenced her for her rich clothing,
And prayed Peace to tell her to what place she was going

In her gay garments, and whom she would greet in them.
"My wish," she said, "is here to welcome spirits   180
Whom so many years I have not seen through hell's darkness.
Adam and Eve and others in hell with them,
Moses and many more, shall now have Mercy.
I shall dance at this, and do you sister!
For Jesus jousted well and joy is already dawning!
Ad vesperum demorabitur fletus, et ad matutinum laetitia.
Love, who is my lover, has sent letters to me
That Mercy, my sister, and I, are men's salvation,
And that God has forgiven and granted to both of us,
Both to me and to Mercy, to be man's surety for ever.   190
Look, here is the patent," said Peace, "*in pace in idipsum;*
And that this deed shall endure, *dormiam et requiescam.*"

"Do you rave?" said Righteousness, "or have you drunk
    deeply?
Do you believe that yonder light can unlock hell's portal
And save men's souls? Sister, never think it!
In the beginning God himself gave judgement;
Adam and Eve and all who followed them,
If they touched a tree and took the fruit and ate it,
Should die, die surely, and dwell in pain thereafter.
Afterwards Adam against his commandment   200
Fed upon that fruit and forsook, apparently,
The love of our Lord and his lore also,
And followed the Fiend's teaching and his mate's frailty
Against Reason: And I, Righteousness, record truly
That their pain shall be perpetual and no prayer help them.
Let them chew as they have chosen, and chide we not, sisters,
For the apple which they have eaten is hopeless sorrow."

"But I shall prove," said Peace, "that their pain may have an
    ending,

And that woe may be weal and all be well at that ending.
For if they had known no woe they could know no happiness,
For no one knows what weal is who has not woe also,   211
Nor what is hunger who has never felt famine.
If there were no night, no man, believe me,
Could tell you truly what day and light are.
No man of rank and riches, in rest and comfort,
Would know what woe is if there were no death in nature.
So God, the beginning of all, in his goodness and pleasure
Became man by a maid for man's salvation,
And suffered himself to be sold to see the sorrow of dying,
Which unknits all care and is the commencing of rest.   220
Till *modicum* meet us, I may well assure you,
No one, I hold, knows what enough is.

"Therefore God in his goodness granted Adam
To sit in solace and in sovereign pleasure;
And then he suffered him to sin and know sorrow feelingly.
To know what weal is he knew woe also.
Afterwards God himself adventured and took Adam's nature,
To suffer what he had suffered in three separate places.
He has been in heaven and in earth and now hell opens
That he may know what woe is who knows joy wholly.   230
So it shall fare with this folk; their folly and their offences
Shall open to them what health is and happiness without
      ending.
No one knows what war is where peace is always,
Nor what is indeed well till *wellaway* teach him."

Then there was one there with two wide eyeballs.
This *beau-père* was called Book, bold in speaking:
"By God's body," said this Book, "I will bear witness
That when this babe was born a star burned in heaven
According in one will all wise men living.

Such a babe was born in Bethlehem city   240
That man's soul shall be saved and his sin banished.
And all the elements," said the Book, "are his witnesses.
The heavens first witnessed that he was creator of all things;
For those who were in heaven took *stella comata*
And tended it as a torch to reverence his nativity.
That light followed the Lord into the lower earth.
The water witnessed that he was God, for he walked upon it.
Peter the Apostle perceived him coming
As he walked upon the water, and knew him well, and
     hailed him:
Jube me venire ad te super aquas.   250
Lo, the sun locked up his light within him
When he saw him suffer who made sun and ocean.
The earth felt heaviness that he should suffer
And quaked as a quick thing and crushed the stone.
Lo! hell might not hold out, but opened when God suffered
And let out the sons of Simon to see him on the rood-tree.
And now Lucifer shall believe, though he be loath to own it.
For Jesus as a Giant comes with an engine hither
To break and to beat down all powers against him,
And to have out of hell whomsoever he pleases.   260
I, Book, shall be burnt, but he shall rise living,
In all the might of a man, and be his mother's gladness,
And comfort all his kindred, and cleanse their sorrow.
All the joy of the Jews will be disjointed and shattered.—
Unless they reverence his resurrection and do the rood honour
And believe in a new law, they lose soul and body."

"Be silent a while," said Truth, "for I hear and see also
That a Spirit speaks to hell and bids unspar the portal.
Attolite portas," etc.
A loud voice from that light cried to Lucifer boldly: 270
"Princes of this place, unpin and unlock it!

For here cometh with his crown the king who is in glory."
Then Satan sighed and said among them:
"Such a light against our leave took Lazar from us.
We are encumbered with care; woe comes to all of us!
If this king come in mankind shall be delivered
And he shall lead them as he likes and lightly shall he bind
    me.
Patriarchs and prophets have prophesied often
That such a Lord and such a Light shall lead them into
    freedom.—

"Check him! chain the gate! fill each chink and cranny! 280
Let no light leap in at loop or chimney!
You, Astoreth, hasten and out with our servants,
Colting and all his kin, that our goods may be hidden!
Set the brimstone boiling; burn it and fling it
Hot upon the heads of all beneath the battlement!
Bring forth the winch-bows and the brazen cannon,
And shatter their shield-wall with shooting madly!
Go, Mahoun, to the catapult and cast out millstones,
Crooked iron and caltrops and encumber them with one
    another!—"

"Now listen," said Lucifer, "for the Lord is known to me,
Both this Lord and this Light; I have long known them. 291
No death nor devil's cunning can daunt him ever.
His way is where he will,—but 'ware danger!
If he reave me of my right, he robs me by violence.
For by right and by reason the wretches with us
Are mine, body and soul, both good and evil.
For he said it himself who is the sire of heaven,
That if Adam ate the apple all should perish,
And dwell with the devils; thus he threatened them.
He who is steadfast spoke this sentence.   300

And since I have seized them for seven hundred winters,
I believe that law will not allow him the least."

"That is so," said Satan, "but there is a sour question.
For you got them by guile and broke the garden fastness,
And in the semblance of a serpent spoke from the apple tree.
You egged Eve to eat the apple
And told her a tale with treachery and lying,
And so you had them out and hither at the ending.—
Goods are not well got where guile is the foundation."

"God will not be beguiled," said Gobelyn, "nor   310
   hoodwinked.
We have no true title, for treason damned them."

"I dread," said the devil, "lest Truth fetch them.
Thirty winters, I wot, he has gone preaching.
And when I saw that it was so, I slipt dream-wise
To warn Pilate's wife what man was Jesus.
The Jews hated him and would have had him to judgment,
And I would have lengthened his life, for I believed that if he
   perished
His soul would suffer no sin about it;
For his body above earth was busy always
In saving men from sin, if they themselves were willing.   320
And now I see where a soul comes hitherward sailing
With glory and with great light, and I know that it is God.
Let us flee," said the fiend, "fast and scatter.
For it were better not to be than to abide his presence.—
For your lies, Lucifer, we have lost our booty!
First we fell through you from high heaven;
For we believed your lies and all leapt forth with you.
Now for your last lie we have lost Adam
And all our lordship, I believe, on land and on water."

K*

Nunc princeps hujus mundi ejicietur foras. 330

Then the Light bad unlock, and Lucifer answered,
"Who art thou, Lord?" said Lucifer: "*Quis est iste?*"
"*Rex Gloriae,*" the Light responded,
"Lord of Might and of Main and all manner of Virtues:
   Dominus Virtutum.
Dukes of this dim place, quick, undo the portal,
That Christ may come in, the King's Son of heaven."

With that breath hell broke! All the bars of Belial,
For all their warriors and wardens, stood wide open.
Patriarchs and prophets, *populus in tenebris,*
Sang Saint John's song, *Ecce Agnus Dei.* 340
Lucifer might not look up, the light so blinded him,
And those whom our Lord loved he lifted into that glory.

Then he said to Satan: "Lo! my soul as restitution
For all sinful souls, to save such as are worthy!
They are mine and of me. I may claim them better.
Although Reason records rightly of me
That if they ate the apple all should perish,
I have not ordained them here in hell forever.
Thy deceit made the deed that they did so evilly.
Thou gottest them with guile against all justice, 350
For thou didst feed falsely those whom I loved.
Thou hast robbed my palace of Paradise in the person of
   an adder,
In likeness of a lizard with a lady's visage,
Against my liking and my leave. The Old Law teaches
That guilers should be beguiled, and in good reason:
Dentem pro dente et oculum pro oculo.
Ergo, soul shall quit soul and sin cancel sinning.
All that man has misdone I, man, shall rectify,

Member for member, by the Old Law of amendment,
Life for life; and by that Law I claim them,   360
Adam and all his issue to be at my will hereafter.
What death destroyed in them my death shall deliver,
And quicken and acquit what was extinguished in sinning.
Good faith asks grace for guile's destruction.
Believe not, Lucifer, that my Law is broken,
For by right and by reason I here ransom my liegemen.
Non veni solvere legem, sed adimplere.
Thou has pilfered my palace against all justice,
Falsely, like a felon. Good faith has taught me
To recover them by right, by ransom and by no other.   370
What guile got grace has conquered.
Thou, Lucifer, in the likeness of a loathsome adder
Gottest by guile those whom God loved.
I, like a living man, who am Lord of heaven,
Requite thy guile graciously: go, guile, against the guiler!
As Adam and all others have died by a fruit tree,
Adam and all others shall live again by the rood-tree.
Guile is beguiled and his guile is upon him.
Et cecidit in foveam quam fecit.
Now thy guile begins to go against thee,   380
And my grace to grow yet greater and wider.
Thy bliss shall be the bitterness which thou hast brewed for
          others.
Thou art doctor of death! Drink what thou madest!
For me who am Lord of Life, love is my potion,
And for that drink to-day I died on earth.
But I will drink of no wide dish, nor of deep learning,
But of the common cups of all Christian people.
Thy drink shall be death and deep hell the bowl.
I fought so that I thirst yet for man's deliverance.
But no drink may moisten me nor moderate my thirsting 390
Till the vintage fall in the vale of Jeosophat,

And I drink righteousness in ripeness, *resurrectio mortuorum*.
Then shall I come as a king, crowned with angels,
And have out of hell the hearts of all men.

"Fiends and fiendlings shall tremble before me,
And be at my bidding wheresoever I wish them.
But my nature shall move me to be merciful to man.
For we are brethren of one blood though not in baptism
    together.
But none who are my whole brethren in blood and baptism
Shall there be damned to death everlasting.   400
Tibi soli peccavi, etc.
It is not the usage on earth to hang a felon
Again if the hanging fail, although he be a traitor.
And if the king of that kingdom comes in season
Where that felon should suffer strangling or otherwise,
Law asks that he give him life if he look upon him.
I who am king of kings shall come in such a season
To give the doom of death and damnation to the wicked.
But if law will have me look on them, it lies in my favour
Whether they die or not die for their evil doing.   410
But if I have in any way bought off their bold offences
I may yet be merciful justly and all my words answered.
And since holywrit wills that I be avenged of all sinners,
Nullum malum impunitum, etc.
These shall be well washed of all their wickedness
In my prison, Purgatory, till *parce* is spoken,
And then my mercy will be showed to many of my brethren.
Blood may see blood both acold and famished,
But blood may not see blood bleed without pity.
Audivi arcana verba quae non licet homini loqui.   420
Then my right and my righteousness shall rule this dungeon
And mercy and mankind be before me in heaven.
I were an unkind king if my kindred were unaided,

And in such an hour when such help is needed.
Non intres in judicium cum servo tuo.
Thus lawfully," said our Lord, "I lead from hence
All those who loved me and believed in my coming.
And thy lies, Lucifer, by which thou didst lead the woman,
Thou shalt abide bitterly!"—Then he bound him in fetters
While Astoreth and all the others hid in corners.   430
They dared not look upon our Lord, the boldest among them
Let him lead forth whom he liked, and left him to his pleasure.

Many hundred angels harped and chanted:
Culpat caro, purgat caro, Regnat Deus Dei caro.
Then Peace played her pipe joyfully:
"*Clarior est solito post maxima nebula Phoebus,*
Post inimicitias clarior est et amor.
After sharp showers," said Peace, "the sun is brightest;
No weather is warmer than after a watery season;   439
No lovers are more loving nor are there lovelier friendships
Than after war and woe, when Love and Peace are masters.
Never was there war in this world nor wretchedness so bitter
That love, if he liked, might not bring it to laughing;
And Peace may put all perils at an end by patience."

"True," said Truth, "you tell us wisdom,
Let us embrace in this bond and both kiss joyfully."
"Let no people," said Peace, "perceive that we have quarrelled
Nothing is impossible with him who is Almighty."
"You say well," said Righteousness, and reverently kissed her,
She Peace, and Peace her, *per saecula saeculorum.*   450
Misericordia et veritas obviaverunt sibi, justitia et pax osculatae sunt.
Then Truth trumpeted the song, *Te Deum laudamus;*
And Love fluted in a loud note:
Ecce quam bonum et jocundum, etc.
These damsels danced till day was dawning,

And men rang to the resurrection; and right at that I wakened.
I called Kit my wife and Calote my daughter:
"Arise and reverence God's resurrection,
And creep to the cross kneeling, and kiss it for a jewel."
God's blessed body it bore to our salvation.   460
It has force to frighten the fiend always.
No grisly ghost may glide where it shadoweth.

PASSUS XIX

SO when I awoke I wrote my vision,
 And dressed myself decently and delayed no longer,
 But went to holy mass and to be houseled after.
 In the midst of the mass when men went to offering
I fell soon again to sleep, and suddenly was dreaming
That Piers the Plowman, painted bloodily,
Came in with a cross before the common people,
And like in all his limbs to our Lord Jesus.
Then I called Conscience to my counsel and asked him: 9
"Is this Jesus the jouster," I said, "whom the Jews crucified?
Or is this Piers the Plowman! Who painted him so crimson?"
Then Conscience cried kneeling. "This is Piers' ensign,
His colours and his coat armour, but he who comes so bloody
Is Christ with his cross, the conqueror of Christians."

"Why do you call him Christ," quoth I, "since Jews call him
    Jesus?
Patriarchs and prophets prophesied often
That all created kinds should come to kneel before him
As soon as men named the name of Jesu.
Ergo there is no name like the name of Jesus,
Nor none so needful to name in the night or day-time.   20
All dark devils are in dread to hear it,
And the sinful are solaced and saved by that title.
You call him Christ. What is the cause, tell me?
Is there more might in Christ; is it a more worthy title
Than Jesu or Jesus, that all our joy comes of?"

"Then consider," said Conscience, "if you can reason rightly,
How knight, king and conqueror may be one person.
To be called knight is noble, for men kneel to him;

To be called a king is nobler, for he can make knighthood.
But to be called conqueror comes of special favour,   30
Both of hardiness of heart and a high gentleness,
To make the free foul thralls if they violate his statutes,
And to make lords of lads in the lands that he conquers.
The Jews who were gentle held Jesu in dishonour,
Both his lore and his law, and are now low villains.
Though this world is wide not one is living
Out of toll or tribute, as tramps and scoundrels.
And those who become Christian because of baptism
Are franklins and freemen by the faith which they have taken,
And are gentlemen with Jesu, for Jesus had baptism   40
And was crowned king of Jews upon the cross at Calvary.
It becomes a king to keep his kingdom steadfast,
And a conqueror to conquer and to give laws and bounty.
And so did Jesus with the Jews; for he justified and taught
      them
The law of life that shall last forever.
He fended them from evils, fevers and fluxes,
And from fiends that were within them and false believing.
Then the Jews called Jesus a gentle prophet,
Also he was king of their kingdom and bore a crown of thorns.
He conquered upon the cross as a conqueror who is noble.   50
No death might destroy him or bring down his sovereignty,
But he arose and reigned and ravished hell.
Then he was called conqueror of quick and dead folk;
For he gave Adam and Eve and many others their deliverance,
Who had lain long years in Lucifer's bondage.
He gave places in Paradise at their departure from the living
With a liberal largess to all his loyal liegemen.
Well may he be called Christ, for conqueror is its meaning.
This has caused his coming with the cross of his passion.
He would advise us with it that whenever we are tempted 60
We may fight with it and defend us from falling into evil.

We see by his sorrow that whosoever loves joy
Must put himself to penance and to poverty of spirit,
And have much woe in this world and a will to suffer.

"But consider more of Christ and how he came by that title.
For to speak faithfully, his first name was Jesus.
When he was born in Bethlehem, as the Book tells us,
And came to mankind, kings and angels
Reverenced him right fairly with this world's riches.
Angels came out of heaven kneeling and singing: 70
Gloria in excelsis Deo, etc.
Kings came after, kneeled and offered
Much gold and myrrh and asked no mercy for it
Nor any goods nor gifts, but acknowledged him the sovereign
Of sand and sun and sea; and so departed
To their kingdoms and their kindred at the counsel of the
          angels.
There was that word fulfilled which you already mentioned:
Omnia coelestia, terrestria flectantur in hoc nomine Jesu.
All the angels of heaven kneeled at his nativity.
All the wisdom of the world was in those three sovereigns. 80
Reason and righteousness and ruth were their offerings.
This is why the wisest who were then living,
The masters and the lettered men, named them *Magi*.
The first offered reason figured by incense;
Then the second king gave a present
Of righteousness in red gold, which is reason's fellow.
Gold is likened to loyalty that lasts forever,
And reason to rich gold, to right and to truth.
Then came the third king kneeling to Jesus,
And presented him with pity, appearing as myrrh.   90
For myrrh means mercy and mild speaking.
These three goodly gifts were granted him together
Through the three kings who came and knelt to Jesu.

"But for all these precious presents our Lord Prince Jesus
Was neither king nor conqueror till he grew by nature
Into the manner of a man of much cunning.
It becomes a conqueror to command such cunning.
He must be wily and wise who would lead a people.
And so Jesus studied more slights than I can tell of.
Sometimes he suffered and sometimes he hid him;   100
Sometimes he fought fiercely and fled at others.
Now he would grant goods or give health with them,
Life and limb, as he liked and listed.
He commenced his course as a conqueror of peoples,
Until he had all for whom he bled piteously.

"At a feast of Jews Jesus in his boyhood
Turned water into wine, as Holywrit tells us,
And then God began graciously to Do Well.
Wine is likened to law and the life of holiness,
But then the law was lacking, for men loved not their enemies.
Christ counselled it, and commanded all men,   III
The learned and the unlearned, to give love for hatred.
So first at this feast, as I before mentioned,
In his grace and his goodness God began to Do Well.
Then he was named and nominated not holy Christ, but
        Jesu,
A keen and cunning youth, called *filius Mariae*.
This miracle was made before Mary his mother,
That she first and foremost should be firm in believing
That he was begotten by grace and by no created being.
He did this deed without wisdom and with one word only,
According to the kind that he came of, he commenced   121
        there to Do Well.

"When he had grown greater and gone from his Mother,
He made the lame leap and gave light to blind folk.

He fed with two fishes and with five wheat loaves
A famished folk of five thousand.
Thus he comforted those in care, and won a greater title,
And wherever he wandered he was called Do Bet.
He dealt the dumb speech and the deaf hearing,
And helped and healed all who asked his mercy.
Then he was called throughout the country by the common
    people,
For these deeds which he had done, *fili David Jesus.*   131
The deeds of David were the doughtiest in his lifetime,
And the maidens sang:
Saul interfecit mille, et David decem millia.
Therefore the country whence Jesus came called him *fili David,*
And named him from Nazareth. No man was so worthy
To be a kaiser or a king of the kingdom of Judaea,
Or a justice over the Jews as this Jesus whom they crucified.
Wherefore Caiaphas and other of the Jews were envious
And day and night devised to kill him.   140

"They killed him on a cross at Calvary on a Friday,
They buried his body and bad soldiers
To stand close and to keep it from comers in the night-time,
So that no friends might fetch him; for prophets told them
That his blessed body should rise from burial
And go into Galilee to gladden his Apostles
And Mary, his Mother; so men had judged of him.
The knights who lay near it knew secretly
That angels and archangels, ere the day had broken,
Came kneeling to the corpse and sang, *Christus resurgens.*   150
Very man before them he went forth arisen.
The Jews prayed all to hold their peace and begged the soldiers
To tell the commune that there came a company of his Apostles
And bewitched them waking, and took away the body.

"But Mary Magdalene met him by the highway
Going into Galilee, in godhead and manhood,
Alive and living; and she cried aloud
In each company where she came, *Christus resurgens.*
Then it was cried that Christ had recovered from his torment:
Sic oportet Christum pati et intrare, etc.   160
For what a woman says is not well considered.
Peter perceived this and persevered further,
And with James and John sought Jesus living.
Then Thaddeus and ten others, with Thomas of India,
Went with them also. And when all were together
In an inn at Jerusalem, and all the doorways fastened,
Christ came in, though all was closed and bolted,
And said to Peter and to the Apostles, *pax vobis.*
He took Thomas by the hand and taught him gently
To feel with his fingers where the flesh was broken.   170
Thomas touched it and his tongue was loosened:
'*Deus meus et dominus meus,*
Thou art my Lord, I believe, O God, Lord Jesus!
Thou didst die and suffer death and shalt judge us all,
And lo! now thou art living in life everlasting!'
Then Christ of his courtesy and his kindness answered:
'Thomas, because thou hast trusted and truly believest,
Mayest thou be blest now and be so always.
And blessed may all those be in body and in spirit
Who never shall see me with their sight as you do now,   180
And believe all this loyally; I love them and bless them.
Beati qui non viderunt, etc.'

"When this deed was done he taught Do Best,
And gave Piers power; and pardon was granted
To all manner of men, with his mercy and forgiveness.
He gave him might to assoil men from all manner of offences

Under covenant that they should come and acknowledge
    faithfully
The pardon of Piers Plowman, with its *redde quod debes*.
So Piers has power by the fulfilling of his pardon
To bind and to unbind both here and hereafter,   190
And to assoil men of all sins save one only.
Soon after he rose on high and went into heaven.
There is his home; and he will come finally
And reward him richly who *reddit quod debet*,
Who pays perfectly as plain truth bids him,
And he shall punish that person who pays badly,
And deal justice at Doomsday to both dead and living,—
The good go to godhead and to great joy,
And the wicked to dwell in woe without ending."

Thus spoke Conscience of Christ and of the cross beside him,
And counselled me to kneel to it; and then there   201
    came, as I imagined,
One *Spiritus Paraclitus* to Piers and to his followers;
In the likeness of lightning he alighted on all of them,
And made them masters of all men's language.
I wondered who he was, and whispered Conscience,
And was afraid of the light, for like fire burning
Spiritus Paraclitus overspread the people.

Quoth Conscience kneeling, "This is Christ's messenger
Who comes from the great God, and Grace is his title.
Now kneel," quoth Conscience, "and if you can, sing   210
And welcome him and worship him with, *Veni, Creator*
    Spiritus."
Then I sang that song and so did many hundred,
And "help us God of Grace," they cried with Conscience.
Then Grace began to go with Piers Plowman

And counselled him and Conscience to gather the commune;
"To-day I shall deal grace and divide it wisely
Among all kinds and conditions who can use five senses.
I give them treasure to live by till their lives' ending,
And weapons to fight with that shall never fail them.
For Antichrist and his army and all the world shall grieve you
And encumber you, Conscience, unless Christ is your helper.
Feigners and flatterers and false prophets   222
Shall come to be curators over kings and barons.
Pride shall be pope and prince of Holy Church,
And Covetousness and Unkindness be cardinals to lead it.
Therefore," said Grace, "before I go I shall give you a
    treasure
And weapons to fight with when Antichrist assails you."
Then he gave to each man grace to guide himself,
That neither pride nor idleness nor envy might encumber him.
Divisiones gratiarum sunt, etc.   230

To some he gave wisdom with words to show it,
And wit to win their livelihood as the world asks it,
As preachers and priests and prentices in law courts,
Who live here loyally by the labour of their pleading,
And by their wit to advise others, as grace will teach them.
To some he gave crafts and cunning eyesight,
And with selling and buying to bring in a living.
He gave lessons in labour, a loyal life and honest,
Some he taught tilling, ditching and thatching,
To win their livelihood with his lore and teaching,   240
Some to divine and to devise and to divide numbers,
Some to use a compass craftily or colours artfully,
Some to see and to say what shall happen,
Both weal and woe, and tell it beforehand,
As astronomers and astrologers and the wise philosophers,
And some to ride and to recover what is wrongfully taken,

And how to have it from them with their hands' ability,
And to fetch it from false men with a violent justice.
He gave some lessons to live in a longing to be hence,
With poverty and penance and prayers for all Christians. 250
He taught all to be loyal and each craft to love the other,
And forbad all boasting and debate among them.
Though some are higher," said Grace, "consider always
That though I have given him the fairest craft, I could have
    put him to the foulest.
Consider well," said Grace, "that grace comes of my favour,
Look that no man blame another, but love all as brothers.
And he who is most the master, be mildest in bearing,
And crown Conscience king, and make Craft your steward,
And let Craft's counsel clothe and feed you.
For I make Piers the Plowman my proctor and steward, 260
And my registrar to receive, *redde quod debes*.
Piers shall be my purveyor and my plowman among you,
And he shall till Truth with a team that I shall give him."

Grace gave Piers a team of four great oxen,
The first was Luke, a large beast and a low-hearted;
And Mark and Matthew, each mighty creatures;
And joined with them John, the gentlest and fairest,
The prize neat of Piers' plow, passing all others.

And Grace gave Piers of his goodness four horses.
All that the oxen eared they harrowed after.   270
One was Augustine and Ambrose another,
Gregory, the great clerk, and the good Jerome.
These four to teach the faith followed Piers' oxen,
And harrowed handily all Holy Scripture
With two harrows that they had, an old and a new.
Id est, vetus testamentum et novum.

For Grace gave him the cardinal virtues
To sow into men's souls, and spoke of them briefly.
Spiritus Prudentiae was the first seed among them.
Whoever ate of that would imagine truly,   280
Before he turned to a task, what his toil would come to.
He lessoned men to buy a ladle with a long handle,
If they would keel the crock and keep the fat from spilling.

The second seed was *Spiritus Temperantiae*.
He who ate of that seed had such a nature
That no meat nor immoderate drinking should make him a
    boaster,
Nor any scold or scorner shake his judgment.
No winning nor wealth in worldly riches
Should move wasted words or idle speaking.
No quaint clothing should come upon his shoulders,   290
Nor any meat to his mouth that Master John had seasoned.

The third seed that Piers sowed was *Spiritus Fortitudinis*.
He who ate of that seed was hardy always
To suffer all that God sent in sickness or affliction.
No lie nor any liar nor any loss of worldly riches
Could make him mourn; for he was minded bravely,
And boldly abode the blows of fortune.
He made all things play through patience, *et parce mihi domine*,
And covered him under the counsel of wise Cato's proverb:
Esto forti animo, cum sis damnatus inique.   300

The fourth seed that Piers sowed was *Spiritus Justitiae*.
He who ate of that seed should be always honest
With God, and never confused, unless guile deceive him.
For guile goes privily, so that good faith is often
Unseen and unserved by *Spiritus Justitiae.*
Spiritus Justitiae does not spare to punish

Those who are guilty and to correct boldly
The king himself if he come into guilt or trespass.
He accounts nothing of a king's wrath; and when he comes to
    the court room
He judges justly; Justice never trembles   310
At a duke or at death; he dickers with no statute
For a present or a prayer or any prince's letters.
He deals equity to all according to his ability.

Piers sowed these four seeds and so harrowed them
With the Old Law and the New Law that love might
    flourish
Among the four virtues and the vices be uprooted.
It is common in all countries that cammocks and thistles
Kill the fruit in the field, if they grow together.
And so do vices kill virtues. "Therefore," said Piers Plowman,
"Harrow all who have the wit to be aided by these doctors,
And who will care for cardinal virtues according   321
    to their teaching."

"Before your grain," said Grace, "begin to ripen
Build a barn, Piers, where you may bring your harvest."
"By God, Grace!" said Piers, "you must give me timber
And ordain that house before you have gone hence."
Grace gave him the cross with the crown of sorrow,
Which Christ donned upon Calvary for mankind's salvation,
With his baptism and the blood that he bled on the rood-tree
He made a mortar and named it Mercy.
With this Grace began to make a good foundation,   330
And wattled it and walled it with his pains and passion.
With all Holywrit he made a roof afterwards,
And called that house Unity, or Holy Church in English.
When this deed was done Grace devised further
A cart called Christendom to carry Piers' sheaves.

He gave good horses for his cart, Contrition and Confession.
He made Priesthood hayward, while he himself went walking
Through the wide world with Piers to till Truth.

Now Piers has gone to plow and Pride has seen him
And gathered a great host to grieve the fellowship   340
Of Conscience and all Christians and the Cardinal Virtues,
To blow them down and break them and bite the roots
    asunder.
He has ordered out Arrogance, the army's marshal,
And his spy, Spill-Love, and one Speak-Evil-Secretly.
These two came to Conscience and to Christian people
And told them tidings that they should take by violence
The seed corn that Piers had sown, the cardinal virtues.
"Piers' barn shall be broken and all who be in Unity
Shall come out, and Conscience and his coupled horses,
Confession and Contrition, and his cart, Believing,   350
Shall be coloured so curiously and so covered under sophistry
That Conscience himself cannot know by Contrition
Or Confession who is Christian or who heathen.
No man among the merchants, with whom money is labour,
Will know whether he wins rightly or with wrong or usury.
With such colours and contrivances I, Pride, come to battle,
With the lord who lives after the lust of the body,
To waste in wealth and wicked living
All the world in a little while through our wit," Pride boasted.

Then Conscience addressed all Christians: "My   360
    counsel is presently
To hasten into Unity and hold us within it,
And pray that there be peace in the barn of Piers Plowman
For I know well enough that we have not strength sufficient
To go against Pride unless Grace is with us."
Then came Natural Knowledge at need of Conscience

And cried and commanded all Christian people
To dig a ditch deep about Unity,
Where Holy Church stood in Unity like the pile of a fortress.
At this Conscience gave orders that all Christians should
   labour
And make a wide moat that might well strengthen   370
And uphold Holy Church and all those who kept it.
Then all kinds of Christians save common women
Repented and revoked sin, save those only.
But false men and flatterers, thieves and usurers,
Liars and inquest-mongers forsworn continually,
Wilfully and wickedly, held with Falsehood,
And were forsworn for silver as they knew surely.
There was no Christian creature with common
   understanding,
Save these shrews of whom I have spoken already,
Who did not in some way help to hold holiness;   380
Some by bead-bidding and some by pilgrimage,
Others through privy penance and pence dealing.
Then water welled forth for wicked living,
Yearning out eagerly from the eyes of many.
The purification of the people and a pure clergy
Made holiness the unity of Holy Church.
"I care not," said Conscience, "if Pride come against us,
The Lord of Lust shall be the loser all this Lent, I wager.—
Come," said Conscience, "come dine, all Christians
Who have laboured loyally all this Lenten season.   390
Here is the blessed bread where Christ's body is figured.
By God's word Grace gave Piers the power
And the might to make it and men to eat it,
As help for their health once monthly,
Or as often as they have need, if they have paid truly
According to the pardon of Piers Plowman, *redde quod debes.*"

"How," cried the Commune, "you counsel us to offer
All that we owe to any before we go to housel?"
"It is both my counsel," said Conscience, "and the Cardinal
    Virtues'
That each man forgive the other in accordance with *pater noster*:
Et dimitte nobis debita nostra, etc.   401
And such shall be assoiled and so houseled."

"Yea, baw!" cried a brewer, "I will not be reasoned!
By Jesu! for all your jangling with *Spiritus Justitiae*,
Nor hear Conscience, by Christ, while I can sell safely
The dregs and the draff and draw at one spigot
Thick ale and thin ale, for that is my notion,—
And no more hoeing after holiness! Hold your tongue,
    Conscience!—
Your *Spiritus Justitiae* is all nonsense."

"Caitiff," cried Conscience, "cursed wretch!   410
You are unblessed, brewer, but if God help you.
Unless you live by the law of *Spiritus Justitiae*,
The chief seed that Piers sowed, you shall be saved never.
Unless Conscience and Cardinal Virtues feed the common
    people
Believe me well, they are lost, life and spirit."

"Then many a man is lost," cried an unlearned vicar.
"I am a curator of Holy Church, but I have encountered no
    man
In all this country who can tell me of the cardinal virtues,
Or who accounted Conscience at a cock's feather.
I can tell you of no cardinals unless they have come   420
    from his holiness.
And we clerks when they come must give them money

For their furs and feed their horses and their followers who
　　rob us.
The Commune *clamat cotidie*, each man to his neighbour,
'The country is the more cursed when cardinals come in it,
And where they lie the longest lechery is greatest.'
Therefore," said this vicar, "by very God, I wish
That no cardinals ever come among the common people,
But let them hold themselves in their holiness and in their home
　　contented,
At Avignon, with Jewish usurers, *cum sancto sanctus eris, etc.*
Or in Rome, as their rule bids them, and have the relics in　430
　　keeping.
And would that you, Conscience, were in the court of the king
　　always,
That Grace, whom you commend so, were the guide of all
　　clergy,
And that Piers with his plows, the newer and the older,
Were emperor of all the world, and all men Christian!
He is but a poor pope who should be the peoples' helper
And who sends men to slay the souls that they should rescue.
But well be it with Piers the Plowman who pursues his duty!
Qui pluit super justos et injustos equally,
Sends forth the sun to shine on the villein's tillage
As brightly as on the best man's and on the best woman's.　440
So Piers the Plowman is at pains to harrow
As well for a waster and for wenches in the brothels
As for himself and his servants, though he is served sooner.
He toils and tills for a traitor as earnestly
As for an honest husbandman, and at all times equally.
May he be worshipped who wrought all, both the good and
　　the wicked,
And suffers the sinful till the season of their repentance!
God amend the pope, who pillages Holy Church,

Who claims that before the king he is the keeper of Christians,
Who accounts it nothing that Christians are killed and beaten,
Who leads the people to battle and spills the blood of Christians,
Against the Old Law and the New Law, as Luke witnesses:
Non occides, mihi vindictam, etc.
Surely it seems that if he himself has his wishes
He recks nothing of the right nor of the rest of the people.
But may Christ in his kindness save the cardinals and prelates
And turn their wit unto wisdom and to welfare of the spirit!
For the Commune," said this curate, "accounts but little
The counsel of Conscience or of the Cardinal Virtues
Unless their sight shows them something profitable.   460
They give not a copper for guile and lying,
For *Spiritus Prudentiae* is guile among the people,
And all the fair virtues become vices in their practice.
Each man has sleights and subtleties to hide his own sin from
    him,
And considers this cunning and clean living."

There was a lord there who laughed and "By this light!" he
    shouted,
"I hold it in right and reason that my reeve should get me
All that my auditor and my other stewards
Give in their accounts and in my clerks' writings.
With *Spiritus Intellectus* they seek the reeve rolls,   470
And with *Spiritus Fortitudinis* I shall fetch it from them."

Then there came a king who took his crown to witness:
"I have the kingly crowning to be the Commune's ruler,
And to keep Holy Church and Clergy from peril.
If I lack enough to live on the law will have me take it
Where I may have it most handily, for I am the head of law.
But since I am the head of all I am also your safeguard,

The chief help of Holy Church and chieftain of the
    Commune.
What I take from you two I take at the teaching
Of *Spiritus Justitiae;* for I judge you severally.   480
So I may boldly be houseled, for I borrow of no man,
And claim from my Commune but what my condition
    warrants."

"On condition," said Conscience, "that you guard faithfu lly
And rule your realm in reason and in truth,
You may take within reason, as the law warrants;
Omnia tua sunt ad defendendum, sed non ad depraedandum."

The vicar said farewell, for he had far to go homeward;
And with that I awoke and wrote my vision.

S I went by the way when I was thus awakened
I walked with a sad heart and a heavy spirit;
I knew not where nor what to eat for dinner.
It was near the high noon when Need came
   toward me.
He greeted me gruffly and called me impostor.
"Could you not excuse yourself as did the king and the others
That you took for your livelihood your clothes and nourishment,
At the teaching and the token of *Spiritus Temperantiae,*
And took no more than Need taught you,
And that Need knows no law and never falls in debt?   10
He takes three things for his life's safety;
Namely, meat, when men refuse him and he has no money to
   buy it,
And nobody to be surety and can pawn nothing.
He gets food in such a case and catches it by ruses—
Surely he does not sin who so wins his nourishment.
And though he comes thus by some cloth and can no better
   pay for it,
Need conceives it quickly and gives him surety.
Lo! if he longs to drink, it is the law of nature
That he drink at every ditch before he die thirsting.
So Need in our necessity may number us in his service,   20
Without counsel of Conscience or the Cardinal Virtues,
And for as long as we shall pursue *Spiritus Temperantiae.*
For by far the first virtue is *Spiritus Temperantiae,*
Before *Spiritus Fortitudinis* or *Spiritus Justitiae.*
For *Spiritus Fortitudinis* fails often.
Many times he does more than measure warrants.
Sometimes he beats men too bitterly and sometimes too little,
And corrects men more grievously than good faith would
   have him.
Spiritus Justitiae judges willy-nilly

After the king's council and Commons' pleasure.   30
And *Spiritus Prudentiae* is proved erring often
In what he holds will happen, if he were not so clever.
It is no wisdom to win nor to imagine wisely.
Homo proponit et Deus disponit and governs all virtues.
But Need is next him, for his nature is humble,
And as low as a lamb from lacking necessity.
Wise men forsook welfare for they would also be needy
And wandered in the wilderness and would not be wealthy.
God left his great joy and his glory in heaven
And came into mankind and took need upon him.   40
So needy was he, the Book says in sundry places,
That he said himself in sorrow on the rood-tree:
'Both the fox and the fowl flee to their coverts
And the finned fishes fleet to rest,
While I must needs remain where Need has taken me,
And suffer much sorrow that shall turn to joy.'
Therefore be not abashed to beg and to be needy,
Since he who wrought all the world was willingly needy,
And none was ever so needy, nor died in such poverty."

When Need had spoken to me so wisely I sunk to slumber,   50
And met with a marvellous dream; that in a man's likeness
Antichrist came against all the crop of Truth,
Dashed it to earth, and turned the roots upward.
Falsehood sprang and spread and sped men's wishes.
In each country where he came he cut Truth down,
And made guile grow where good had fallen.
Friars followed that Fiend, for he gave them clothing.
The religious reverenced him and rang for him in their belfries.
All the convent came forth to welcome that tyrant
With all their followers as well—except the fools only.   60
These fools were liefer far to perish
Than to live longer since loyalty was so injured.

L

The false Fiend Antichrist took all folk into his kingdom.
They cursed the counsel, whether from clergy or unlearned,
Of all mild men and holy who held misfortune lightly,
Who defied all falsehood and all folk who used it.
They cursed any king who accused them of treachery.

Antichrist soon had hundreds at his banner,
And Pride bore it boldly before him,
With the lord who lived after the liking of the body. 70
They came against Conscience, the keeper and warden
Over the Christian commune and the cardinal virtues.
"I counsel," said Conscience then, "that you fools come
   with me
Into the Unity of Holy Church and hold yourselves within it.
Let us cry to Nature that he come to defend us,
Fools, from this Fiend's arm, for the love of Piers Plowman.
And let us cry to all the commune that they come into unity
And abide there and do battle against Belial's children."

Then Nature heard Conscience, and, coming from the planets,
Sent forth his foragers, fevers and fluxes, 80
Coughs and cardiacles, cramps and toothaches,
Rheums and Saint Radigunds and raging itches,
Boils and botches and burning agues.
Frenzies and foul evils, the foragers of Nature,
Had pricked and priedupon the polls of the people,
So that a legion lost their lives shortly.
Then there was "Alas and help! here comes Nature,
With dreadful death to undo us all!"
The lord who lived in liking loudly shouted
After Comfort, his comrade, to come and bear his banner. 90
"Alarm! Alarm!" cried that lord, "each look out for himself!"
Before a minstrel had piped these men had encountered,
And before an herald of arms had named the champions.

Age the hoar rode in the vanguard
And bore the banner before Death; by right he claimed it.
Cruelly came Nature with many keen weapons,
With pokes and pestilences from which the people perished.
His cramps and corruptions killed many.
Death came driving after and dashed to powder
Kings and knights, kaisers and pontiffs,   100
Laity and learned; he let none withstand him
Whom he hit evenly; they never stirred after!
Many a lovely lady whom knights loved dearly
Sorrowed and swooned as Death struck her.

Then Conscience kindly and courteously sought Nature
To cease this strife and to see if the people
Would leave their privy pride and be better Christians.
So Nature ceased and sought amendment.
Then Fortune began to flatter the few remaining.
He promised long life and sent Lechery thither.   110
Among all manner of men, wedded and unwedded,
And gathered a great host to go against Conscience.
This Lechery laid on with laughing gestures
And with privy speech and painted language,
And armed himself in idleness and in high bearing.
He bore a bow in his hand with many bloody arrows,
That were feathered with fair promises and many a false
    seeming.
His soft stories incensed often
Both Conscience and his company, who were the Church's
    teachers.

Then Covetousness came and contrived craftily   120
How he might overcome Conscience and the cardinal virtues.
He armed himself in avarice. He was an hungry huntsman.
His weapons were wiles in winning and hiding.

His leering and lying misled the people.
He sent Simony to assail Conscience,
Who preached before the people; they made him prelate
     among them
To hold them with Antichrist and have revenues in keeping.
To the king's counsel he came as a baron
And kneeled to Conscience in court before all men.
He caused Good Faith to flee and Falsehood to linger,   130
And bore down boldly with many a bright noble
Much of the wit and wisdom in Westminster palace.
He jogged towards a justice and jousted in his ear
And overturned truth with 'take⁄this⁄in⁄recompense.'
He hastened after to the hall of the arches.
He turned civil law to simony and so bribed the officials.
For a mantle of minever he made honest marriage
Dissolve before death, and divorced many.

"Alas," said Conscience, and cried: "Would Christ of his
     goodness
That Covetousness were a Christian, he is so keen a fighter,
So brave to suffer while his bags are with him!"   141

Then Life laughed aloud and let his clothes dangle.
He armed himself in haste with words of ribaldry,
He judged holiness a jest and generosity a waster,
Looked on Loyalty as a churl and on Liar as a freeman,
And accounted Conscience and Good Counsel folly.
So Life rallied at a little fortune,
Pricked forth with Pride, and prized no virtue,
Nor cared that Nature cuts down and comes finally
To kill all earthly creatures save Conscience only.   150
Life leapt aside and caught a lady for his mistress,
"Health and I," he said, "and haughtiness of heart
Shall deliver you from all dread of death and infirmity.

You shall hold sin a straw and sorrow in forgetfulness."
This living pleased Life and his lady, Fortune,
And they begat in their glory a gad-about finally,
One who has wrought much woe; Sloth was his name.
He grew with wondrous eagerness and was soon at manhood,
And was wedded to one Despair, a wench of the brothels.
Her sire was a sizar who never swore truly,   160
One Tom-Two-Tongue, taken at each inquest.
Sloth was wary of war and wielded a stone sling
That cast dread and despair a dozen miles about him.
Then Conscience took care, and called Age to him,
And bad him prepare for the fight and fright Despair from
    them.

Age had good hope, and hastily shrived himself,
Drove off Despair and dared Life in battle.
Life fled for fear and sought physic to help him,
He besought him for succour and got salves and syrups.
He gave physicians the gold that gladdened their spirits,   170
And they gave him against Age a glass helmet.
Life believed that Leachcraft would lead Age captive,
And drive away Death with drugs and powders.

Age adventured against Life and at last so battered
A physician in a furred hood that he fell in a palsy,
And that Doctor died three days after.
"Now I see," said Life, "that surgery is no physic,
And may not help a mite to remove Age from me."
Yet he hoped for good health and held his heart merry,
And rode thus to a revel with riches and merriment,   180
The Company of Comfort, men have called it sometimes.—

But Age was soon after me, and walked on my brain pan.
He made me bald before and bare on the crowning.

He walked so heavily on my head that it will be seen forever.
"Sir-ill-mannered Age," I said, "woe be with you!
How long has your way been upon the heads of the people?
If you had acted courteously you would have asked permission."
"Yes, dear sluggard!" he said and struck me harder.
He hit me under the ear so that I am hard of hearing.
He buffeted me about the mouth and beat out my teeth.   190
He gyved me in gouts; I could not walk freely.
And this woe that I was in moved my wife also.
She wished heartily that I were already in heaven.
The limb that she loved was no longer able.
Age and she had enfeebled it together.

As I sat in this sorrow I saw Nature passing
And Death drawing near; dread seized me.
I cried Nature of his courtesy to give my care an ending.
"Lo, Age the hoar has beset me sorely!
Avenge me, if it be your will; for I would go hence."   200
"If you will be avenged walk into Unity
And hold yourself there always till I send for you.
And look that you get in some craft before you come thence."
"Counsel me, Nature," quoth I, "what craft is best to study."
"Learn to love," said Nature, "and leave all others."
"How shall I come by goods to clothe and feed me?"
"If you love loyally," he said, "you will lack never
For meat or worldly wearing while life is with you."
Then at counsel of Conscience I commenced to travel
Through Contrition and Confession, till I came to Unity.
There Conscience was constable to save Christian livers.   211
They were sadly besieged by seven great giants,
Who held hard with Antichrist against Conscience.

Sloth assaulted it with his sling and made a sorry passage;
A thousand proud priests passed in with him,

With cut suits and piked shoes and soldiers' daggers;
All came against Conscience; Covetousness led them.
"By Mary," cried a cursed priest from the coast of Ireland,
"I count no more of Conscience if I catch the silver
Than I do when I drink a draught of good ale."   220
So said sixty others from the same country.
They shot at him and shot again a sheaf-full of curses,
Broad hooked arrows, God's wounds and nails,
And almost had Unity and Holiness at mercy.

Conscience cried, "Help, clergy, or else I perish,
Through imperfect priests and prelates of Holy Church."
Friars heard him cry and came to his assistance,
But were unskilled in their craft and Conscience forsook them.
Then Need came nearer and told Conscience
That those came from Covetousness and to have cures   230
    in the parish.
"Perhaps since they are poor and patrimony fails them
They will flatter and be officious to folk who are wealthy.
Since they have given themselves to cold and to common
    poverty,
Let them chew as they have chosen, and charge them with no
    duties.
Those are looser in lying who have livelihood by almsdeed
Than those who labour for a livelihood and lend it to beggars.
Since friars have forsaken the felicity of mortals
Let them be as beggars, or live by angels' feeding."
But when Conscience heard that counsel he began laughing
And comforted friars kindly and called them hither.   240
He said: "Sirs, assuredly, you are all welcome
To Unity and to Holy Church. But one thing I pray you.
Hold yourselves in Unity and have no envy
Against learned or unlearned, but live by your statutes.
I shall be your bail that you shall have bread and clothing

And all other necessaries; nothing shall fail you
If you will leave logic and learn loving.
For love were friar Dominic and friar Francis holy.
For love they left their lordships in land and college.
If you covet any cure Nature can teach you   250
That God made measure in all modes of creation.
He set in all things a sure and certain number,
And named them by their names and numbered the stars:
Qui numerat multitudinem stellarum, et omnibus eis, etc.
Kings and knights who guard and shelter
Have officers under them, and each of them a quota.
Their wages in war are written in numbers.
Others have no wages, though they work truly.
All others in the war are held robbers
Who pillage and pick armour, and in all places are cursed.
Monks and masters and all men of religion   261
By their order and their rule have a stated number.
The law of learned and unlearned equally
Is a fixed number for a fixed order; but friars are the exception!
Therefore," quoth Conscience, "common sense shows me
It is not good to give you wages; you grow out of number.
Heaven has an even number and hell is without number.
I wish heartily that you were all in the register
And numbered by the notary, none more nor missing."

Envy heard this and had the friars to schooling,   270
To learn logic and law and contemplation also,
To preach from Plato and to prove by Seneca
That all things under heaven ought to be in common.

Yet he lies, as I believe, who gives the laity such doctrine.
For God made man a law, and Moses taught it:
Non concupisces rem proximi tui.
This is ill observed in English parishes.

Parish priests and parsons are for the peoples' shriving,
And are named curators to know and to heal
All people in their parishes, to put penance upon them   280
And to shame them in their shrift; but now shame has
     forced them
To flee to the friars, as false men to Westminster.
These borrow and bear it thither, and then bid their creditors
Fervently for forgiveness, or for longer mercy.
But while they are in Westminster it is wasted already.
They make themselves merry with the money of others.
So it fares with many folk who go to friars' shriving,
As sizars and executors who will give these friars
A pittance to pray for them; and make themselves merry
With the residue and the remainder for which others   290
     have laboured,
And so leave the dead in debt till the Day of Judgement.

On this account Envy hated Conscience.
He sent friars to philosophy and founded their colleges,
While Covetousness and unkindness went against Conscience.
Conscience held himself in Unity and in Holy Church,
And made Peace porter to pin the gateways
Against all tale-tellers and tattlers in Idleness.
Hypocrisy and he gave hard battle,
And wicked wounds to many wise teachers   299
Who accorded with Conscience and the Cardinal Virtues.
Conscience called a Doctor well acquainted with shriving.
"Go, salve the sick whom sin has wounded."
Shrift took sharp salve and made men do penance
For many misdeeds that they had there committed,
And saw that Piers was paid, *redde quod debes*.

Some disliked this leachcraft and sent letters broadcast
To find a surgeon in the city who had softer plasters.
    L*

Sir Love-to-Live-in-Lechery lay there groaning,
Afraid to die famished from fasting on Friday.
"There is a surgeon in this city who is soft in handling,   310
And knows far more physic and fairer plasters;
One, friar Flattery, is physician and surgeon."
Contrition said to Conscience, "Let him come to Unity,
For here is many a man hurt by Hypocrisy."
"We have no need," said Conscience, "and I know no better
    doctors
Than parson or parish priest, penitencer or bishop,
Except Piers the Plowman, who has power above all men,
And may give indulgences, unless debt forbid them.—
Yet I will suffer it," said Conscience, "inasmuch as you
    desire it.
Fetch the friar Flatterer, and let him physic your wounded."

The friar heard of it and hastened eagerly   321
To a lord for a letter and his leave for absolution.
Then like a curator, with his case of letters,
He came boldly before the bishop, and his brief with him,
To hear confession in all cou ntries where he came in his travels.
He came where Conscience was and knocked at the portal.
Peace unpinned it, for he was porter to Unity,
And asked in haste what he was seeking.
"In faith," said the friar, "your profit and your welfare.
I would consult Contrition. Therefore I come to your city."
"He is sick," said Peace, "as are many others.   331
Hypocrisy has hurt them and they will hardly recover."
"I am a surgeon," he said, "and make salves also.
Conscience is my good friend, and can tell my ability."
"I pray you," said Peace, "before you pass further,
What are you called ? I pray you, do not hide your name."
"Certainly," said this fellow, "Sir *Penetrans-Domos*."

"Then go your way," quoth Peace," by God, for all your
 physic,
Unless you can work in some craft you shall not go further!
I knew one once, not eight winters before you,   340
Came with such a cope into the court where I was living,
And was leach to my lord and to my lady also.
And at last this limitour, when my lord was absent,
So salved our women tha t some were with children."—
But Courtesy counselled Peace to give him free entrance:
"Let in the friar and his fellow, and give them fair welcome.
He may see and hear and so it may happen
That Life through his lore will leave Covetousness
And dread Death, and withdraw from Pride,
And accord with Conscience, and each kiss the other." 350

Thus through this pleading they entered the city
And came to Conscience and greeted him kindly.
"You are welcome," said Conscience, "And can you heal
 our patients?
Here is Contrition," said Conscience, "my cousin, wounded;
Comfort him," said Conscience, "and care for his bruises.
The plasters and the powders of the parson bite sorely.
He lets them lie overlong, and is loath to change them.
From Lent to Lent he lets his plasters bite him."
"That is overlong," said this limitour, "I believe I shall
 amend it."—
Then he groped about Contrition and gave him a plaster 360
Of "a privy payment, and I shall pray for you,
For all that you are holden for all my lifetime,
And make you my lady in mass and in matins,
And like a friar of our fraternity for a little silver."
So he crept and gathered and glossed over his shriving,
Till Contrition had forgotten his crying and weeping,

And waking for his wickedness, as he was wont formerly.
For this comfortable confessor he left contrition wholly,
Which is the sovereign salve for all our sins.

Sloth saw it and so did Pride.   370
They came with a keen will to grieve Conscience.
Conscience cried again and bad Clergy help him,
And called on Contrition to keep the portal.
"He lies dreaming," said Peace, "and so do many others.
The friar with his physic holds this folk enchanted,
And plasters them so easily that they dread no sinning."
"By Christ," said Conscience, "I will become a pilgrim
And walk as wide as all the world endures
To seek Piers the Plowman; by him shall Pride perish.
He shall find friars a maintenance who flatter as beggars 380
Grieving me, Conscience;—grant Nature to avenge me
And send good hap and good health till I have Piers the
   Plowman."—
So he cried for grace, till I began to waken.

EXPLICIT PIERS PLOWMAN

The following notes have no more ambitious aim than to explain allusions that may puzzle the modern reader, and aid him in grasping Langland's allegorical and literary conventions and in holding the thread of the argument firmly in hand.

Page 3, l. 1. IN A SUMMER SEASON. The entire dream setting of the poem is a mediaeval convention. The "I" may be a fictitious character. His dream is not necessarily of himself.

Page 3 l. 13. I LOOKED UP AT THE EAST. The East and the Sun are biblical symbols of God.

Page 3, l. 17. A FAIRFIELD FULL OF FOLK: the world, which lies midway between heaven and hell.

Page 4, l. 44. ROBERT'S CHILDREN: a common expression of reproach, the allusion now being lost.

Page 4, l. 54. WENT TO WALSINGHAM: the site of a celebrated shrine of the Blessed Virgin.

Page 4, l. 61. THEY COVETED THEIR COPES: they sought the clothes and accompanying dignity of the religious orders.

Page 6, l. 104. THESE ARE CALLED CARDINAL: the four active or moral virtues, prudence, temperance, justice, and fortitude.

Page 6, l. 114. COMMON WIT: the natural intelligence unenlightened by revelation.

Page 6, l. 123. THEN A FOOL CAME FORTH: the dreamer himself. In the ensuing allegory the angel counsels moderation on the part of the crown; the "glutton of language" would welcome more stringent measures by the crown; while all the Commons in any case agree to loyalty.

Page 7. l. 146. A RABBLE OF RATS. This fable refers to events following the Good Parliament (1376). The king, Edward III, is the cat. The rats are certain nobles, desiring to depose the king (to "bell the cat"), but lacking the power and courage to put their plan into effect. The poet sympathizes with the desire of the nobles to bring pressure on the rulers, but refuses to go so far as to favour the deposition of the aged king and the establishment of a regency.

Page 8, l. 161. BEARING BRIGHT CHAINS: the chains of office worn as insignia by the officials of the city.

Page 8, l. 182. A MOUSE OF IMPORTANCE. While it is not sure that any individual is here intended, the speaker clearly voices the opinion of the poet.

Page 9, l. 185. THERE WOULD STILL COME ANO-THER: probably John of Gaunt.

Page 9, l. 209. WHAT THIS DREAM MAY MEAN. An affectation of innocence is the custom of medieval poets who use the dream setting for their poems.

Page 10, l. 225. DIEU VOUS SAVE, DAME EMME: a popular song.

Page 10, l. 231. AND SEVEN TIMES MORE. This apparently refers to the seven ensuing Passus, or 'steps', comprising the first long section of the poem.

Page 11, l. 12. TRUTH'S DWELLING. Truth is here used by Langland to signify God, as elsewhere to signify the true way of life.

Page 11, l. 19. A MODERATE COMFORT. Note that Holy Church begins by stating the necessity of supplying man's physical needs, though favouring moderation in place of luxury.

Page 13, l. 85. HOW I MAY SAVE MY SOUL. This is the 'argument' of the poem.

Page 14. l. 105. KNIGHTED TEN. There are nine orders of angels in heaven; Lucifer and his followers formed a tenth order.

Page 14, l. 109. TRUTH BY KNOWLEDGE OF THE TRINITY: the first of Langland's many statements that not only God but the true way of human life is tri-une. Hence his later presentation of Do Well, Do Bet and Do Best.

Page 15, l. 127. W R O N G. This character is synonymous with Lucifer or Satan.

Page 15, l. 138. H O W T R U T H D E S C E N D S: an allegorical manner of asking how God made man in his own image.

Page 17, l. 184. M A L K I N. The reader need not look for an allusion hidden behind this name, a diminutive of Matilda.

Page 18, l. 5. O N T H Y L E F T S I D E. The left is symbolical of evil.

Page 18, l. 18. I W O N D E R E D W H O S H E W A S. The political allusion at this point seems to be to Alice Perrers, mistress of the king.

Page 18, l. 20. M E D E. This word contains a pun. Mede in Middle English signifies both reward and bribe. Passus II-IV elaborate this conceit, the meaning of the word changing frequently between reward and bribery.

Page 19, l. 43. F L A T T E R Y : an important character in Langland's poem, since in his opinion at the root of all ill lies a flattering view of sin, which keeps men from repentance.

Page 19, l. 60. A S S I Z A R S A N D S O M P N O U R S. Sizars are jurors; sompnours are servants of the ecclesiastical courts.

Page 20, l. 62. A D V O C A T E S O F T H E A R C H E S : the lawyers.

Page 20, l. 70. A C H A R T E R : an imaginary presentation of the Seven Deadly Sins and a few of their myriad branches. The passage is highly conventional.

Page 21, l. 110. I N W I T N E S S W H E R E O F. The charter is signed by the devil and a number of rascals whose names probably refer rather to notorious professions than to individuals.

Page 21, l. 115. I N T H E D A T E O F T H E D E V I L : a parody of *anno Domini*.

Page 22, l. 139. A N D M I G H T K I S S A K I N G. It is the function of the king to give just rewards.

Page 23, l. 170. F A L S E H O O D S A T O N A N A S S I Z E R.

This familiar type of grotesque imagery shows the individual dominated by a sinful or daemoniac 'idea'.

Page 23, l. 176. P R O V I S O R S: either a purveyor, or one who sued to the court of Rome for an ecclesiastical living before the death of the actual incumbent.

Page 24, l. 192. M U L T I T U D E S O F M E N: another instance of allegorical realism. Guile is an abstraction, while the beguiled are actual persons.

Page 25, l. 234. A N H A L F Y E A R A N D E L E V E N D A Y S: a parody of legal phraseology.

Page 28, l. 55. K I N D: Nature.

Page 29, l. 63. B U T G O O D M E N A R E N O T G R A V E R S: The next sixty-three lines are a digression in the story but not in the argument. The poet shows typical cases of public bribery (Mede).

Page 32, l. 158. A S C O M M O N A S A C A R T W A Y. The satirist lists the rascals most commonly found on the main highways of medieval England.

Page 32, l. 183. L O V E - D A Y S. These are days set apart for the arbitration of legal disputes.

Page 33, l. 212. I N E V E R K I L L E D A K I N G: a reference to the death of Edward II.

Page 33, l. 213. S I X T Y T H O U S A N D: the number given by the poet to the English army in France.

Page 34, l. 218. T H E K I N G C A M E T O F R A N C E. The ensuing passage makes transparent references to the wars of Edward III in France.

Page 37, l. 316. D I R E C T R E L A T I O N. The following passage is a good example of the symbolic treatment of philology popular throughout the Middle Ages.

Page 39, l. 384. R E G U M: the Book of Kings.

Page 40, l. 412. O N E C H R I S T I A N K I N G. The fervent imagination of the Middle Ages was haunted by millenial visions which produced much writing similar as literature to the prophetical books of the Old Testament. Here Langland reflects this tradition. Even in his farthest visions, however, he never becomes wholly individualistic. Law and punishment are to exist even in an entirely pacific world.

Page 40, l. 428. B A S E L A R D S: short swords.

Page 41, l. 436. D I N G U P O N D A V I D: to sing the Psalms.

Page 41, l. 451. B Y S I X S U N S A N D A S H I P. This seems a literary imitation of the many occult prophesyings of the times.

Page 43, l. 17. H I S K N A V E C A T O. Reason's servant is Cato because a text ascribed to Cato was commonly used in elementary school instruction. The passage is a playful allegory on systematic education.

Page 43, l. 18. T O M T R U E ⁄ T O N G U E. Picturesquely compounded names, the natural development of an allegorical style, are easily carried to unexampled lengths by Langland.

Page 43, l. 27. W A R Y N W I S D O M. This character and Witty signify the learned and shrewd distortion of the law. Langland fails later, however, to be entirely consistent in his use of these figures. The name Waryn is shifted about.

Page 44, l. 50. T H E N P E A C E C A M E T O P A R L I A ⁄ M E N T. Although the story of Peace interrupts that of Lady Mede, it is an essential part of the allegory. His complaints lead to a typical example of the use of bribery in law.

Page 47, l. 122. T I L L L O R D S A N D L A D I E S L O V E T R U T H. This passage follows a familiar type of medieval jesting. Reason will only yield when a great number of impossibilities become true.

Page 47, l. 124. T H E P U R F L I N G S O F P E R N E L: the finery of a worldly woman.

Page 47, l. 129. A S S A I N T B E N E T B A D. These are references to the monastic rules, of which the greatest is that of Saint Benedict.

Page 47, l. 136. G A L I S : Galicia, or Spain, in which lies the shrine of Saint James.

Page 47, l. 140. O R F O R F E I T H I S F E E , I F T H E Y F I N D I T A T D O V E R . He will be penalized on embarking from England.

Page 50, l. 1. T H E N I A W O K E . The several occasions on which the dreamer awakes mark the chief transitions in the poem. The previous section has dealt only with public affairs; the ensuing section deals with man's moral and religious life as a whole. The first hundred lines of this Passus afford the chief sketch of the dreamer, Long Will. He is a scholarpriest, who makes a living by performing too irregular religious services in the houses of the welltodo in London. His 'Will' is not that of God. Although he argues plausibly with Conscience, he recognizes in the end his personal guilt and so prepares himself for repentance.

Page, 50, l. 2. K I T : the poet's wife.

Page 50; l. 2. L O L L E R : an idle and lazy beggar.

Page 52, l. 62. C R O W N I N G : an allusion to the tonsure of the religious orders.

Page 52, l. 69. B O N D M E N A N D B A S T A R D S . Note that despite his sympathy with the poor, Langland is always a staunch supporter of the established ranks of society and the Church.

Page 52, l. 83. S I M O N ' S S O N : a person guilty of simony.

Page 53, l. 117. A N D R E A S O N M A D E R E A D Y . Since the moral law is primarily the law of reason, it is Reason who delivers the systematic sermon on the duties of the social orders from the lowest to the highest.

Page 54, l. 132. P E R N E L : a woman of doubtful virtue.

Page 54, l. 136. H E W A R N E D W A T T . This man should see, says Reason, that his wife wears inexpensive hats.

Page 55, l. 166. S E E K S A I N T T R U T H . In the poet's fable this means to seek God and to live a good life.

Page 55, l. 170. A N D W I L L B E G A N T O W E E P .We now have seven characters representing the Seven Deadly Sins. Nevertheless the central figure is still Long Will, who should be considered as confessing his own sins in the same spirit in which the seven notorious characters confess theirs.

Page 56, l. 200. G Y B H A D M I S F O R T U N E . Like most of Langland's minor characters, Gyb is unknown to the historian.

Page 58, l. 249. L I M I T O U R S : friars limited as to the districts in which they could work.

Page 58, l. 253. T O S H O W T H E I R S H R I F T S T O T H E M : to come to them for confession.

Page 58, l. 255. P O S S E S S I O N E R S : the regular clergy.

Page 60, l. 301. S I R H A R V E Y : the personification of Avarice.

Page 60, l. 313. S I M ‑ A T ‑ T H E ‑ H E D G E S . The hedges were the scenes of much petty thievery.

Page 62, l. 356. F O R L O V E O F T H E C R O S S : a pun, referring to the cross figured on the coin and to the cross of Christ.

Page 62, l. 362. I L E N D M E N W H O W I L L L O S E A L I P O F F E A C H N O B L E : I lend men whom I can cheat by having the coins in which they are paid pared at the edges.

Page 62, l. 365. D I D Y O U E V E R L E N D L O R D S . Avarice declares that he has acted much like a pawnbroker, selling his goods again to the original owners at greatly advanced prices.

Page 64, l. 432. W A R N E R : the gamekeeper.

Page 64, l. 438. A R A K E R O F C H E A P S I D E : a street cleaner.

Page 68, l. 535. I T E M I S S A E S T : the last words of the Mass.

Page 69, l. 579. T H E R E W A S A W E L S H M A N T H E R E . This character stands for the man who can still make restitution for his sin. The ensuing character, Robert the robber, is the man who, since he cannot make full restitution, must place all his hope in God's mercy.

Page 70, l. 602. HE HAD LAIN WITH LATRO: he had been a robber.

Page 71, l. 625. IN OUR GARMENT: Christ in his Incarnation.

Page 71, l. 630. DEEDS DONE IN OUR ARMOUR: the same meaning as the above.

Page 72, l. 647. A PILGRIM IN PAGAN CLOTHING: Langland's symbol for the vanity of the merely external observances of religion.

Page 72, l. 668. CRIED A PLOWMAN: This is Piers Plowman in his simplest guise as the faithful layman.

Page 73, l. 696. THAT YOU LOVE OUR LORD. The next twenty lines depict the Ten Commandments, the first laws for the faithful to follow, in terms of a day's journey across a medieval countryside.

Page 74, l. 722. CRENELLATED WITH CHRISTENDOM. The faithful, after observing the moral law, must espouse the Christian faith and charity.

Page 75, l. 756. SEVEN SISTERS. These are the ascetic and Christian virtues. Hence the monastic imagery.

Page 76, l. 773. MERCY IS A MAIDEN: the Blessed Virgin.

Page 77, l. 4. HALF AN ACRE TO HARROW: Langland's typical symbol for man's moral duties in a fleeting world.

Page 78, l. 51. IN A CHARNEL AT CHURCH. The bones of rich and poor in the churchyard are hard to distinguish from each other.

Page 79, l. 89. SO I WRITE MY WILL. The writing of imaginary testaments became a convention of medieval poetry.

Page 85, l. 245. MATTHEW WITH THE MAN'S FACE.

This is the customary symbol for the author of the First Gospel.

Page 87, l. 320. UNLESS HIS WAGES ARE HIGH:
referring to the labour unrest following the Black Death.

Page 88, l. 334. THUS SAID SATURN. The following is
a parody of astrological prophecy.

Page 89, l. 14. AS LEGISLATORS OF BOTH LAWS:
the Canon and the Civil Law.

Page 89, l. 26. TO HELP HOSPITALS. There follows a
representative list of the chief philantropic activities of the
wealthy in the Middle Ages.

Page 91, l. 77. THE CLERK OF HISTORY: Vincent
of Beauvais.

Page 94, l. 167. THEIR SINS ARE COVERED. Since
these persons are lunatics, they cannot be held morally re-
sponsible. They lack free will.

Page 96, l. 246. THE PRIEST AND PERKIN. In the
foregoing passage Piers, or Perkins, supports a text apparently declaring salvation to be wholly a matter of personal
merit. The quarrelsome priest notes that this position takes no
account of the doctrine of pardons. The issue between the two,
however, seems not doctrinal, for the dreamer later asserts his
belief in the orthodox doctrine of pardons, glancing as a satirist only at the abuses in practice. The poet shows no infidelity
to the Church, which also acknowledges the obligation to
Do Well.

Page 99, l. 2. SEEKING FOR DO WELL. Note that the
previous Passus has virtually identified the search for Truth
with that for Do Well, Do Bet and Do Best. The knowledge
of Truth, or God, is made man's ultimate goal.

Page 99, l. 18. "THIS MAN IS AMONG US." This is intended as a somewhat frivolous answer. The true priest must
seek for truth in life and in the writings of the Church, and
not rely on the words of the superficial.

Page 101, l. 70. A TALL MAN LOOKED MUCH AS I DO. This begins the biographical feature of the Life of Do Well. The poet means that at a tender age a person reaches self-consciousness, or thought.

Page 101, l. 79. ARE THREE FAIR VIRTUES. For an exposition of Langland's tripartite system, see the Introduction.

Page 102, l. 105. ONE TO BE KING. The king is judge between the laity and the clergy.

Page 102, l. 115. WIT APPROACHED US. Wit signifies Thought refined by experience rather than by education (Study).

Page 104, l. 2. IN A CASTLE: the human body. The allegory in this Passus proceeds from birth and schooling to marriage.

Page 104, l. 7. ANIMA: the soul.

Page 107, l. 84. THE POUK: SIR PRINCEPS HUIUS MUNDI: the Devil.

Page 110, l. 179. IMP AN ELDER: to practice grafting.

Page 110, l. 201. THOUGH THEY RIDE TO DUNMOW. According to an ancient tradition any married couple who could come a year after marriage to Dunmow and truthfully swear that they were happy, could carry away gratis a flitch of bacon.

Page 115, l. 121. IMAGINATION SHALL HEREAFTER ANSWER. This somewhat naive parenthesis refers to the chief character of Passus XII. Curious as art, the line well indicates the highly self-conscious plan of the poem.

Page 117, l. 154. MY COUSIN, CLERGY. The word "clergy" in Langland means both learning and priesthood. In the pilgrim's life, just as Study follows Wit, Clergy naturally succeeds Study. The progression is Will, Thought, Wit, Study, Clergy (Learning) and Imagination. Since learning is chiefly of the Scripture, Clergy's wife is given this name.

Page 117, l. 174. I WROTE HER MANY VOLUMES. The foremost study of the learned was of course of the Scriptures. Theology and later the secular branches of learning are presently mentioned in turn by Study.

Page 123, l. 364. "CONTRA," CRIED I. From here to the end of the Passus we have a too rash and radical objection by the young scholar against his wiser teachers. He discourages an implicit trust in learning.

Page 126, l. 432. CULORUM: the gloss, or note, upon the Scriptural text.

Page 129, l. 8. THE LAND OF LONGING. Here commences a common variant of the story of the Prodigal Son in terms of medieval student life.

Page 130, l. 34. RECKLESSNESS. This figure becomes far more important in the latest version of the poem than in the version used here. Many of the speeches later given to Recklessness are originally assigned to the pilgrim. Apparently after Langland had at first deliberately painted his hero as reckless, he felt the errors of the character to be so grave that he put the same words into the mouth of Recklessness himself.

Page 133, l. 143. TROJANUS, WHO HAD BEEN A TRUE KNIGHT. The story of Trajan was well known during Langland's age. Naturally variants were extremely common. Thus the *Legend of Saint Erkenwald*, the great patron of Saint Paul's in London, in many details minutely follows the account given by Langland of Trajan and Gregory. This legend is not only in the metre but in the general style of Langland, suggesting that it is either his own work or that of a close follower. The fate of the righteous heathen was one of the chief questions of the age. Langland follows closely on the path of Dante, giving a less drastic and dogmatic answer to the problem of wholesale heathen damnation than a naive view of the subject might lead one to suppose.

Page 134, l. 155. LO, YOU LORDS. The next 350 lines

consist in a continuous speech by Scripture on the familiar themes of charity, poverty and the duties peculiar to the clergy.

Page 134, l. 158. SARACEN: a term applicable to any heathen whatsoever.

Page 151, l. 1. IMAGINATION. This speaker in Passus XII represents the culmination of the intellectual life. Trained by Study, Clergy, Scripture and Reason, the pilgrim at last is shown reality in its true form and proportions. Imagination carefully corrects all the errors of the pilgrim's past, which sprang rather from excessive and misplaced zeal than from positive evil (deadly sin). This canto is thus a systematic recapitulation of the argument of Passus X-XI.

Page 151, l. 11. YOU MEDDLE WITH MAKING POEMS. Imagination holds that the poet's duty is to save his soul and not to create literature. Since the saving truth has many times been stated in books, further books are merely ornaments.

Page 152, l. 43. FELICE: probably the proud and unhappy wife of Guy of Warwick.

Page 152, l. 44. ROSAMUND: the mistress of Henry II.

Page 154, l. 99. YOU WILL NEVER BLAME LOGIC. Imagination again rebukes the impatience and romanticism of the pilgrim, who has scorned logic, law, money and good works, relying wholly upon grace.

Page 162, l. 21. UNLESS VIX AID HIM. This may be merely a reference to the words, Vix justus sit secures. It has been suggested that it also refers to the five wounds of Jesus Christ (VIX).

Page 163, l. 31. PATIENCE CAME AS A POOR CREATURE. This character remains conspicuous from here to the end of the poem. The statement that he is similar in appearance to Piers Plowman indicates his importance. He naturally introduces the theme of the inner, contemplative and ascetic life, the subject of the Life of Do Bet.

Page 163, l. 41. CLERGY CALLED FOR MEAT. This figure in this Passus is called 'Clergy', 'Master', and 'Doctor'. He represents the Clergy possessed as they are with the most palpable human faults, but nevertheless, as Imagination has shown, essential in society as established by God's will.

Page 164, l. 59. MEAT OF MISERERE-MEI,-DEUS: that is, the spiritual food of the Psalms.

Page 165, l. 102. SAINT ADVISA. The saint was fed by a delicious bread from heaven. The reading of the manuscript, however, is doubtful at this point.

Page 166, l. 133. "I HAVE SEVEN SONS," SAID CLERGY. Here Clergy confesses the strength of the mystical element in religion, relying on the words of Piers Plowman (Christ). The ascetic side of Christianity receives additional support from the abrupt and visionary appearance of the Plowman himself in the second paragraph. The "seven sons" are the seven liberal arts.

Page 167, l. 163. EX VI TRANSITIONIS. This quotation and the four lines following are, so far as I know, incapable of a clear interpretation. They may well be intentionally obscure. Their general purport, however, is definitely to assert the mysterious power of the more spiritual and mystical element in religion. "Love is without fear."

Page 170, l. 238. MY NAME IS ACTIVA VITA. The pilgrim is led to the contemplative life by the confession which Activa Vita makes of the inevitable frailty and corruption of his own life. The letter part of this Passus is devoted, in slightly hidden form, to the confession of the Seven Deadly Sins.

Page 170, l. 240. I AM A WAFER-SELLER. Active Life is figured as a poor wafer-seller incompetent on his own account to win salvation. The name and idea reflects the biblical symbol that man shall not live by bread alone.

Page 170, l. 260. TWO POLLS IN THE MIDDLE:

an allusion to the physical form of the pardon, with the two
heads·(polls) of Peter and Paul upon the seal.

Page 173, l. 332. YOUR BEST COAT, HAUKYN: Name-
ly, the body, which is both the requisite of the active life and
the source of its weakness.

Page 179, l. 1. "I HAVE BUT ONE WHOLE SUIT."
This Passus and the following are introductory to the Life of
Do Bet, or Life of Contemplation. Passus XIV deals with the
rewards of the ascetic life, while Passus XV continues the
theme with reference to those who do, or who should, practise this life, as notably hermits, the monastic orders and the
clergy as a whole.

Page 179, l. 6. I HAVE WASHED IT IN LENT: a reference to Lenten penances which chastise the body.

Page 189, l. 293. BUT I SHALL PARAPHRASE IT. The
latter part of this Passus is developed from the *Speculum His-
toriale* of Vincent of Beauvais.

Page 190. l. 321. THE PASS OF ALTOUN: Alton, in
Hampshire. A scene once notorious for robberies.

Page 192, l. 16. "I AM A CHRISTIAN CREATURE."
The prologue to the inner or contemplative life is properly in-
troduced by a psychological analysis of the soul. Langland's
source here is Isidore of Seville.

Page 199, l. 209. THE PLOWMAN PERCEIVES MORE
DEEPLY. From this point on, the symbol of Piers frequently
stands for God, and also for the Church so far as it is divinely
inspired. Thus thirteen lines further on the symbol almost certainly refers to the Pope himself. "Petrus, id est Christus."

Page 204, l. 371. LUSHBORGH: a spurious coin.

Page 206. l. 419. SARACENS MAY BE SAVED: a nota-
ble passage in developing the transitional relation between Do
Well and Do Bet. Langland here stresses the thought that
heathens may Do Well and have at least some conception of

the Fatherhood of God, or the First Person of the Trinity. It remains for the faithful and zealous Christian, however, to Do Better or to Do Best.

Page 210, l. 546. THE RED NOBLE: a gold coin.

Page 210, l. 554. AS THE TEMPLARS DID. This order of knights was abolished through charges of pecuniary corruption.

Page 211, l. 591. METROPOLITANUS. The figure of Christ as an archbishop continues the typical symbolism of the poem which images the Life of Do Best as that of a bishop.

Page 212, l. 603. THE SYRIAN EPISCOPATE. This alludes to the bishops of sees in countries under pagan rule who either by choice or necessity lived in Christian countries. Such bishops became unpopular in England.

Page 215, l. 3. WHAT IS THE MEANING OF CHARITY. Throughout this section of the poem Charity is regarded as the good principle of the soul. Piers Plowman is progressively the symbol for Christ—a symbol somewhat veiled in Passus XVI, more open in Passus XVII, where Piers is blended with the Good Samaritan, and wholly clear in Passus XVIII, describing the crucifixion and harrowing of hell. Cf. Introduction.

Page 215, l. 23. PROPPED WITH THREE PILES. Observe that each of the three sections on the three aspects of the soul begins with an allegorical fable regarding the Trinity. This is of course the second section, the Life of Do Bet.

Page 218, l. 95. BUT TWO LIVES ALLOWED BY OUR LORD. Langland here explains his less usual division of life into three parts, by adjusting his views to the more common division into two parts, the active and the contemplative. The three states mentioned in this paragraph, namely marriage, widowhood and virginity, are allegorical of Do Well, Do Bet and Do Best. Widowhood is especially appropriate to the life of contemplation, since this consists largely in meditation on the world as widowed by the death of its lover, in other words, by the crucifixion.

Page 222, l. 225. I AM FAITH. The theological virtues, faith, hope and charity, are here allegorized as Abraham, Spes (Moses) and Piers Plowman (Christ).

Page 224, l. 280. GOD CAME AS THREE PERSONS. This interpretation of the visit of the three angels to Abraham is equally familiar in scholastic comment and medieval art.

Page 225, l. 312. A LEPER LAY THERE. This leper is the soul of the just heathen in hell, awaiting the 'harrowing of hell' by the coming of Christ.

Page 227, l. 5. HIM WHO HAS THE SEAL IN KEEPING: a symbol to express the relation between the Mosaic and the Christian Law. The Old Law is the document, the New Law is the supernatural ratification, without which the document has no final validity. Note that the Mosaic Law is here given not as the Ten Commandments but as the twofold command, quoted by Christ, to love God and one's neighbour.

Page 228, l. 49. WE SAW A SAMARITAN. This interpretation of the parable of the Samaritan is familiar in patristic comment and medieval art. It shrewdly recapitulates Langland's story of Abraham and Spes.

Page 229, l. 69. HE UNBUCKLED HIS TWO BOTTLES: symbols of the Sacrament.

Page 229, l. 73. THE NEW MARKET: the Last Judgement.

Page 230, l. 108. ON CARO, MY COURSER: a symbol for the Incarnation.

Page 230, l. 117. HOPE WILL KEEP THE HOSTELRY: namely, the Church.

Page 236, l. 285. HE WHO MURDERS A GOOD MAN. This discussion of murder as the supreme sin artistically precedes the account of the most wicked of all murders, the crucifixion.

Page 237, l. 324. THERE ARE THREE THINGS. The homely similes of the scolding wife, the leaky roof and the smoky fire are commonplaces of the old homiletic literature.

Page 239, l. 15. FAITH CRIED FROM HIS WINDOW, "A FILI DAVID!" This is one of the many passages in Passus XVIII which are vividly duplicated in the Christian art contemporary with Langland. The entire passage also preserves many of the traditions of Anglo-Saxon poetry.

Page 239, l. 21. THE FRUIT OF PIERS PLOWMAN: the souls in hell.

Page 239, l. 23. WILL JOUST IN PIERS' ARMOUR: that is, Christ in the human body will fight against Satan.

Page 242, l. 116. SECUNDUM SCRIPTURAS. Much of this Passus is a poetical adaptation of the Apocryphal Gospel of Nichodemus, which had long been popular with the Anglo-Saxon poets.

Page 242, l. 117. A WOMAN AS I THOUGHT. This story of the so-called Four Daughters of God is a commonplace of medieval allegory. A fine version occurs, for example, in the Coventry Mystery Play.

Page 247, l. 242. AND ALL THE ELEMENTS. This passage brings the medieval conception of the four elements, earth, air, fire and water, into relation with the Incarnation.

Page 247, l. 256. THE SONS OF SIMON. Langland derived this episode from the Gospel of Nichodemus.

Page 249, l. 315. TO WARN PILATE'S WIFE: an allusion to an incident familiar through the Passion Play, as, for example, in the Play of Coventry.

Page 255, l. 15. "WHY DO YOU CALL HIM CHRIST." The hundred and twenty-five lines following relate Langland's idea of the three states of the soul to the threefold divisions in the life of Christ. Thus the passage serves as a transition between the Life of Do Bet, dealing with the Incarnation, and the Life of Do Best.

Page 260, l. 155. BUT MARY MAGDALENE. This passage marks a forward step in the chronological sequence. DoWell described the Creation. Do Bet dealt with the history of the world from Abraham to the Redemption. Do Best deals with the history of the Church beginning with the Resurrection and continuing to Langland's own times.

Page 260, l. 184. AND GAVE PIERS POWER. Here, as several times previously, we note that Piers signifies the Church's Authority and even in a more specific sense, the Pope. The first word spoken by Piers in the poem is "Peter." Piers, Perkin and Peter are all forms of one name. The significance of Peter in reference to the Pope should be observed.

Page 261, l. 201. ONE SPIRITUS PARACLITUS. The Holy Spirit as the Divine guide of the Church, operating according to the promises of Christ, becomes the central force in the Life of Do Best, just as Christ himself is the centre of the Life of Do Bet, and God the Father of the Life of DoWell.

Page 261, l. 214. THEN GRACE BEGAN. Grace is commonly used as a name for God the Holy Spirit.

Page 262, l. 231. TO SOME HE GAVE WISDOM. The Holy Spirit is also often named wisdom by the Fathers. The realist in Langland shows nowhere more surprisingly than in the ensuing passage, which describes the gifts of the Holy Spirit in terms of the vocations of men.

Page 264, l. 277. THE CARDINAL VIRTUES: These are the active virtues as distinguished from the theological virtues of faith, hope and charity. From this distinction it becomes clear that by the Life of Do Best Langland means the second or higher stage of the active life.

Page 265, l. 323. BUILD A BARN. By the barn, or Unitas, Langland means the Church.

Page 267, l. 392. GRACE GAVE PIERS THE POWER. Piers clearly signifies here the clergy, who alone have the power to celebrate the Sacrament.

Page 268, l. 416. AN UNLEARNED VICAR: another modest mouthpiece for the opinions of the poet.

Page 269, l. 433. HIS PLOWS, THE NEWER AND THE OLDER: the New and Old Law.

Page 270, l. 472. THEN THERE CAME A KING: one of the many passages in which this final section of the poem harks back to the beginning. Do Best, being the just govern-ance of man, is occupied with secular as well as with ecclesi-astical rule.

Page 272, l. 1. AS I WENT BY THE WAY. This and several other passages in the last Passus bring to a conclusion the biographical theme of the poem, which is to trace the life of a Christian man from his birth and his youth spent in stu-dies to his old age.

Page 274, l. 79. THEN NATURE HEARD CON-SCIENCE. In Langland's view Nature and her planetary influences always fight on the side of God. He often uses the word Kynd (Nature) to signify God.

Page 277, l. 157. SLOTH WAS HIS NAME. Medieval authors use 'sloth' with a highly comprehensive meaning. It includes both physical sloth and the lazy neglect of religion.

Page 280, l. 274. YET HE LIES, AS I BELIEVE: a point-ed denunciation of medieval communism. Langland is politi-cally a conservative.

Page 282, l. 312. ONE, FRIAR FLATTERY. Like the first section of the poem, the last ends with Langland's direst warning: through false confessors the people have lost the sense of sin. In the last passage the poet refers to what he regards as the failure of the friars to live up to their high promises as reform-ers in religion.

Page 284, l. 382. TILL I HAVE PIERS THE PLOW-MAN. Although it has been suggested that the poem is unfin-ished, no foundation whatever exists for this theory. The poem definitely deals with this world, or the field of folk. Heaven is not on earth nor is the celestial city to be established within the mortal life of man. Hence the pilgrim passes out of our view still yearning and groping his way towards a Divine City built not in time but in eternity.

THE END